Trinity in Process

TRINITY IN PROCESS
A Relational
Theology of God

Joseph A. Bracken, S.J., and
Marjorie Hewitt Suchocki, editors

CONTINUUM • NEW YORK

1997
The Continuum Publishing Company
370 Lexington Avenue, New York, NY 10017

Printed in the United States of America

Library of Congress Cataloging-in-Publication Data

Trinity in process : a relational theology of God / edited by Joseph A. Bracken,
  Marjorie Hewitt Suchocki.
    p.   cm.
  Includes bibliographical references and index.
  ISBN 0-8264-0878-8 (alk. paper)
  1. Trinity History of doctrines. I. Bracken, Joseph A.
II. Suchocki, Marjorie.
BT111.2.T77 1997
231'.044—dc20   96-22538
                                                                              CIP

Contents

Introduction

Thomas Aquinas opens his great *Summa Theologiae* with the magnificent questions on the being of God. He moves us through question, discussion, and answer, carefully developing the metaphysical basis of his work. But when he reaches the twenty-seventh question, it is as if he encounters an intermezzo, breaking the rhythm of the great harmonies he has developed. And within this interlude, he shifts from metaphysical to confessional categories as he addresses the questions and answers of God as trinity. Completing this section, he then returns to the metaphysics of his first twenty-six questions in order to complete his discussion of God.

The intermezzo-like quality of the trinitarian confessional questions fits Thomas's metaphysically based epistemology, which argued the two routes of nature and grace for knowledge. The metaphysical questions were developed according to the first category; whereas, the trinitarian questions evoked the categories of grace. The issue this raises so sharply is the compatibility between metaphysical and confessional categories in discussions of God. Nowhere is this issue stronger than in the doctrine of the trinity.

As Thomas so clearly shows, the classical Christian doctrine of God is based upon the metaphysical assumption that substance is an ultimate category, with substance being that which requires nothing other than itself in order to exist. Confessional categories existed in some tension with this, since they dealt with God's relation not only to the world, but within the divine life itself. The inward relations correlated with the external relations—e.g., the internally generative God is the externally creative God who brings forth a world; the internally generated wisdom is the external pattern for God's creative and redemptive activity, and the internally unitive Spirit is the externally reconciling Spirit. This correlation, in turn, creates tension with the fundamental substance metaphysics that undergirds the doctrine of the totally self-sufficient God, whose inner life can in no essential way be related to other than God's self.

In our own day, the metaphysics of substance has been radically brought into question. In a sense, substance metaphysics parallels Newtonian physics, and just as Newtonian physics is relativized by particle physics, even so, substance metaphysics is relativized by contemporary relational metaphysics. The erosion of substance metaphysics has caused many to eschew the metaphysical task entirely, but if metaphysics attempts to answer the question, "What must be the case in order for the world to exist as we experience it?" then this task is essential not only to philosophy, but to theological discussions of God.

The process philosophy of Alfred North Whitehead relates directly to the physics developed in the early twentieth century. Whitehead, himself a physicist and mathematician, developed his philosophy to reconceptualize the structures that account for existence. These structures were, of course, thoroughly relational, in keeping with the discoveries of physics. The import for Christian theology has been monumental with respect to the doctrine of God. If relationality, far from being an inferior accident of finite existence, is instead the sine qua non of all existence whatsoever, then the tension between God and the world is resolved. The question is not how a totally self-contained and self-sufficient reality can relate to anything outside of itself, but rather, how one can reinterpret creation, providence, redemption, and eschatology under the new relational paradigm.

Perhaps the most intriguing possibilities for utilizing a relational metaphysics for Christian theological development rests with reconsideration of that anomaly of substance metaphysics, the intrarelationality of God's own self, and its issuance into God's relations with the world: the doctrine of the trinity. The resources within process thought are various. Whitehead posits a triad of principles in what he calls the "category of the ultimate," and these are "one," "many," and "creativity." In narrative form, these principles express the foundational fact that "the many become one, and are increased by one." All three principles are essential for any and every existent reality: To exist is to experience the energy or influences of that which is other, and to integrate these feelings into a new configuration. This process of becoming takes place through creativity, which is the transmission of feeling between entities, and the integration of feelings within the becoming entity.

One, many, and creativity are, therefore, ultimate terms as a unified triad.

Whitehead posits a further triadic structure within his complex notion of God. God is the unification of a primordial and
consequent nature, with these natures being roughly equivalent to
the mental and physical poles that characterize all entities. The
internal complexity of any entity, including God, is that it is both
other-created (through the many as prehended through the physical pole), and self-created (through the mental pole), with unity
being achieved as the many are integrated into the self at the
direction of the mental pole. Thus, God is a creative unification of
the many prehended through the consequent nature into the unity
of the primordial nature. This, of course, is the primal instantiation
of the category of the ultimate (one, many, and creativity) named
as the first triad.

Can these metaphysical triads, whether considered
abstractly or as concretized in God, be at all congruent with the
Christian sensitivity of an ultimate triunity within God? Process
thinkers have not been eager to leap to an answer. Norman
Pittenger was the first to give attention to the trinitarian possibilities in a 1967 essay arguing that God's love required internal
relationality, but he made no strong use of Whiteheadian categories to make this point.[1] This was followed in 1970 by Anthony
Kelly's article, "Trinity and Process: Relevance of the Basic
Christian Confession of God."[2] Kelly suggests that "trinity" is the
ultimate process, providing a paradigm for all human processes.
He did not yet explore process categories as a way to illumine
the trinitarian doctrine itself. This was first done by Lewis S. Ford
in his 1975 article, "Process Trinitarianism," in which he correlated the triadic structure of God with the trinity.[3] John B. Cobb,
Jr.'s 1975 *Christ in a Pluralistic Age* gave a more tentative answer
that equated God's primordial nature with Logos, or the Son, and
God's consequent nature with the Spirit, or the kingdom of
God—a binitarian rather than trinitarian view.[4] Schubert Ogden's
1980 article, "On the Trinity," roughly parallels the "Father" with
the inclusive essence of God, the "Son" with divine objectivity,
and the "Spirit" with divine subjectivity.[5] My own 1982 chapter
on the trinity in *God–Christ–Church* objected to the equation of
metaphysical principles with "persons" in God, and dealt instead
with the trinity as the way God is experienced in history.[6] The
major sustained development of process implications relative to

the trinity was done by my colleague in this volume, Joseph Bracken, who utilized a Hartshornean variation of Whiteheadian metaphysics.[7]

In the 1990s, however, interest in the possibilities of process metaphysics for exploring and illumining the Christian doctrine of the trinity has grown markedly. If the doctrine of the trinity is an inherently relational depiction of God, should not an inherently relational philosophy be helpful in expressing this doctrine? This volume brings together contemporary voices in this venture. Clearly, there is no unanimity—the process structure is triadic, but not trinitarian, leaving much room for creative interpretation. The many, in this instance, are not necessarily one! But there are themes and directions developed that together constitute a significant contribution to contemporary trinitarian discussion.

The importance of such trinitarian discussion is varied, ranging from speculative to pragmatic interests. The origins of trinitarian thinking in Christian history were also pragmatic as well as speculative, rooted as they were in soteriology. This remains the pragmatic concern. We live in an age when human society is being torn apart by ethnic rivalries and issues of difference of race, religion, gender, sexual orientation, and physical abilities. Individualism apparently only admits of community when that community is made up of like individuals. However, at the heart of the Christian doctrine of the trinitarian God is a quite different image. Whatever else it says, trinitarian doctrine maintains that an irreducible diversity is necessary for the ultimate unity—or that the ultimate unity is itself communal in nature, in and through an irreducible diversity.

Christian doctrine suggests that humanity is created in God's image. If God is such that the deepest image of God in human society is attained not by an individual alone, nor by societies made up of like-minded and like-looking individuals alone, but only through a society that becomes community through its embrace of irreducible differences, is there not a different force at work for peace in the world? Can we envision communities that not only embrace diversity within themselves, but that understand themselves to be but one irreducible community, whether religious or national, among valuable others?

The model of a trinitarian God, irreducibly diverse yet one, suggests a world community of irreducibly diverse communities, each of which is itself richly created in and through the irreducible diversity of its members. The model of God as triune offers a new model for creating community in a world that too often answers difference with destruction in the name of homogeneous unity.

There is a further pragmatic value to the understanding of God as triune. From Feuerbach's day to our own, we have been made keenly aware of our penchant to attribute our own favorite prejudices and biases to God. We make God in our image. Feminists have struggled with the issue through the blatant attribution of maleness to God that has marked the patriarchal Christian tradition, and, of course, this has clearly happened in relation to the notion of God as a Father and Son as well as Spirit. But rather than concede maleness irrevocably to the image, can we not use the image of "trinity" to break us of our tendencies to such idolatry?

None of us, neither male nor female, is triune. I have already pointed to the essentially communal imagery connected with the doctrine. Given the unity of God, however, God is no more like a conventional human community than God is male or female. The notion of God as triune forces us beyond our human categories in our speech about God, and thus can break our captivity to the categories. "God" can be freed from the cage of our projected selves, echoing once more the "I am God, and no man" of Hosea 6. "Trinity" says not only that an essential diversity is required for ultimate unity, but that the reality of God so surpasses our categories and limitations that all our statements about God are necessarily relativized by our own experience, and, therefore, are finally metaphors for the God who is more than we can fully comprehend. "Trinity" taken seriously can burst its bindings of maleness and take us beyond itself to the God who, in fact, is more than we are and not reducible to our own small categories.

The different ways of portraying trinity through process categories in this volume are valued as voices in a dialogue that is intended to produce not uniformity, but creative differences. The first three essays utilize classical Whiteheadian scholarship and tend toward an emphasis upon the economic as opposed to an immanent trinity. Although the Christian experience of God in history can be interpreted in a trinitarian fashion, the dyadic Primordial/Consequent Whiteheadian categories tend toward a binitarian rather than trinitarian structure of deity. We begin with John B. Cobb, Jr., who sets out his perception of various models of the trinity, and various possibilities within process thought for addressing the issue of God's relationality. His own preference for a binitarian (God as transcendent and immanent) rather than trinitarian model is tempered by his exploration of a twofold rather than singlefold immanence of God in the world. David Ray Griffin follows, arguing that the application of the love revealed in Jesus Christ requires an understanding of divine power as persuasive and evocative, and historically this power has been experienced triadically. Lewis S. Ford also locates the trinity primarily in history as the Christian interpretation of God. Philosophical categories—neither Whitehead's nor any others—do not yield any essential tri-unity to God.

The next five essays utilize a neo-Whiteheadian model in that they explore aspects or adaptations of Whitehead that differ significantly from traditional Whiteheadian scholarship. All five argue for an immanent as well as economic trinity, moving beyond a dyadic structure of God. Joseph Bracken and Gregory Boyd emphasize a tripersonal notion of God, while Philip Clayton, Roland Faber, Marjorie Suchocki, and Bernard Lee emphasize the unity of a complex God. For all five, the world is involved within the trinitarian life of God. However, for Bracken and Boyd, God's inclusion of the world supplements the triunity of God; whereas, for Clayton, Faber, Suchocki, and Lee, the prehended world is in some sense constitutive of God as trinity. We conclude with Joseph Bracken's summary of four major issues that emerge as central for the present and the continuing discussion of process trinitarianism. The dialogue is rich and diverse. We invite you into the process.

MARJORIE HEWITT SUCHOCKI

NOTES

1. Norman Pittenger, *God in Process* (London: SCM Press Ltd., 1967).

2. Anthony J. Kelly, "Trinity and Process: Relevance of the Basic Christian Confession of God," *Theological Studies* 31 (1970). Pittenger wrote a reply to this article, arguing that priority in any doctrine of God must be on God's relation to creation (see "Trinity and Process: Some Comments in Reply," *Theological Studies* 32 (1971).

3. Lewis S. Ford, "Process Trinitarianism," *Journal of the American Academy of Religion* 43 (1975).

4. John B. Cobb, Jr., *Christ in a Pluralistic Age* (Philadelphia: Westminster Press, 1975).

5. Schubert Ogden, "On the Trinity," *Theology* 83 (1980).

6. Marjorie Hewitt Suchocki, *God–Christ–Church: A Practical Guide to Process Theology* (New York: Crossroad, 1982).

7. Joseph A. Bracken, *The Triune Symbol: Persons, Process and Community* (Lanham, MD: University Press of America, 1985) and *Society and Spirit: A Trinitarian Cosmology* (Cranbury, NJ: Associated University Presses, 1991).

The Trinity and Classical Whiteheadian Metaphysics

John B. Cobb, Jr.
The Relativization of the Trinity

· 1 ·

There are four main types of trinitarian doctrine. The trinities that result from these are quite diverse. Within each type are further differences. Debates, sometimes heated, exist among advocates of the several types, and many present their own doctrine as the doctrine of the trinity. Nevertheless, there is a widespread view that what matters is that the Christian come up with some trinitarian doctrine. How the three are understood is viewed as less important than that there be three.

Until recently, the names of the three were not much in dispute. They were "Father," "Son," and "Holy Spirit." The question was to what these terms referred and how they were related to one another and to the One. However, feminists have now made the question of how the three are named a central topic of discussion. Referring to God in this traditional way confirms the widespread sense that God is male—if not exactly a male, nevertheless, male or masculine in nature and character. Feminists argue that once this is recognized as a projection of patriarchy, Christians should reject this language or at least balance it with feminine language.

Those who insist on retaining the obviously male terminology respond in two ways. Some deny that this language implies that God is masculine. They emphasize that God is so completely transcendent of all that we can say or think that we must not allow the language we use about God to shape our understanding of who God is. That defense implies that the only reason for retaining masculine terminology is that it is traditional, and that until recently, masculine language was also supposed to function generically.

Other defenders of traditional language offer the stronger justification that the Second Person of the trinity was incarnate in male form. They can also claim that the First Person is to be related to more as we relate to a father than as we relate to a mother, or even that the characteristics of the first person are, in fact, more masculine than feminine. These are important claims that require discussion and debate.

Although I do not myself believe that God is more like human males than like human females, this essay is not primarily about the issue of sexist language. This concern will be woven into a discussion of the trinity that was going on before the issue of language was raised. The positions considered were problematic quite apart from their sexism.

The four types of trinitarian doctrine are as follows. First, the Eastern doctrine in which the three are really conceived as three divine persons. Second, the Augustinian doctrine in which, whatever use is technically made of "persons," God is conceived monotheistically as one person within whom three aspects or modes can be distinguished. Third, a nonmetaphysical trinity in which the three are differentiated within the horizon of human experience or language. Fourth, an "economic" trinity in which the discrimination of three functions does not necessarily imply much about differentiations within the divine life itself.

I do not find any of these types of trinitarian doctrine satisfactory. Each has strengths the others lack, but each also has features that advocates of the others rightly reject. I can find no way to gather all the strengths into a single consistent doctrine omitting all the weaknesses. In short, I know of no convincing or adequate doctrine of the trinity.

Since there are many profoundly different trinitarian doctrines among devout Christians, and since this diversity does not interfere with agreement on a wide range of important theological and practical matters, the question arises as to what is truly important about the trinity. Do all these types of trinitarian doctrine satisfy this criterion? Does it not matter much which doctrine one adopts as long as one affirms a trinity of some sort? What, indeed, is the importance of that affirmation in general? What is lacking in a unitarian position? Would a binity or a quaternity do as well?

Sometimes it is said that the importance of the trinity is Christological. Certainly, in the formation of the doctrine in the early church, most of the discussion centered on Christology. The need was to differentiate what was incarnate in Jesus from the "Father" to whom Jesus prayed. The danger was that this differentiation would result in a denial that what was incarnate in Jesus was truly God. The declaration that, indeed, what was incarnate in Jesus was of one substance with the Father was the happy solution of this problem. My critical comments about the various doctrines of the trinity do not entail any challenge to the importance of this achievement of the early church. I share with the early church its view of the importance of the doctrine of the incarnation. My formulation of this doctrine is not in substantialist terms, and this difference is important, but that is not the issue with which we are dealing here.

Once the binity was worked out in the Christological debates, the status of the Holy Spirit could be settled rather easily. It could simply be declared that it, too, was of one substance with the Father and the Son. This was done, and I regard that, too, as a sound doctrine. What it excludes and rejects needs to be excluded and rejected: that is, any view that in the experience of the Holy Spirit we are experiencing a reality inferior to, or other than, God.

Why, then, all the problem about the doctrine of the trinity? First, there is a real question as to why the church must say that the divine reality experienced in the Holy Spirit differs from the divine reality incarnate in Jesus. What would be lost if the church affirmed that it was the Holy Spirit that was incarnate in Jesus? There were Spirit Christologies in the early church that seemed quite as satisfactory as the Logos Christology. Why will the Binity not suffice?

Second, does "Father" refer to God in general; whereas, the other two refer to God with a certain qualification? Or are Father, Son, and Spirit really three co-equal ways of referring to a unity that can better be referred to as the Godhead? "Father" seems to function ambiguously in these two ways throughout the history of the church.

Third, are other ways of identifying the divine, which, in the Bible seem to have the same status as these, denied equal status? In particular, does "Wisdom" have a subordinate status to Son and Spirit; or is it another name for the Word, which is identified with the Son? Is there any reason, other than custom, not to add Wisdom to the consubstantial aspects or modes of God, ending up with a quaternity instead of a trinity?

It is apparent that differentiations within God and in the ways God works in the world can be made in many ways. Are we to assume that all but one of these are erroneous? Or can we acknowledge that, indeed, there are many ways of making distinctions within God's own being and also within the divine activity in the world. Different doctrines of the trinity select from among these. They are not to be judged as right and wrong but rather as more or less continuous with Biblical language and liturgical usage, more or less coherent, more or less illuminating of our experience now, more or less helpful in directing our energy and thought.

If proposals for trinitarian doctrine can be taken in this more relativistic sense, then I am freed to enter the discussion. A process theologian finds helpful resources for doing so in Whitehead's conceptuality. But there is no one doctrine of the trinity that is dictated by that conceptuality. I propose more than one possibility. But, first, we reflect briefly on the four main types of approaches thus far developed.

• 2 •

The trinity took its original form in the speculations of the Eastern church. There, theology as a whole was organized in terms of the work of God as Creator, Redeemer, and Transfigurer.[1] These three activities of God were clearly distinguished, and each was understood to stem from a distinct *hypostasis* or *prosopon*. These were imaged or conceived on the analogy of human persons. This trinitarian doctrine did affirm, in quite a strong sense, three persons. Since this theology began with three distinct persons, the challenge was to clarify their unity. This unity was crucial to the coherence of theology as a whole. The clarification could be made in two ways. The three persons could all be coequal hypostasizations of the one Godhead. Or the relations of the three persons could be depicted as so intimate that they constituted a social unity.

Process thought is indebted to the work of theologians who followed this latter path. Whitehead attributed to them the one fundamental metaphysical improvement on Plato. They taught that the three persons are constituted by their mutual relations so that their very existence is involved in these relations. They do not exist as separate persons who are subsequently and contingently related to one another. The relations are internal to what they are.

Therefore, as Joseph Bracken has shown,[2] one Whiteheadian doctrine of the trinity can follow, and in some ways deepen, this Eastern path. For Whitehead, the unity of a society is not identical with the unity of a single actual entity, but most of the entities we think of as individuals are, in fact, societies. Hence, to affirm that God is a society of three persons does not deny God's oneness in a very genuine sense.

The problem with this doctrine in either its traditional Eastern form or in that of Bracken is not conceptual. The problem is with the evidence in favor of the reality of three distinct persons in God. The doctrine appears to be a solution to a set of problems created in a centuries-long debate. Its tritheistic tendency, however carefully qualified, does not fit well with the far more radically monotheistic perspectives of the Jewish authors of Scripture, and it has been a profound offense to Jews ever since its development. If this offense were essential to faith in Christ, we would have no choice but to live with it and work with it, but many Christians have found that they could faithfully develop their Christology and their thought of God without any tendency to tritheism. Furthermore, it is not required for the explanation of any phenomena in the world including Christian experience.

· 3 ·

Although I regard the tritheistic tendencies in the Eastern formulation as undesirable, we must acknowledge that the doctrine of the trinity in the East is an integral part of its total theological understanding. The same cannot be said for the Western formulation stemming chiefly from Augustine. Here, the doctrine is an unneeded appendage to theology.

Augustine cannot be faulted, on the other hand, for any tendency to tritheism. In terms of what we mean by "person," God is for him one person. His doctrine of God begins with this one person. His task is to find a way to make sense of threeness within this one person. Hence, rather than three persons comprising a close social unity, Augustine and the Western tradition generally offer us one person within whose interior life a threefold distinction can be made.

Here, again, there is no conceptual problem for a Whiteheadian to follow suit. Whereas classical theology embodies a tension between its trinitarian speculations and its doctrine of the divine simplicity, Whitehead rejects the idea of divine simplicity and offers us clear and important distinctions within the divine life. The most important is between the Primordial and the Consequent Nature. At one point, Whitehead speaks also of the Superjective Nature, thereby providing us a ready-made trinity in a monotheistic context! If one objects to the term "Nature," one could shift to "person" as long as this is meant in the Augustinian sense rather than the Eastern or modern one.

Furthermore, the Augustinian approach offers an opening, at least in principle, to the use of feminine imagery in speaking of God. Since "Father" and "Son" are used to refer to features of the divine life that have no close analogy to creaturely fathers and sons, these features can be referred to as "Mother" and "Daughter" just as well. Indeed, what is important is to have three terms applicable to God, and since one knows that all such language is symbolic or metaphorical, the Augustinian tradition allows Sallie McFague to offer "Mother," "Lover," and "Friend" as ways of identifying the members of the trinity. Unfortunately, this possibility, valuable as it is in certain respects, only highlights the artificiality and arbitrariness of the discussion of the doctrine of the trinity in the West.

The primary problem with the Western tradition of trinitarian speculation, then, is that it is inauthentic. That is, it does not respond to any real problem in Christianity. There is little connection between Augustine's trinitarian doctrine and the course of the discussion that led up to the dogmatic decision about the trinity. The relations to the Biblical uses of the terms Father, Son, and Holy Spirit are tenuous. The immanent trinity is connected loosely or not at all to the economic trinity, that is, to the ways God works in the world. Lacking this connection, the distinctions are cast in at terms of the relations of the intrapersonal three. The Son is "begotten" by the Father; whereas, the Spirit "proceeds" from him and, in the West, from the Son. The only real reason for retaining the doctrine—other than number mysticism—is that the church once declared that God is three in one, so that some way of showing how three can be one is required.

Actually, the Augustinian trinity is not only inauthentic but also theologically damaging in its account of the Holy Spirit.

Whereas, in the East, the Holy Spirit was understood authentically as that Spirit that transfigures the lives of Christians, in Augustine, It is the unity of Father and Son. This means that, whatever terminology is used, It or He has a secondary role within God and little or none in the world. The creedal change in the Western church to asserting that the Spirit proceeds not only from the Father but also from the Son confirmed and furthered its practical subordination in Western theology.

Thus, the West, while technically maintaining the doctrine of the trinity, abandoned its two main reasons for being. It could not function to integrate Western theology. It could not function to assure the believer that the Spirit encountered in the church—and indeed more broadly in the world—is truly God. It functioned chiefly in two negative ways: first, as a conceptual puzzle that distracted theologians from important questions; second, to change faith, for many, from trust in the God known in Jesus Christ to acceptance of unintelligible speculations by a sacrifice of the intellect.

• 4 •

A third way of thinking of the trinity has recently gained extensive influence, especially because of the brilliant work of Juergen Moltmann.[3] In this formulation, the second person of the trinity is the human historical Jesus, rather than the preexistent divine reality incarnate in him. Since this Jesus addressed His heavenly Father, this "Father" is the first person. Since the New Testament also testifies to the Spirit at work in the church and the world, this is the third person.

This way of thinking of the Father, the Son, and the Holy Spirit has much support in the New Testament, although it was not identified there as trinitarian. The possibility of basing the doctrine of the trinity upon it arises today because of the rejection of "metaphysical" theology. Since the whole classical formulation of the doctrine of the trinity, East and West, was "metaphysical" in the now rejected sense, this is a drastic move.

"Metaphysical" here means referring to deity in a realistic fashion; that is, as One who exists apart from human belief, experience, and history. When this referential character of theological language is denied, then "Father" can mean whatever

Jesus experienced as "Father" without any judgment about its ontological status. The "Spirit" is that experience of believers that they describe with that term. And Jesus is, of course, the human, historical Jesus with no thought of a divine preexistent reality being incarnate in Him. It is remarkable how far one can go in transposing language originally developed for metaphysical assertion into this nonmetaphysical context.

As a process theologian, I cannot make this move. I hold to a "metaphysical" understanding of God. That is, I believe that God is a cosmic reality whose nature is little affected by the opinions of human beings or by how human beings formulate their religious language. If viewing the human Jesus as a member of the trinity accorded to Jesus the status of being God, or a God, in this metaphysical sense, it would be both nonsensical and contrary to the creeds, which declare him to be not only of one substance with God but also of one substance with humanity. As I read the classical creeds, trinitarian doctrine dealt with the preexisting divine reality that was incarnate in Jesus rather than the human, historical Jesus as such. The Christological debate was about the relation of this divine reality in Jesus to his human nature.

The situation is similar with regard to the Holy Spirit. For me, it is appropriate to refer to the spirit present among believers as a member of the trinity only if it can be understood as the presence of the one true, and metaphysically real, God. Trinitarian doctrine dealt with the relation of the divine that was present among and within the believers to that which was incarnate in Jesus, not with the direct historical influence of Jesus, and of testimony to him, upon events among believers.

My point here is not to object to this nonmetaphysical talk of Father, Son, and Spirit. Nor, from my relativistic perspective, do I object to reflections about the three entities that are identified in this nonmetaphysical context as "Father," "Son," and "Holy Spirit." However, this whole process continues the inauthenticity of the Western tradition. These are referred to as the Trinity only because that idea is around, and the theologian must give some content to it.

What is now proposed as Trinity does not fulfill the function of traditional trinitarian doctrine. That doctrine has had quite another role in both East and West. It came into existence because of what is now dismissed as metaphysical thinking. To continue to speak of trinitarian doctrine when the original problematic has been dismissed is confusing.

The artificiality of this approach to trinity is apparent also in the treatment of biblical sources. Much of what is said about Father, Son, and Holy Spirit is read from the New Testament texts. However, these texts do not single out these three terms from other ways of speaking of God. We have noted that Wisdom, in particular, is prominent in the scriptures, not only in the wisdom literature but also in both the synoptic Gospels and Paul. If we were to develop our doctrine from the Bible in a demetaphysicized way, we would at least include this term in the heart of what we said about God. Its omission results from its neglect in the metaphysical tradition. One is committed to three, even if the three in question differ radically from the three that were earlier dealt with in the traditional doctrine of the trinity.

A second problem with this move is that it commits theology to sexist language. If Father, Son, and Holy Spirit are ways of talking about God, metaphysically understood, then the language must be recognized as contingent and inadequate. To some extent, this has been acknowledged in both East and West. The situation is then, in principle if not in fact, open to the discussion of alternative terms to refer to that in God to which these patriarchal terms have referred. However, if language is itself the horizon of life and thought, this freedom is lost. "Mother" or "Father and Mother" cannot be substituted for "Father." We cannot ask whether God is really more like a father or more like a mother or has characteristics of both types, because the meaning of "God" is inseparable from the language that speaks of God.

• 5 •

The fourth approach to the doctrine of the trinity has a long tradition behind it, but it has become more prominent recently as a solution to the feminist critique. This approach begins with the economic trinity, naming it in terms of three different types of activity of God in the world. The resulting names for the "persons" of the immanent trinity are then, also, derived from the three functions. One such set of terms is "Creator," "Redeemer," and "Sanctifier."

The claim made in this approach is that the theological account of the work of God in the world can be well ordered under these three headings. It is less clearly implied that these three ways of acting in the world express differentiations in God as well. Process theology affirms strongly that God does work in the world creatively, redemptively, and sanctifyingly. Hence, a Whiteheadian can be fully open to exploring how well the approach to the trinity works.

There are theologies in which these distinctions work well. Consider, for example, a theology that identifies creation with a once-for-all *creatio ex nihilo;* redemption with forensic justification brought about by Jesus' atoning death; and sanctification with the transforming work of God in believers. Here, we have three categorically different modes of divine working, and this type of theology may acknowledge no other. Given these doctrines, to trace these differences in the economic trinity back into distinctions within God is plausible. It may be believed that that in God which creates, that which incarnates, and that which sanctifies are quite distinct. God is, then, Creator, Redeemer, and Sanctifier.

For theologians of this stripe, then, the terms Creator, Redeemer, and Sanctifier can be viewed as synonymous with Father, Son, and Holy Ghost and as valid alternatives to these sexist terms. This would bring us back to the classical question of how the three are one and would be open to both Eastern or Western answers. Although it would not resolve the problems in the doctrine, it would show that a nonpatriarchal discussion is possible.

However, this is not process theology. Process theology sees creation primarily as an ongoing process of bringing novel order and ordered novelty into being out of the settled past. It now seems that the Big Bang identifies a creative "singularity," and, if so, it is a remarkable instance of God's creative working. However, process theologians remain more interested in God's universal creative activity than in what happened fifteen to twenty billion years ago.

This universal creative activity cannot be sharply distinguished from redemption. When creatures allow it to be effective, it is the transformation of what has been into that which now can be. There are many times and places where the possibilities are extremely limited, but over the ages, the transformation brings into being creatures who are capable of much greater richness of experience. The process of transformation works in them what is at once new creation and redemption. The redeeming work in and through Jesus Christ is historically unique in its character and it is continuous with what happens elsewhere.

One effect of this creative and redemptive working is the assurance of being loved and affirmed by God. This assurance opens us to being transformed in new ways. This may be called sanctification. However, the process of sanctification is not discontinuous with the creative and redemptive transformation worked elsewhere. We may, of course, focus on the distinctions between what God does everywhere, what God does in Jesus, and what God does among those who believe in Jesus. Given the continuity of all of this activity of God, however, there can be no movement from this economic trinity to an immanent one. If the proponent of this type of trinitarian doctrine does not care about an immanent trinity, then this is no objection. However, the great gap between the resultant position and the classical doctrines should be acknowledged.

We could argue that the development of traditional doctrine itself justifies this indifference to the immanent trinity. The ancient church, despite its emphasis on the distinctions among the three persons, also asserted that all three divine persons are involved in all *ad extra* acts of God except the incarnation. Although creation is the act most commonly associated with the first person, the second and third persons are also understood to be involved. Even if the point is arbitrarily maintained that only the second person is incarnate in Jesus, the first and third persons are involved in redemption. Moreover, certainly all three persons are involved in sanctification.

This doctrine weakens every attempt to establish a close connection between an economic trinity and an immanent one. If we argue that it implies that only the economic trinity matters, then we can connect the modern functional trinity to the ancient doctrine. Nevertheless, the tradition never drew this conclusion. Indeed, the doctrine of the trinity was primarily the doctrine of the immanent trinity. If we cannot move from a distinction of three functions of God in the world to some underlying distinctions in God, the distinction of the functions hardly counts as a trinity at all.

• 6 •

Should we, then, simply reject trinitarian thought and affirm a unitarian view? Certainly we should affirm the unitarian emphasis on the unity of God, but there is a danger in emphasizing only that.

Monotheism, when unqualified, tends to present us with a transcendent supernatural being who is externally related to the world. Juergen Moltmann has shown the close connection between this kind of monotheism and a monarchical view that is remote from the New Testament and has supported authoritarian styles in church and society.

Monotheism in this monarchical sense is quite opposite to process theology. To whatever extent trinitarian thought has modified this monolithic, authoritarian view, it is to be strongly affirmed. Hence, there are good reasons for process theologians to share in making proposals about how to think of God as trinity. At the same time, it is important to repeat that such proposals are not to be viewed as true and false but, rather, as more or less successful in performing the roles that trinitarian doctrine may help theology perform. Accordingly, I offer two proposals, the first, following immediately, and the second, more briefly, thereafter.

Process theology affirms that God is truly immanent or incarnate in the world. God, like everything else that participates in constituting creaturely events, is also transcendent. That is, God is not exhausted by God's immanence in any event or in all creaturely events together. We can, therefore, distinguish God in God's transcendence and God in God's immanence in this world. The difference is real. But one is not more God than the other.

This distinction can provide us with a Binity that is real both ontologically in terms of the nature of God and experientially in terms of how God is known by human beings. This double reality is analogous to that of the trinity when it is understood as both immanent (characterizing God's own being) and economic (operative in the world). In the case of this binity, the distinction between what God is from the divine point of view and how God is found in the constitution of the world is real in itself. It is like the economic trinity in the sense that encountering God as an Other and discovering God within ourselves are phenomenologically and existentially different. Like this traditional doctrine of the trinity, this doctrine of divine binity is the insistence that despite both the ontological and the experiential differences, there is only one God, that the God who is within is no less God than the God who is beyond.

I believe that this binitarian doctrine is more important than trinitarian doctrine. Nevertheless, it does not exclude a trinity. An authentic trinitarian formulation would follow if we can identify a distinction in the ways that God works in the world that points to, or stems from, a distinction within the divine life.

I have argued above, from the perspective of process theology, that the distinction between creation, redemption, and sanctification does not express an immanent differentiation within God. However, there are other ways of differentiating God's working in the world. Is there any distinction made in the Bible that implies a difference either in the way God is present or in the element of the divine life that is present?

The most promising candidate for a distinct mode of God's working is to be found in Paul's treatment of spiritual gifts. The distinction between the charismatic gifts and experiences of which Paul speaks and the ordinary creative, redemptive, and sanctifying work of God was recognized by Paul. It proved to be of great importance in the life of the early church.

Furthermore, the revival of interest in spiritual gifts in the twentieth century has had enormous historical consequences. The charismatic movement has influenced most of the oldline churches. It has also generated new denominations. A major task for the church in the twenty-first century will be to heal the rift between the declining oldline churches in which spiritual gifts play little role and the growing Pentecostal churches in which they are emphasized. Trinitarian reflection relevant to this task is authentic theology.

Spiritual gifts appear to be "paranormal." That is, they are somewhat discontinuous with that universal, transformative working of God in the world that is creative, redemptive, and sanctifying. They are not essential to the Christian life, and Paul warned against giving them too high a priority. But Paul certainly did not oppose them or minimize them. They include spiritual healing, working miracles, prophecy, distinguishing spirits, ecstatic speaking, and the interpretation of ecstatic speaking (I Cor 12). Paul never questioned their occurrence in his congregations or their genuineness.

What difference might there be in the way in which God works in these paranormal cases and the way God is present everywhere? In Paul's writings, the answer seems to be that God gives special capacities and experiences to different members of the Christian community. The question for me is whether Whitehead offers us a way to think of God's acting in human life other than the one that has been in view thus far that might illumine paranormal religious experience.

At the very end of *Process and Reality*, Whitehead proffers a suggestion with little explanation or development. I must take full responsibility for my speculations as they take off from his comments and seek to make contact with Paul's discussion of spiritual gifts as well as their role in church history. My intention is to be consistent with what little Whitehead says and likewise be relevant to the actual phenomena.

Whitehead speaks of a fourth phase in the cosmic process in which the Consequent Nature of God "passes back into the temporal world and qualifies this world so that each temporal actuality includes it as an immediate fact of relevant experience." It is "the particular providence for particular occasions" (*Process and Reality* 351).

Process and Reality as a whole was written without this phase of cosmic process clearly in view. The role of God in the world throughout the book is primarily that of the Primordial Nature. This provides both the novel order and the ordered novelty, which move the world toward more complex and richer patterns. As we analyze how this works in theological language, we can speak of creation, redemption, and sanctification as human beings open themselves to the lure of God and allow it to work within them. The process formulation of these functions of God in the preceding section can be understood without reference to the fourth phase.

There are serious problems with introducing the fourth phase into theology. There are practical problems in the church, because the particular providence has often been appealed to as justification for many actions on the part of believers that are disruptive of the healthy life of the church. The early church decided for institutional order rather than charismatic authority for reasons that deserve our sympathy. The oldline churches have, for similar reasons, been inhospitable to the twentieth century charismatic movement.

There are also theological problems to which Donald Sherburne, among others, has called attention.[4] If, in Whiteheadian terms, an individual prehends God's Consequent Nature, and if this includes knowledge that is not accessible through prehensions of past occasions, then we can explain apparent cases of paranormal knowledge. Or, if we do not go this far, but think only of the initial aim as derived, in part, from the Consequent Nature, then what God calls for in each moment will take account of events of which we are otherwise unaware. This would explain some rare instances in which people seem to act rightly without knowing the reasons for so acting, but it would leave us perplexed by the large number of instances in which it seems God could have guided us away from unknown dangers or into response to the unknown needs of a friend and, apparently, has not done so. The problem of theodicy that seems otherwise greatly reduced for Whiteheadians would be exacerbated.

In addition, there are philosophical problems internal to Whitehead. As presented, the fourth phase seems to be quite distinct from the influence of the Primordial Nature in the world, identified as the second phase. That would mean, in technical terms, that creatures had two separate prehensions of God, one of God's conceptual feelings and one of God's physical or propositional feelings. This seems to be in conflict with Whitehead's general position that each entity in an occasion's actual world is felt in a single complex but consistent way.

We can avoid many problems by ignoring or denying the paranormal elements in the relation of God to human beings. This would be continuous with most practice in the oldline churches. It is made easier by the obvious exaggeration and confusion in the claims made for spiritual gifts. Nevertheless, the price has been high. One reason for the decline of the oldline churches is that they have largely excluded the richness of experience and the intensity of feeling to which the paranormal contributes.

More broadly, the culture as a whole has suffered by its exclusion of the paranormal in general. As David Griffin has shown, the denial of action at a distance associated with mechanical models has truncated scientific explanation on the one hand and suppressed much real human experience on the other. It has contributed to destructive forms of dualism. It still blinds the dominant culture to much that is genuinely occurring within it and drives those who know of these occurrences to suppose they belong to a sphere separate from ordinary experience. Griffin has shown that Whitehead's conceptuality can overcome these problems.

To do so requires the affirmation of some kind of action at a distance, a doctrine to which Whitehead's conceptuality is open. This makes it possible to understand how emotions, or even thoughts, in one psyche can affect emotions or thoughts in another. The problem then arises: Why are most of us most of the time unaware of the content of other psyches in this way? In other words, the problem is no longer to explain remarkable instances of mental telepathy. The problem is to explain why vivid instances are so rare.

The explanation can be developed along the lines in which we explain musical genius. All of us have some capacity for music, but there are genetic differences that affect the extent of this capacity. Whatever the capacity, a great difference is made by good teaching and extensive practice. The combination of differences in genetic gifts, environmental support, and personal commitments lead to an enormous range in performance.

Similarly, it may be that all of us are somewhat affected by events at a distance. However, some are genetically more sensitive to these events than others are. The encouragement to develop this sensitivity varies greatly, and so does the amount of time and effort given to its cultivation. This results in enormous differences in the ability to discern particular features in the distant environment.

The implication of this account is that there is a discontinuity between "action at a distance" and the effects of contiguous events. In technical Whiteheadian language, the former are instances of hybrid physical feelings; whereas, pure physical feelings connect an occasion immediately only to contiguous occasions. Both are present in all. Whereas the latter are a prominent, even dominant, feature of all experience, hybrid feelings of remote occasions may be peripheral for most people most of the time and never enter clear consciousness for them. The possibility of their playing a significant role in conscious experience is much greater in some people than in others.

Although some people are remarkably gifted along these lines, it is important to recognize that they are not infallible. Even for the most gifted, the clarity of knowledge gained in this way does not match that of ordinary sensory experience. Discrimination of what is actually being felt at a distance from all the other elements in the psychic life is far from perfect. Error is extensive and pervasive.

Ecstatic religious experience, or gifts of the Spirit, seem to introduce a similar distinction with respect to the experience of God. In addition to the universal or creative activity directed toward attaining what value is possible in each moment, there is also a "particular providence for particular occasions." Both affect every occasion, but, for the most part, the effects of the latter are peripheral and vague. One may be somewhat conscious of what Whitehead called a rightness in things partly conformed to and partly disregarded (Process and Reality 66) or what Heidegger identified as the call forward (*Vorrufen, Sein und Zeit* 290). These express a dim awareness of the immanence of the Primordial Nature. Most people, on the other hand, may never be conscious of their prehension of the Consequent Nature of God.

There are, however, a variety of religious experiences that are best explained by reference to this nature. The belief that we are accepted and affirmed by God does not depend on this experience, but to whatever extent this is an experience as well as a belief based on indirect evidence, the prehension of the Consequent Nature is involved. This is true of the sense of the divine presence in general.

The most important question is whether the derivation of the initial aim of each occasion involves the Consequent Nature. Whitehead does not say, and it is very doubtful that he had this in view in most of his writing. Nevertheless, it is hard to understand the particular providence for particular occasions in any other way. Also, systematically to assert that both the Primordial Nature and the Consequent Nature are involved in an integrated way fits the overall conceptual scheme. Now, the question is what difference this makes in the understanding of the initial aim.

If the Consequent Nature is involved, then, in principle, we should assume that the aim is affected by a knowledge of what is happening in the world not otherwise available to the occasion. If a landslide is developing on the road ahead, but the driver has no normal way of knowing of this, the initial aim might, nevertheless, call her to stop the car rather than proceed. If a friend needs one's help urgently, but one has no normal way of knowing this, the initial aim might, nevertheless, prompt one to telephone. In contrast, if the Consequent Nature is not involved, the ordering of possibility in the Primordial Nature would not involve the relevance of events not otherwise accessible to the occasion.

There are numerous accounts of guidance that suggest precisely this kind of working of particular providence. The problem, already noted, is that there are far more cases when admirable and devout people are totally unaware of any such guidance. Does this mean that God plays favorites or is capricious? Or should we blame those who do not receive this guidance for being insufficiently spiritual?

If sensitivity to the particularity of the aim is analogous to sensitivity to noncontiguous events, we may be able to understand what happens without being forced to answer either of these questions in the affirmative. It may be that the Consequent Nature does affect the initial aim in all cases, but that people differ greatly with regard to sensitivity to it. This difference may be partly genetic. It may be that environment also affects the extent to which there will be attention to the cultivation of whatever sensitivity there is. It may also be that personal discipline plays a role as well as what is occurring in an individual's life at the precise moment.

Whatever the factors that lead a few to be dramatically affected by this unusual type of guidance, the primary consequence of the role of the Consequent Nature is not of this dramatic sort. Its involvement does imply a much more pervasive sense that as we are sensitively responsive in each moment, we may be formed by a wisdom that is greater than our own. Looking back, we may see something at work in our lives of which we were unaware at the time. We may express gratitude to God for leading us in ways that at the time we did not understand. We may perceive God's guidance more reliably over such periods of time than when we try consciously to identify it in a single moment.

I do not attempt to give an account of the still more dramatic instances of spiritual gifts. It is my assumption that, insofar as they are authentic, they are continuous with those of which I have been speaking. The physical feeling of God's physical pole, including elements in God's experience not otherwise accessible, is relevant to explaining at least some of the ecstatic phenomena associated with the Spirit.

My interest here is not to make a case for the authenticity of one or another supposed gift of the Spirit. My interest is only to show that there is a range of religious phenomena that, from a Whiteheadian point of view, is best explained in terms of what Whitehead calls the fourth phase of the cosmic process, the flooding of the Consequent Nature back into the world. Thus, there is a distinct element in religious experience that correlates with a distinct "nature" of God. The difference here is both economic and immanent.

I have focused on the more extravagant "gifts of the Spirit" in order to indicate the discontinuity with that part of experience of

God that is understandable without appeal to the Consequent Nature. However, once we have introduced discussion of the Consequent Nature, we can see that it colors all of our experience of God. It is at work also in the less spectacular process that forms the fruits of the Spirit. Indeed, it is present in that process that brings life out of the inanimate world.

In the discussion above, we noted that action at a distance and the efficacy of contiguous events are both present in every occasion. We did not note that the hybrid feelings that allow for action at a distance also operate in the prehension of contiguous occasions. In a similar way here we can say that both the Primordial Nature and the Consequent Nature participate in constituting every occasion, and that the work of the Consequent Nature is far from limited to paranormal experience.

Just as, in the discussion above, we noted that, especially for conscious experience, the perception of noncontiguous events is usually negligible; so here we may assert that the prehension of the Consequent Nature is usually negligible as far as conscious awareness is concerned. But also, just as affirmation of the reality of action at a distance allows explanation of much that is otherwise denied or placed in the category of sheer mystery, so also affirmation of the reality of the role of the Consequent Nature allows us to explain extraordinary types of religious experience that are otherwise ignored or else elevated to supernatural status. At the same time, just as the authentic elements in parapsychological phenomena are difficult to distinguish from confusion and self-deception, so also the authentic elements in ecstatic religious phenomena are hard to distinguish from the many that can better be understood as delusory.

I launched on this inquiry to supplement the binity of God as transcendent and God as immanent with a distinction in the ways God is immanent. I had already discussed at length the way God works always and everywhere, transformatively, in the world. I had interpreted creation, redemption, and sanctification as expressions of this work. All of this can be understood in terms of the presence of the Primordial Nature in the world. We can think of this, in traditional terms, as the Logos or the Word. Whitehead, in *Adventures of Ideas*, calls it Eros.

To point to a different mode of God's activity in the world, I turned to the ecstatic, the "gifts of the Spirit." Here the term Holy Spirit is clearly appropriate. I then argued that the Spirit that is dramatically present in these gifts is also pervasively present throughout. It, too, is present in the creative, redemptive, and especially the sanctifying work of God. Love, joy, and peace are fruits of the same Spirit as glossolalia and prophecy and spiritual healing, although, in these cases, the role of the Primordial Nature is more prominent.

Much can be affirmed with this doctrine of the trinity that is continuous with traditional trinitarian theology. It allows us to say that all the "persons" are acting in all *ad extra* work of the trinity, while distinguishing their contributions. It corresponds to much of the biblical language and also to that of Christian worship. It offers a generally satisfactory way of organizing what we need to say of God and God's activity in the world.

On the other hand, this formulation differs from most of the tradition in important ways. It does not allow us to exclude the Spirit from incarnation in Jesus. It distinguishes the Word and the Spirit in a way that is different from the way it distinguishes them jointly from the Father. It offers little basis for such language as begetting and proceeding in the distinction of the "Persons."

• 7 •

However much can be said in favor of this formulation of the trinity, it is, emphatically, not the only way to make theologically significant distinctions in God. Other Biblical language can be used that draws the lines differently with equal justification. Consider, for example, Sophia or Wisdom, a topic of current importance. Is it really appropriate first to develop a doctrine of the trinity leaving Wisdom out and then try to fit it into one of the established slots? Considering that the Bible has more to say about the Wisdom of God than about either the Word or the Spirit, this approach must be seen as brought about by contingent, historical developments that are not normative for us. If we do try to make Wisdom fit, I suggest that She transcends and subsumes the labored distinction between Word and Spirit. It is, then, quite simply, Wisdom that names the creative, redemptive, and sanctifying work of God in the world. It is Wisdom that is incarnate in Jesus. If we are still driven to make further distinctions, we could work with Paul's language of the Wisdom and the Power of God.

In terms of current issues, we could approach God with the distinction of God's masculine and feminine attributes as an organizing principle of our thought. Or we could distinguish what is impersonal in God from what is personal. We can analyze our doctrine of God into three elements as has been traditionally done, or into two. We could also use a fourfold distinction as one text in Whitehead suggests: The Primordial Nature, the Superject of the Primordial Nature, the Consequent Nature, and the Superject of the Consequent Nature.[5] This could be translated easily into theological language. We could then, if we wished, add a fifth name for what unites all these.

My point in these comments is not to favor a binity, a quaternity, or quintity. It is only, again, to relativize the threeness of God. The absolutization of this threeness is not biblical. Christian experience does not require it. Commitment to threeness distracts from truly important theological questions and it has led to a great deal of obscurantism. When trinitarian thought of one sort or another is recognized to be a good way of organizing our thought about God, corresponding to real distinctions within God, the trinity plays an eminently positive role in Christian theology. As long as the "doctrine of the trinity" asserts only this, it can be an admirable doctrine.

This attitude leaves open the continuing work of seeking trinitarian language that is not patriarchal. I have indicated my judgment that the substitution of Creator, Redeemer, and Sanctifier does not work well. I have mentioned the extensive role of Wisdom in the Bible and the appropriateness of identifying Wisdom as the divine that is incarnate in Jesus as well as the divine immanence as a whole. If trinity is important for traditional reasons, we could build a nonpatriarchal trinity around Her.

God as originative source we might identify as Mother/Father; God as immanent, as the Wisdom of God; and God as our loving companion, receptive of all that we do, as the Compassion of God. In Whiteheadian terms, this would pair off with the Primordial Nature, the union of the second and fourth phases of the cosmic process, and the Consequent Nature. Reflection about God and God's relation to the world could be organized fruitfully in this way as well.

Again, my concern is not to argue strongly for one trinity or another. My concern is to recognize the usefulness and authenticity of threefold formulations of what we experience and know of

God alongside others, while showing that more than one such formulation is possible. Which formulation is best for us now is a topic for discussion and debate.

One part of the discussion should be its relevance to what God is really like. Another part should be its continuity with biblical and liturgical language. Still another, and perhaps most important of all, is how the proposed language affects those who use it. My interest is not to announce the conclusion to which I hope such a discussion would lead. It is to open up the most honest discussion possible of all of these matters. Where that will lead is less important than the process of getting there and the tentative spirit in which any conclusion is adopted.

NOTES

1. I learned the importance of the difference between East and West in this regard chiefly from Lynn Lorenzen for whom it functioned as a central principle in the organization of her dissertation, "The Trinity Reauthenticated" (Claremont Graduate School, 1994). Working with her on this dissertation renewed my interest in the Trinity and led to my agreement to write for this volume.

2. See Joseph A. Bracken, *The Triune Symbol: Persons, Process and Community* (Lanham, MD: University Press of America, 1985); and *Society and Spirit: A Trinitarian Cosmology* (Cranbury, NJ: Associated University Presses, 1991).

3. See Juergen Moltmann, *The Trinity and the Kingdom*, Margaret Kohl, trans. (San Francisco: Harper & Row, 1981).

4. See Donald W. Sherburne, "Decentering Whitehead," *Process Studies* 15 (2): 83–94.

5. See *Process and Reality*, 32. Here Whitehead distinguishes the objective immortality of the Primordial Nature and the objective immortality of the Consequent Nature. I take it that objective immortality is equivalent to, or at least entails, what Whitehead elsewhere calls the Superjective Nature.

David Ray Griffin
A Naturalistic Trinity

In this essay, I discuss the notion of God as trinitarian from the perspective of the contrast between supernaturalistic and naturalistic theism. By "supernaturalistic theism" I mean the doctrine that, because God created the world *ex nihilo*, or out of absolute nothingness in the sense of a complete absence of finite existents, God can completely determine the events in the world. In the traditional version of this supernaturalism, held by most theologians from Augustine to Calvin, God did, in fact, completely determine all events in the world, including the movements within the sinner's soul. In more recent times, many supernaturalists have held that God, after creating the world and imposing a system of "natural laws" upon it, allows events, at least for the most part, to unfold as they will. The idea that there is some freedom from God's (potentially) all-determining power is especially applied at the human level. God is said to have voluntarily limited the divine power in order to allow human beings to be genuinely free. By retaining the traditional doctrine of divine omnipotence, however, these theologians imply, and sometimes explicitly assert, that God can intervene in the world now and then, interrupting the normal cause–effect of relations in order to bring about some event unilaterally. One problem with both of these versions of supernaturalistic theism, I have argued at considerable length, is that they create an insoluble problem of evil, making it impossible to reconcile belief in the divine goodness with the world's evil in a plausible way.[1]

The crucial presupposition of this supernaturalistic version of theism is the traditional (albeit nonbiblical) doctrine of *creatio ex nihilo*, according to which what exists necessarily is simply God, so the fact that God is now related to a realm of finite, nondivine entities is due entirely to the divine will. This doctrine was adopted over against the Platonic and biblical doctrine of creation

out of chaos—the view that our particular world was created by
bringing its type of order out of a chaotic realm of finite existents.
That Platonic–biblical doctrine would suggest that although our
particular world exists contingently, because of a divine decision,
*it embodies causal powers and principles that are inherent in the
very nature of things and thereby not overridable, even by God.*
The rejection of this idea was the most important and fateful implication of the decision by traditional Christian theologians to affirm
the doctrine of *creatio ex nihilo.*

A naturalistic theism, by contrast, affirms the Platonic-biblical
view. It holds that God is related to the universe, in the sense of a
realm of finite existents, naturally, not merely voluntarily. What
exists necessarily and, thereby, naturally is not simply God, but
God-in-relation-to-a-universe. God is essentially not a Solitary
One, but Soul of the Universe. God does not, accordingly, essentially have a monopoly on power, because power is also inherent
in the realm of finitude. Although what we normally call "the laws
of nature" are fully contingent, with the most basic of them (the
laws of physics) having been chosen by God at the creation of our
particular universe (perhaps some 15 billion years ago), these laws
reflect more basic causal principles that obtain necessarily. In the
version of naturalistic theism that I hold, which is based on the
philosophy of Alfred North Whitehead, these underlying causal
principles include the notion that each unitary event has the
twofold power to exercise some degree of self-determination and
to exert causal influence upon subsequent events. Because this
twofold power of worldly events lies in the very nature of things,
it cannot—supernaturalistic theists to the contrary—be overridden
or interrupted by God. God cannot create a universe such as ours
instantaneously, unilaterally prevent evil events, infallibly reveal
divine truths, or inerrantly inspire sacred scripture.

To call this version of theism "naturalistic," it should be clear,
does not mean that our particular world was not freely created. It
does not mean that God is not distinct from the world. It does not
mean that God is not a conscious, personal, purposive Being. And
it does not mean that God does not influence the world; indeed,
in the version I hold, God, being omnipresent, directly influences
every event in the universe. All that the word "naturalistic" denies
is supernaturalism, understood as the doctrine that God, by virtue
of essentially having a monopoly on power, can act coercively;
that is, can unilaterally determine events in the world. This denial

is expressed in Whiteheadian theism with the distinction between God and creativity, with "creativity" understood as the aforementioned twofold power of self-determination and causal influence. This version of theism holds that this twofold creative power is eternally embodied not simply by God alone, but by God and a universe of finite events. This means that God necessarily always acts persuasively, never coercively.

Given this distinction between the supernaturalistic and naturalistic versions of theism, we can entertain the possibility that the manifold reasons that have brought trinitarianism into disrepute may have resulted less from the idea that God is threefold than from the form this idea took in a supernaturalistic context.

Accordingly, in developing a naturalistic trinity, I begin with two versions of economic trinitarianism. The temporal economic trinity refers to God's activity at the beginning, middle, and end of the world. The epistemic economic trinity refers to three ways in which God is known to us: through the creation, through the revelation of the biblical tradition and especially Jesus, and through our direct experience. After that, I move to a discussion of the immanent trinity.

1.   NATURALISTIC THEISM AND THE TEMPORAL TRINITY

The temporal trinity can be formulated in terms of God as Creator, Revealer–Redeemer, and Consummator. What has this to do with naturalistic theism, the essential idea of which is that God works in only one way in the world, the way of persuasion? It could have everything to do with it. The ideas that all three *personae*, or aspects, of the trinity are equally divine, that they are really one, and that the trinitarian God has been especially revealed in Jesus of Nazareth, could be taken to mean: The way God acted in Jesus is the way God has acted in creating the world and the way God will act in sanctifying the world and bringing it to consummation.

What notion do we get of the divine modus operandi if we take Jesus not only as a special instance of God's saving activity but also and thereby as a special revelation of the divine modus operandi in general? On one reading of Jesus's life, at the center of Jesus's preaching of the kingdom of God was the message and example of nonretaliatory, suffering love. Only by loving your enemies, forgiving them, returning good for evil, can you imitate

the nondiscriminating love of your heavenly Father. Jesus' suffering on the cross, with the prayer of forgiveness to those who crucified him, was the final and ultimate expression of his living out
of the message he preached. The early Christians saw themselves
as called to imitate Jesus in one and only one way: to follow the
way of the cross while proclaiming the love of God. One is to follow the way of love, the way that relies upon the persuasive
power of preaching and example, and when necessary is willing
to suffer and die.

One stimulus for the formulation of the doctrine of the trinity
was the rejection of Marcionite and Gnostic dualisms, according to
which the creator of heaven and earth, spoken of in the Jewish
Scriptures, was not the God and Father of Jesus. Another stimulus
was the rejection of Arianism, according to which the Divine
Being itself was not incarnate in Jesus, because Jesus obviously
suffered; whereas, the Divinity (Arius held) could not suffer. If
these dualisms are rejected, so that the Holy One who created the
universe also is held to have acted in an especially redemptive and
self-revealing way in Jesus of Nazareth, then it would seem that
we should regard the world as having been created through the
power of persuasive-suffering love. Furthermore, the application
of this idea of divinity to the consummation of the world would
have meant that the ultimate victory of God's reign over the forces
of evil would be attained by this same method, that of persuasive
and suffering love. In this way, the doctrine of the economic trinity would have been a way of formulating naturalistic theism.
Whether we talk of God's activity in creating, sustaining, revealing,
redeeming, sanctifying, or consummating, God always acts in one
and the same way, a way that no more coercively violates the
power or freedom of the creatures than Jesus' activity violated the
freedom of His hearers.

Further support for the notion that God's activity in the creatures is in no way a supernatural, unilateral incursion into the
world, but a fully natural part of what is going on all the time,
could be drawn from the associated doctrine that God's incarnating activity in Jesus did not violate Jesus' freedom or full humanity, but depended upon his free human response, and, in fact,
resulted in his being more rather than less free and human. If in
this special instance the divine's incarnating activity does not
destroy the integrity and freedom of the one in whom it is incarnate, this would surely be true of all other instances of divine

incarnating activity. And if this special act of the trinitarian God, through which the nature of God is revealed, is an act of incarnation, then God's creating and consummating activities must also be acts of incarnation. Accordingly, the doctrine of the trinity, along with the associated doctrine of the incarnation of this trinitarian God in Jesus, would support naturalistic theism. God always and everywhere works persuasively, by becoming incarnate to some degree in the creatures, this degree depending upon the free response of the creatures.

2.   SUPERNATURALISM AND THE TEMPORAL TRINITY

The above development, of course, is not what happened, especially in Western Christianity. To the extent that God was regarded as working persuasively in Jesus, this modus operandi was regarded as an exception, not the chief exemplification, of the general rule. God in creating the universe was not understood as working persuasively; the Platonic doctrine that God persuasively brought order out of a realm of chaos was explicitly rejected. God was said to have created the world *ex nihilo*, with the *nihil* interpreted in such a way as to make clear that the world had no power of its own with which it could resist God's subsequent control of it. God's creative and providential activity was understood as unilateral control, not persuasion, as the creatures had no inherent power vis-à-vis God.

The reverse side of this view was the denial that God's relation to the world involved any suffering on God's part. How could it, if the creatures had no power vis-à-vis God by which they could initiate any activity? Far from taking Jesus' suffering as a revelation of the deepest truth about divine power, these theologians explicitly denied that when Jesus died on the cross, God the Father suffered. To have said such a thing would have been to commit the heresy of "Patripassianism." One of the original motivations for the doctrine of the trinity was, in fact, to guard against this heresy: Before it had been agreed that the Logos or Son, which was incarnate in Jesus, was of the same stuff as ("consubstantial with") the Father, the distinction between the Father and the Son or Logos was thought helpful to explain how Jesus could have suffered and yet been the incarnation of a divine being or element. However, after the Council of Nicaea in 325 declared against Arianism that

the Logos was *homoousion* with (of the same essence as) the
Father, but without rejecting Arius' nonbiblical view that divinity
cannot suffer, it was necessary to distinguish within Jesus between
that which was divine in him (the second person of the trinity) and
that which was merely human. All the suffering was, of course,
assigned to the merely human part. Jesus' death on the cross was
no longer taken as a revelation of a deep truth about the very
nature of the divine reality of the universe and how it saves and
acts in general.

Neither Jesus' persuasive activity, of preaching and offering
himself as an example, nor his suffering, accordingly, was taken as
a revelation of the way in which God creates and sustains the universe. The way of persuasion and suffering is for mere creatures; the
creator of heaven and earth—the Lord of Hosts is his name!—has
quite another modus operandi, a way free from the need to wait for
a response from the other, and certainly free from all suffering.

The divine side of Jesus' nature—or rather, the divine nature
of Jesus, for he was said to embody two natures in one unified
person—was assigned its paradigmatic exemplifications in accord
with this notion of divine action. Not his preaching, in which he
sought to persuade others to follow his vision of the divine purpose, but his performance of miracles, in which he was thought to
coerce the forces of nature, was taken to be the sign that he was
the Son of God. The ultimate revelation of his divinity was taken
to be not his crucifixion, in which he willingly suffered because of
the sins of others and advocated forgiveness rather than retalia-
tion, but his being raised from the dead, which was taken as the
miracle *par excellence*. (I have heard supernaturalist defenders of
divine omnipotence argue that God could have stopped Hitler's
tanks and bombs, because, if God raised Jesus from the dead, God
can do anything!) To these miracles in the middle and end of his
ministry was added the miraculous beginning, the virgin birth.

By focusing on these elements, supernaturalistic theology
lifted Jesus out of the stream of humanity. Although the Council of
Chalcedon insisted that it protected Jesus' full humanity, it did not:
It said that God's presence in Jesus was ontologically different
from God's presence in the rest of us. Because Jesus was not
essentially like the rest of us, the main point of his life could not
be exemplary. Faith in Jesus as the Son of God and God's Christ
came to mean not the *imitatio Christi*, following the way of the
cross, but believing and existentially appropriating the fact that

Jesus had done for us what we could not do for ourselves. Any suggestion that salvation involved following Jesus' own way, thereby putting into practice the sermon on the mount, was branded as heretical (Pelagianism, "works righteousness"), on the grounds that this would involve trusting in our own power rather than gratefully accepting the salvation that God had already uni-laterally provided for us. The cross is not an example and symbol of the way God works through each of us to bring about our sal-vation, but a unique, once-for-all act in which God achieved our salvation unilaterally, outside of us.

The doctrine of the trinity was used to support this view of Jesus as the great exception to—not the chief exemplification of—the way in which God normally acts in the world. The notion that Jesus was not essentially different from God's other prophets in regard to God's presence in him was rejected as the heresy of "Ebionism." Against Ebionism, the orthodox asserted that God was not present in Jesus only in the way God had been present in the prophets, that is, as Holy Spirit, but uniquely: Only in Jesus was God present as Word (*Logos*), as eternally begotten Son. The traditional trinity, hence, in no way supported a naturalistic the-ism, according to which God's incarnating activity in Jesus would be paradigmatic for God's universal modus operandi, a mode that is not incompatible with the freedom and causal powers of the creatures.

Even many modern liberal Christologies retain the notion that God's essential way of acting in the world is essentially different from what one would gather from taking Jesus's life as the best clue to this modus operandi. They deny that Jesus manifested any supernatural powers, such as performing miracles or being omni-scient. But they say that the incarnation involved a "kenosis," or self-emptying. The biblical basis for this doctrine is the hymn in Philippians 2:5–11, which says that Jesus, "though he was in the form of God, . . . emptied himself, taking the form of a servant, being born in the likeness of men." The modern kenotic theolo-gians take this to mean that Jesus was the incarnation of the sec-ond person of the trinity, but that the incarnation meant temporarily giving up divine powers. The nature of deity, there-fore, is really hidden in Jesus' life and death, not revealed; we have to learn from some other source the kind of power God has. This kenotic theology thereby provides a further example of the fact that traditional trinitarianism has been supernaturalistic.

The main question in this essay is whether we can understand the doctrine of the trinity as a way of formulating a naturalistic theism according to which God exclusively uses the way of persuasion at the beginning, middle, and end. We have thus far seen that traditional theism was supernaturalistic in regard to God's activity both as creator and Redeemer–Revealer. The same is true of its view of God's activity as consummator. Indeed, it has been God's expected eschatological activity that has been preeminently pictured in supernatural, coercive, and even violent terms. In comparison with it, in fact, God's activity in Jesus has been seen as primarily persuasive. The miracles involved coercion, to be sure, but primarily coercion of physical nature. Their effect upon the human audience was a form of persuasion: People had freedom to decide what to think of the miracles and their agent, and how to respond to his message. Although those trying to find a precedent for war in Jesus' own activity have pointed to his use of a reed whip in cleansing the temple, even the strongest advocates of just-war theory, nuclear deterrence, and Armageddon theology have granted that God's method of acting in Jesus was primarily persuasive. But, they say, that was only a temporary strategy. Jesus said that we should forgive seventy times seventy. Whereas many have interpreted this to mean that we should forgive indefinitely, forever, and that in so doing we would be imitating God's endlessly patient love, supernaturalist theology has said that God's forgiving patience runs out. As Billy Graham put it in *World Aflame*: "God has offered his love and mercy and forgiveness to men. . . . However, when that love is deliberately rejected, the only alternative is judgment."[2]

Supernaturalism has said, in effect, that the method of suffering love is not God's only or even primary method for overcoming evil. Jesus died softly on the cross, but he held a big stick in reserve. As one author put it in a critique of pacifist theology: Christ may have acted nonviolently during his life, but "Jesus will at the end bring all criminals (sinners) to judgment by violent means (overthrowing the armies of the Antichrist by force and casting sinners into hell).[3] As a book entitled *Armageddon* puts it:

> In His first coming to earth, Jesus Christ was born in a stable . . . in a time of comparative peace. . . . The second coming of Jesus Christ to earth will be no quiet manger scene. It will be the most dramatic and shattering event in the entire history of the universe. . . . Cities

will literally collapse, islands sink, and mountains disappear. Huge hailstones, each weighing a hundred pounds, will fall from heaven. . . . The rulers and their armies who resist Christ's return will be killed in a mass carnage."[4]

No more Mister Nice Guy!

Although Jesus had said that we should abstain from revenge in order to be like God (Matthew 5:44–48), Paul explained that it was because vengeance belonged to God alone (Romans 12:19). The supernaturalistic Christian consciousness has understood this to refer primarily to God's defeat of evil by destroying the evildoers at the end of history. Many modern theologians, of course, do not take these apocalyptic pictures literally. And yet, the dualism between the modus operandi of Jesus and that of God the Father has ingrained in the Christian mind, especially in the West, the idea that evil can only be overcome, or at least contained, by the threat and occasional use of coercive violence, and that persuasive love will never overcome it. For example, Reinhold Niebuhr, himself no supernaturalist, uses for antipacifist purposes the imagery of the Antichrist at the end of history as symbolic of the truth that human evil will not be overcome in history but will, in fact, accumulate.[5] Likewise, William Temple, in his justification of war, claimed that God had two modes of dealing with the world. The method of love supplements, rather than abolishes, the method aimed at establishing justice and law, and those who will not acknowledge love must be treated according to the other method.[6]

Not only the defeat of evil was seen as requiring supernatural power. The same was true to an extent of the final salvation of the righteous. Just as Jesus' resurrection was taken as the ultimate supernatural stamp of approval upon his life, so our own resurrection from the dead would require supernatural agency. Those who have stressed that the biblical doctrine is resurrection of the body, not immortality of the soul, have done so in part to stress that continued life after bodily death is not a natural power of the soul but depends upon God's supernatural act.

God's consummatory activity in bringing the world to its goal, like God's creative activity in bringing the world into existence, has neither been understood in terms of persuasive-suffering love nor as a process essentially continuous with our present way of being influenced by God. Insofar as the three-foldness of God's activity in the world has been understood as the temporal threefoldness of beginning, middle, and end, it has reflected and supported a supernaturalistic understanding of divine activity. The fullness of the divine power may be quiescent now, says this supernaturalism. In the end God, however, will step in with that omnipotent power with which he created all things in the beginning.

3. THE EPISTEMIC TRINITY AND NATURALISTIC THEISM

Understanding the economic trinity in temporal terms is supported by the anti-Marcionite affirmation that the Redeemer God of the New Testament is the God of the Old Testament who created the world and gave the law, and also by later doctrines that construed the world in terms of the ages of the Father, the Son, and the Holy Spirit. However, the idea of God's threefold manifestation in the world was probably understood originally more as an epistemic than as a temporal threefoldness. The language of "Father, Son, and Holy Spirit" certainly fits three temporal periods less naturally than it does three ways of knowing God: through nature, through historical events, and through immediate experience. How could a trinitarian understanding of God in this epistemic sense be relevant to naturalistic theism? The idea that God has acted in creating and sustaining the natural world and in the revelation in Jesus in the same way in which God acts in our immediate experience is fully compatible with naturalistic theism's view that God works persuasively always and everywhere. Although a Christian view of divine activity should be dialectically based on all three forms of revelation (natural, historical, and individual), with each informed by the other two, we know our own experience with an immediacy that we do not have in regard to the rest of the world (as a whole or in its parts) and to past historical events. Through this direct experience of ourselves, we have an overwhelming conviction that we are partially free. This conviction is, in fact, a hard-core common-sense notion,[7] which we inevitably presuppose in practice even if we try to deny it verbally. Because we cannot deny it consistently, its denial makes no sense. On this basis, we can only assume that, if there is a Holy Spirit acting upon or within us, it does so in such a way as not to violate our freedom. Furthermore, when we examine our experience with the question in mind, "In what way, if at all, do we have a direct experience of deity?" a plausible answer (especially for those whose vision has been shaped by taking Jesus as a special revelation of deity) is that we do so in the experience of normative ideals. In Whitehead's words: "There are experiences of ideals—of ideals entertained, of ideals aimed at, of ideals achieved, of ideals defaced. This is the experience of the deity of the universe."[8] These ideals, which can be moral, aesthetic, religious, or cognitive (for example, the importance of being logical),[9] have an insistent nature about them: we should not violate them. And yet we remain free to violate them: we have the experience "of ideals defaced." If this be our direct experience of deity, then the deity of the universe operates persuasively and incarnationally. Insofar as we actualize the ideals, we create ourselves out of those ideals. They and, therefore, the deity in which they were lodged become literally incarnate in us.

If we generalize this idea of the divine modus operandi to Jesus (recognizing that we derived it in part by interpreting our own experience in the light of the impact of Jesus), we get a notion of God's activity in him that involves a real presence of God in him, but that is in no way supernaturalistic, that in no way violates his freedom and full humanity.

Likewise, if we generalize this idea of the divine modus operandi to the creation at large (recognizing that we had derived the notion of divine activity that we applied to Jesus and ourselves in part from our reflection upon the world as a whole), we come up with the suggestion that God works in the creation in general, including what we normally think of as inanimate nature, by presenting ideals. Working out this perhaps initially startling suggestion would require us to conceive of natural entities in such a way that they are patient of ideals. If this line of thought were developed, we would have a theism that is fully naturalistic, seeing God as acting in one and the same basic way in ourselves, Jesus, and nature.

This line of thought, of course, was not developed. As mentioned earlier, traditional theology insisted that God's active presence in Jesus was not analogous to the presence of God as Holy Spirit in the rest of us. The "Ebionite" christology, and the "Pelagian" soteriology implicit in it, were rejected. Equally rejected, in the modern period, was the view that God works in nature by becoming incarnate in it. Such doctrines were quite prevalent in the sixteenth and seventeenth centuries, in philosophical theologies inspired by Platonic, Neoplatonic, Hermetic, Pythagorean, and Cabalistic roots. Moderns such as Marin Mersenne, Robert Boyle, and Isaac Newton, however, launched an attack upon this outlook, claiming that it was degrading to speak of God as immanent in matter. They portrayed matter instead as hard, impenetrable, devoid of any inside, thereby portraying God as absolutely transcendent over nature, controlling its motions from without. Insofar as this natural philosophy became associated with what came to be called "natural science" and the "modern scientific world view," theologians were reluctant to challenge it. In modern theologies, accordingly, the ideas of nature as divine creation and of the Holy Spirit as present in all things have been faint or totally absent. One practical implication is that these modern theologies have provided no obstacle to the total exploitation of nature for human profit—a result that was not unintended by the founders of the modern world view.[10]

Traditional economic trinitarianism was completely supernaturalistic. The naturalistic possibilities within neither the temporal nor the epistemic trinity were developed. In each case, the three modes of God's activity in the world were, in the popular versions, understood as involving different ways of acting. In rigorous theological discussions, it was sometimes stated that God works the same way in all events, but this was a thoroughly supernaturalistic way, in which all freedom and natural causation of the creatures were denied either explicitly (Luther, Calvin) or in effect (Thomas).[11]

4.   NATURALISTIC THEISM AND THE IMMANENT TRINITY

What about the doctrine of the immanent trinity, the idea that the divine reality is, in itself, somehow triune, somehow three while still being one? It did nothing to mitigate traditional theism's supernaturalism in the ontological sense (which is the sense we have been discussing). And it increased its epistemological supernaturalism (an idea introduced here), the view that the nature of God cannot be known apart from supernatural revelation. In fact, the idea that God was three in one was often held up as the chief example of a truth that not only could not be known apart from revelation, but that, once revealed, still could not be understood. For that reason alone, such a trinitarianism could not be a feature of a theology commended on the basis of its ability to make sense of our experience in an intelligible way. It also creates an insurmountable barrier between the Christian and other religious visions of reality, including the other biblically based traditions.

However, following the lead provided by Whitehead's distinction between God and creativity, we can formulate an immanent trinity that is fully intelligible, that takes seriously the idea that God's character was revealed in Jesus and his cross, and explains why God's activity in the world, whether as creator, redeemer, or consummator, is always persuasive, incarnating, suffering love. Further virtues of this trinity are that it should not, in principle, be objectionable to other biblically based monotheists, and that it should provide a point of contact with some major nonbiblical religions, such as Hinduism and Buddhism.

Creativity is the ultimate reality of the universe. It is not an actuality but that ubiquitous reality embodied by every actuality. Because it is not an actuality, it is not on the same level as God, who is actual. The distinction between God and creativity is not, therefore, a dualism of two cosmic actualities, as in the best-known form of Zoroastrianism and various forms of Gnosticism. Rather than standing over against God, creativity finds in God its primordial embodiment, and God gives it its primordial characterization. We can think of the creativity embodied in God as the first aspect of God's threefold nature. God's way of characterizing creativity provides the second and third aspects. On the one hand, God's eternal purpose to evoke creatures with the richest possible form of experience into being characterizes the Divine Creativity as Creative Love. This side of God's nature includes the primordial potentials for the universe, those mathematical, geometrical, and valuational forms that give creatures their particular shapes. These primordial potentials are envisaged with appetite for their actualization; this Creative Love is the divine eros, which initiates all motion. On the other hand, once creatures have been evoked into being, God responds to the experiences of the creatures with sympathy (literally: feeling with). This is the Responsive Love of God. When the creatures undergo torment, this Responsive Love takes the form of divine suffering; when they delight in their existence, this Sympathetic or Responsive Love means divine joy. The use of the term "suffering love" to refer to this side of the divine love does not mean that it always involves suffering as opposed to delight, but that it is always ready to share whatever suffering the creatures undergo.

The threeness immanent within God, therefore, consists of Divine Creativity, Creative Love, and Responsive Love. The latter two dimensions refer to the dual way in which the creativity embodied in God is eternally characterized. Creativity, which is always *experiential* creativity, being the creativity of moments of experience, takes two modes. There is the creativity involved in self-creation, or self-determination, in which the many become one: a moment of experience creates itself by appropriating influences it has received from the experiences of others. In God's experience, this creative appropriation of the experiences is always characterized by Responsive Love, never by hate or indifference. Creativity in its second mode is the creative influence that a momentary actuality, once it has completed its self-creation, exerts upon others: the one becomes incarnate in the many. This is outgoing creativity. It is creativity as causal efficacy upon others. In God's case, this creativity is always characterized by Creative Love, never by destructive hate or indifference. God's influence upon others is always aimed at evoking the best from them.

The two dimensions of the divine love are not unrelated to each other: God's outgoing creativity in every moment is informed by love not only because it is based only upon God's eternal loving purpose to create the most satisfying world possible, but because it is also based upon God's Responsive Love to the previous state of the creatures' experience and upon God's anticipation of sympathy with their experience in future moments. With this perfect sympathy as an eternal feature of God's experience, there can be no separation between God's good and the good of the creatures. Because the internal appropriation of the creaturely experiences with perfect sympathy, identifying with their weal and woe, is an eternal characteristic of Divine Creativity, there can be no distinction between the Divine good and the good of the creatures. God could not possibly be less than perfectly good, in the sense of willing and seeking the good of the whole world and each of its creatures.[12]

Although God eternally embodies creativity, it is equally presupposed that not all creativity is embodied in God. For there to be a one, there must be a many. Creativity as it is involved in self-creation is always a process by which many become one: the experiences from a multiplicity of past experiences are synthesized into a new unity of experience. Accordingly, the very nature of creativity entails that there has always been a plurality of actualities. There could never have been God alone, a Solitary One: the very meaning of being one is to be a creative unification of a many. The creation of our world could not have been creation *ex nihilo*, in the sense of creation out of absolute nothingness. Divine Creativity presupposes the eternal existence of a plurality of finite actualities.

The eternal existence of finite embodiments of creativity is required by the idea that Creative and Responsive Love are eternal characterizations of Divine Creativity. God could not eternally be Responsive Love unless there were others to which to respond, for love is an essentially relational category. Therefore, if God is Love, reality must be inherently social. Traditional supernaturalism, which insisted upon creation out of absolute nothingness, used the immanent trinity to avoid this truth. It agreed that love eternally characterized God's nature and that love, a social relation, needs an object. It claimed, however, that the other members of the trinity provided each of the divine "persons" with adequate objects. The doctrine thereby did, as Jews and other Unitarians complained, verge on affirming three divine beings. This is an illustration of the way in which trinitarianism not only reflected but increased the supernaturalism of traditional theism. Divine Creativity, Creative Love, and Responsive Love, by contrast, no more constitute three distinct or quasidistinct beings than do the energy, basic life purpose, and basic attitude to others that we can distinguish, as abstractions, within our own unified experience. If Divine Creativity is eternally characterized by Responsive Love, then God has never been without a plurality of creatures to love.

Creative Love no less than Responsive Love requires objects. The outgoing mode of creativity, through which causal influence is exerted upon others, is as essential to creativity as its responsive, self-creative mode. Traditional theism was also supernaturalistic here, denying that God was essentially creative; thereby, making the realm of finite beings a purely contingent, arbitrary matter, dependent upon an act of will. Thomas Aquinas said that this truth could only be known by supernatural revelation, granting that reason suggests the eternal existence of nondivine beings as well as the Divine One. This is another example of how ontological supernaturalism leads to epistemic supernaturalism.[13] Naturalistic theism follows Whitehead in holding that a rational theology "requires that the relationships of God to the World should lie beyond the accidents of will, and that they be founded upon the necessities of the nature of God and the nature of the World."[14] The triune nature of God, in which Divine Creativity is eternally characterized by Creative and Responsive Love, requires a world of finite experiential embodiments of creativity, just as such a world requires a God who relates to it in this dual way.

This does not mean that our world has always existed, or even that there has always been some world or other, if by "world" we mean a well-ordered set of actualities. The plurality of finite things may well be a "chaos," in which there are not even forms of order as high as an electron, or even a quark. Our world would, accordingly, not have been created out of absolute nothingness, in the sense of a complete absence of finite beings; it would have been gradually formed out of a chaotic state of such beings. And those beings—those extremely primitive, brief, momentary events—would have embodied some iota of creativity. They would have had some iota of the twofold capacity to determine their own inner state, in response to their environment, and to exert causal efficacy upon others. There is some freedom even in chaos. God's creative causal efficacy on them, therefore, would not have been coercive, in the sense of totally determining their inner and outer states, but persuasive, influencing them to actualize their creativity in a way that would lead to a desirable order.

5. THE CREATIVITY CONNECTION

The preceding section points to the connection between the immanent and the economic trinities. It is because the immanent trinitarian nature of God requires that creativity be embodied in the creatures, so that they are not *mere* creatures but partially self-creating creatures, that the various distinctions we make in regard to God's activity in the world (creation, redemption, revelation, and so on) cannot involve different modes of divine operation. Divine activity cannot alternate between coercion and persuasion. Nor can it always be coercion, as traditional theism in its rigorous form said. The creativity of the creatures is nonoverridable, noninterruptible, in either its self-determining phase or its phase of causal efficacy. The immanent trinity provides, thereby, the basis for naturalistic theism and its economic trinity. God's activity at all stages of the world must be exclusively persuasive.

If this view were to become pervasive, the doctrine that God is trinitarian would no longer seem intellectually incoherent and practically irrelevant, as it has to most thoughtful people in the modern period. It would, instead, be a shorthand way of saying that the ultimate power of the universe, which we as religious beings seek to imitate and which we can trust, achieves its purposes through exclusively peaceable means. I believe that this is the God we have. I also believe that more than ever, this is the God in whom we need to believe.

NOTES

1. See David Ray Griffin, *God, Power, and Evil: A Process Theodicy* (Philadelphia: Westminster, 1976; Lanham, MD: University Press of America [reprint with new preface], 1991), and *Evil Revisited: Responses and Reconsiderations* (Albany: State University of New York Press, 1991).

2. Billy Graham, *World Aflame* (Minneapolis: The Billy Graham Evangelistic Assn., 1965), 218.

3. Ranald Macaulay, "Review of *Nuclear Holocaust and Christian Hope*" (by Ronald J. Sider and Richard K. Taylor), in Jerram Barrs, *Who Are the Peacemakers: The Christian Case for Nuclear Deterrence* (Westchester, IL: Good News Publisher: Crossway Books, 1983), 55–61.

4. John F. and John E. Walvoord, *Armageddon: Oil and the Middle East Crisis* (Grand Rapids, MI: Zondervan Publishing House, 1976); quoted in Robert Jewett, *Jesus Against the Rapture* (Philadelphia: Westminster, 1979), 16.

5. Reinhold Niebuhr, *The Nature and Destiny of Man* (New York: Charles Scribner's Sons, 1949), II: 316n. 17, 318.

6. William Temple, York Diocesan Leaflet, 1935; discussed by Charles E. Raven, *The Theological Basis of Christian Pacifism* (New York: Fellowship Publications, 1951), 51.

7. I have discussed hard-core common-sense notions in the introduction to David Ray Griffin *et al.*, *Founders of Constructive Postmodern Philosophy* (Albany: State University of New York Press, 1993), 23–29.

8. Alfred North Whitehead, *Modes of Thought* (New York: The Free Press, 1968), 103.

9. *Ibid.*, 6, 11, 26.

10. See Carolyn Merchant, *The Death of Nature: Women, Ecology, and the Scientific Revolution* (San Francisco: Harper & Row, 1980), 193.

11. See the chapters on Luther, Calvin, and Thomas in my *God, Power, and Evil.*

12. See my article, "The Holy, Necessary Goodness, and Morality," *Journal of Religious Ethics* 8(2), 330–49, or chapter 8 of *God and Religion in the Postmodern World* (Albany: State University of new York Press, 1989), esp. 142–45.

13. Like the immanent trinity of traditional theism, this doctrine of the contingency of the creation was "above reason" in the strong sense, meaning that it could not be understood even after it had been revealed. If God is perfectly simple, as St. Thomas insisted, so that the divine will and the divine essence are identical, and if the divine essence is eternal and hence necessary, how could the divine will to create a world be any less necessary than the divine essence itself? See my chapter on Thomas, entitled "Divine Simplicity and Theological Complexity," in *God, Power, and Evil.*

14. A. N. Whitehead, *Adventures of Ideas* (New York: Free Press, 1967), 168.

Lewis S. Ford
Contingent Trinitarianism

In an earlier essay on "A Process Trinitarianism" I sought to translate some of the concerns of the classical doctrine of the trinity into the conceptuality of Whitehead's philosophy.[1] I remain convinced that the twofold problem of transcendence and immanence of God and the world, for which the trinity is often used, can be better handled in process terms. I identified God the Father with the primordial envisagement, God the Son with the Logos, the entirety of the primordial nature, and the Spirit with the inverse of the consequent nature.

Obviously, this is not the only way in which Whitehead's metaphysical features can be correlated with the divine personae, as other essays in this anthology indicate. I am particularly drawn to Marjorie Suchocki's proposal, originally developed for the Cobb festschrift.[2] On the whole, however, my proposal seems to have stood the test of time, if our purpose is to find a reasonably satisfactory way of expressing trinitarian issues in terms of the necessary principles proposed by Whitehead's own philosophy.

On the other hand, I question whether that purpose is an appropriate purpose for process theism. The whole enterprise now seems to me to be fundamentally bankrupt. It has neglected one of the most novel and important features of process thought; namely, the ascription of contingency to God. Divine contingency is most evident in its temporalistic character, since the capacity to be influenced by temporal actuality is the capacity to be influenced by that which could have been otherwise.

Classical theism lacks the alternatives this contingency affords. Since God is then conceived as wholly eternal and necessary, every divine feature must be equally necessary. Necessity and eternality go hand in hand. Anything that is eternal could never be otherwise than what it is, and so has at least a de facto necessity, even if ultimately arbitrary. Classical theism did not have the opportunity to conceive the divine *personae* as contingent. Process theism should not simply foreclose that opportunity in blind imitation of past limitations.

Let us review my original conception in greater detail as an example of a metaphysical trinitarian proposal. Then I seek to show that such necessary trinities should be replaced by contingent ones, giving an example of a contingent trinitarian proposal. A contingent trinity may better reflect the traditional sense that the trinity should be considered a revealed doctrine. That which is revealed may be incapable of being rationally ascertained. If the trinity cannot be rationally ascertained in terms of necessary principles, precisely because it could have been otherwise, then it may only be known through revelation, or at least not by reason alone.

MY METAPHYSICAL TRINITARIAN PROPOSAL

Some trinitarian projects have sought to express God's simultaneous transcendence of, and immanence in, the world. Increasingly, however, the artificiality of these attempts is being called into question, for it is by no means evident that this problem demands a triunity of principles for its resolution. Thus, Cyril C. Richardson has criticized the classical formulations of the trinity as imposing an arbitrary "threeness" upon our theological thinking, and proposes instead a basic twofold distinction between God as Absolute and God as Related.[3] For Richardson this is a basic paradox,[4] but Hartshorne has removed the contradictory element by reconceiving the distinction in terms of the abstract and concrete dimensions of God's nature and experience.[5]

Now, a twofold solution is quite adequate for the classical problem of God's transcendence of, and yet immanence within, the world. From the perspective of Whitehead's theism, however, there is a double problem (cf. *Process and Reality*, 347), the other aspect consisting in the world's transcendence of, and immanence within, God. As Whitehead argues, "It is as true to say that the World is immanent in God, as that God is immanent in the World. It is as true to say that God transcends the World, as that the World transcends God (*Process and Reality*, 528).[6] Only a threefold solution seems able to meet this problem, in which the third element speaks to the way the world is immanent in God.

Here we need a series of distinctions. The *Logos* is the totality of divine aims that apply to all kinds of creatures, human and non-human, terrestrial and extraterrestrial. The creative word specifically addressed to the human situation to bring about its transformation is the Christ. Christians find this creative word most fully actualized in the life, death, and resurrection of Jesus.

Too often these distinctions have been ignored with the result that Jesus is given a pre-existent subjectivity, which is identified with the second member of the trinity. The fourth gospel assumes just such a pre-existent subjectivity (John 17:1–5). According to process principles, however, it is extremely difficult to admit distinct subjectivities within God. Subjectivity lies at the heart of actuality. It is a process of unification, whereby the many initial prehensions of an occasion become one final satisfaction, one being. Since each subjectivity, as an act of becoming, results in one being, there must be as many beings as there are subjectivities.

Although the trinity has been traditionally understood as "three persons (i.e., three subjectivities) in one substance (i.e., one impersonal substratum), the original formulation need not be so understood. *Una substantia*, insofar as it translates Aristotle's *ousia*, signifies one actuality, one concrete determinate entity. *Persona* (as in *dramatis personae*) did not mean "person" in our sense but the mask through which an actor spoke, indicating the specific role being performed. Hence, the phrase could be construed as meaning "one actuality in three aspects," aspects that are formally distinct (distinct, but not separable).[7]

This interpretation, which may well have been the original meaning of the formula, insists upon a stricter notion of monotheism than the "social trinity" can allow. The social trinity may well have arisen because Christians experienced God in terms of distinct subjectivities, because the *personae* constitute different ways in which the one divine subjectivity was mediated to them. Thus, the means could have been experienced in terms of the properties of the source. Yet the ascription of subjectivity to the *personae* disrupts the divine unity, especially in the context of process thought. Moreover, a social trinity tends to undermine the coherence or interdependence Whitehead requires of his basic elements, including God and the world. Interdependence guarantees metaphysical stability, for no element can exist without the others. It is the very opposite of substantial independence, requiring nothing other than itself to exist. A social trinity can satisfy God's concern with sociality, short circuiting God's dependence on the world and its inhabitants for the divine experience and social interaction.

Thus, the trinity I propose is a single subjectivity as one actuality with three formally distinct natures, Father, Logos, and Spirit. As the totality of the divine possibilities, the Logos may be interpreted as corresponding to the primordial nature of God. This primordial nature is the outcome of a single nontemporal concrescence: for the primordial instance of creativity "achieves, in its unity of satisfaction, the complete conceptual valuation of all eternal objects [all forms of possibility]" (*Process and Reality*, 32).

In this proposal, I correlate the Father with the primordial envisagement and the Son or Logos with its outcome in the primordial nature. This nicely agrees with the formula that the Son is "begotten of the Father before all worlds" in a purely nontemporal concrescence. Although this was obviously a live concern for the early church, it seems more of a bit of excess cultural baggage today. Other metaphysical proposals may wish to sacrifice this correlation to achieve different perceived advantages.[8] The Spirit cannot simply be identified with the consequent nature, which is God's receptive activity whereby God experiences the temporal occasions of the world. In one sense, the Spirit and the consequent nature are opposites, since the Spirit makes it possible for God to be immanent in the world (in the guise of ordinary divine aims), while the consequent nature makes it possible for the world to be immanent in God (through God's ongoing experience of the world).

We cannot directly experience God's experience of us, but the particular aims provided for our ongoing experience form a specific response to our past actions. Most of the time, preoccupied with practical affairs, we hardly notice the aims and values that guide our activities. Occasionally, we may become sensitive to these values, but usually as directives for our own existence, as moral intuitions. Only rarely do we experience these values in terms of the dynamic source from which they spring. Only a living person experiencing a whole series of divine aims, sensitive to the way in which these shift, grow, and develop in response to our changing circumstances can become aware of their source as dynamic and personal, meeting our needs and concerns.[9] Jesus, full of the Spirit, knew God personally in this intimate way. Divine personality, communicated by the Spirit, requires a dynamic responsiveness that only the experience of God's consequent nature could supply.

Usually the Spirit in traditional trinitarian formulations is assigned the role of uniting the other two persons. That role is unnecessary if the *personae* are interdependent aspects of a single actuality. Moreover the Spirit, in terms of its necessarily intimate connection with the consequent nature, has a different role to play. The primordial envisagement transcends the world, but its outcome in the primordial nature as Logos is (partially) immanent in the world. The double problem Whitehead saw becomes evident (*Process and Reality* 347). The world itself transcends God in the sense that each achieved actuality is something for itself alone and also something upon which the divine experience depends. The world is immanent in God by means of the consequent nature, which in interaction with the primordial possibilities supplies the specific aims of the Spirit upon which we depend.

WHITEHEAD AND CLASSICAL THEISM

In classical theism God, is customarily conceived as purely necessary. As perfect, without beginning or end, God's eternal necessity was contrasted to the contingency of the world. Process theism conceives of God as having abstract necessary features, but also as contingently responding to the temporal world, giving ultimate meaning to its finite (and contingent) endeavors. The classical tradition, however, has somewhat indirectly recognized an element of contingency with respect to the trinitarian debate, even if not with respect to God. The debate whether trinitarian speculation is properly philosophical or theological was settled by Aquinas in favor of theology. However, the trinitarian speculation has been philosophically interesting right from the start, when it was expressed in terms of Logos and *substantia*. It is one of the most philosophical of the doctrines of the church, if not the most philosophical. At least this has been true whenever all that which pertains to God has been conceived as purely necessary.

On the contrary, I submit that there is an element of brute facticity at the heart of trinitarian thought. If we don't wish to go behind it, there is the classical formulation of the doctrine itself, put forth by the authority of the believing community. Or we can consider the fundamental problem that gave rise to the doctrine.

Either way, we are confronted by historical contingencies, largely masked by the philosophical abstractions in which the doctrine became increasingly expressed. This contingent element must be ignored if God is conceived as purely necessary. Then the trinitarian persons must also be considered as necessary, and if necessary, then eternal, to contrast with the contingency of the world. After all, all the properties of deity are attributed to each person, and each is differentiated from the others only in terms of its innertrinitarian relation (The Son is not the Father, etc.). However, if God were to have both necessary and contingent features, we should have to reconsider how these features are to be distributed among the persons. Could it possibly be that while God is everlastingly necessary, that (some of) the persons could possibly be deemed contingent?

This raises the question whether the trinitarian members should be regarded as persons or *personae*. Obviously, there are strong pastoral reasons internal to the Christian tradition for remaining faithful to the time-honored understanding of the trinity in terms of persons; however, there are also strong arguments for abandoning this approach for *personae* understood as aspects of the divine, particularly for those committed to process theism. There is always the danger of tritheism, which the Christian church has usually been able to overcome, at least to the extent of being able to persuade itself that it is strictly monotheistic. Certainly, it has always been strictly monotheistic in intention, however much popular thought, poetry, hymns, etc. have strayed from this ideal. But looked at in cold logic, without the subtle qualifications and the pervasive assurance of monotheistic intent, the doctrine of the trinity looks suspiciously like the worship of three Gods. If religions can be understood as more or less effective strategies of reconciliation with God, then one tradition is peculiarly burdened if it must insist on a trinity of persons as constituting that God, while other traditions expressly deny such complications in the name of divine unity. We may also wonder, "how will it play in Tau Ceti?" assuming that there is intelligent life elsewhere in the universe.

The basic formula, *una substantia in tres personae*, one actuality [manifest] in three roles, is often understood as "one substance in three persons." This interpretation was possible because the underlying substance need not be essentially subjective in order to be the actual divine unity. Also, the three persons could be conceived as subjectivities inhering in that one substance. Traditionally, a single subjectivity was not necessarily a distinct, separate actuality. That possibility, however, is precluded by Whitehead's metaphysics. Each subjectivity is a concrescence whereby its experience of the world is unified into one synthesis. This is both the culmination of subjective experience and the production of new being. By this self-creative act, the past efficient causal influences are unified together so that they may be rendered effective. Every being (unity) is the outcome of its act of becoming (unification), which makes the act of becoming or subjective concrescence more fundamental than its product. Being is effective as objectively immortal, but only because its subjective unification has been completed. (Unification ceases with the attainment of unity.) Thus, no being is subjective, and no becoming can be objectified. In this vision, subjective becoming is ontologically more fundamental than objective being. Thus, God, at least for Whitehead, is conceived as a single everlasting concrescence. Since each concrescence is a distinct actuality, and each subjectivity is a distinct concrescence, any social interpretation conceives of God in terms of three distinct actualities, raising the suspicion that "those Christians really worship three Gods."

This result is not substantially altered by reconceiving the divine concrescence(s) as personally ordered societies. Hartshorne assumes that there is only one such divine society, but Joseph Bracken postulates three. If there are several, divine unity must be sought in the underlying field. If this field is purely objective, then it violates the reformed subjectivist principle, according to which there can be no "togetherness" that is not derivative from "experiential togetherness" (*Process and Reality*, 189f), a principle closely cognate to the ontological principle. If this field is understood in terms of Jorge Nobo's proposal that creativity and the extensive continuum are aspects of each other,[10] then God as unity enjoys subjectivity. However, subjectivity seems to be imperious. Either God as a unity is subjective, and the *personae* are objective aspects, or the divine persons are subjective, and the comprehensive unity is objective.

The issue of divine sociality arises in Gregory Boyd's synthesis of conservative evangelicalism and Hartshornean theism.[11] Roughly speaking, God conceives God before creation in classical terms, but since creation in process terms. Boyd appreciates sociality as a positive value, but argues that the "necessary actuality" of God prior to creation possesses sociality in the relations between the eternal trinitarian persons. To sort out this issue, we must attend to some meanings of "sociality."

THREE MEANINGS FOR SOCIALITY

Sociality simply means the need for interrelatedness among entities. The indeterminateness of this definition can be resolved differently:

(1.) Sociality may mean nothing more than bare relatedness. In that case *any* beings may be related. But then sociality does not require any subjective interaction within the trinity. It is enough if the *Personae*, as necessary aspects of the one divine actuality, are related to one another. In my metaphysical example, the Father and the Son are strongly interrelated, because the primordial envisagement requires the primordial nature as that which it engenders, and the primordial nature requires its envisagement as its source.

(2.) Sociality may apply to relations between actualities. Those features that pertain to an actuality by itself are not social, only those it acquires solely from others. Only other actualities and their properties can be truly other to it. Applied to the trinity, this means that the Persons can enjoy sociality only if they are distinct actualities, which would be tritheism.

(3.) A more intense form of sociality requires that one benefit from the others. Otherwise, what purpose is achieved by engaging in social relations? A social being must be capable of being enriched, and the other must be capable of providing the one with something it does not already possess. This is possible only if what it provides is something new. But the eternal Persons can neither enrich nor be enriched. Their sociality can only be sham.

This form of sociality is a great boon, which the God of process theism establishes not within godself but with the world. God and the world are, thus, interdependent. Here the relata are not only related to one another, but require one another. The world requires God for its order, while God requires the world for its experience. This is one of the ways in which things cohere.[12]

Whitehead's refusal to identify creativity with God is in part based on his sense of interdependence. Both God and all occasions of the world require their measure of creativity. If God were creativity as such, the occasions could not be empowered short of being themselves divine. God, like all other actual entities, depends on creativity for empowerment. Without creativity, no concrescent unification could be possible. Creativity, on the other hand, is dependent upon actualities for whatever determinateness it might achieve, as well as for its very existence (*Process and Reality*, 7). If creativity were dependent on God, and not vice versa, Spinozistic determinism would prevail. If God were dependent on creativity, and not vice versa, a pluralistic pantheism without any centering principle would prevail.

THE INTERDEPENDENCE OF NECESSITY AND CONTINGENCY

For our purposes, the most important interdependence pertains to necessity and contingency. Necessity is rendered concretely actual by contingency; whereas, contingency is rendered possible by necessity. To be possible, every contingent actuality must exemplify the metaphysical principles, and, thereby, be subject to necessity. Necessity, however, is quite abstract, and requires contingent factors to flesh out its actuality. We accept these principles quite readily for the finite actualities of the world, because we take them to be primarily contingent (although with some necessary features). Traditionally, however, God as wholly necessary has been contrasted to the world as wholly contingent.

Whitehead finds that the interdependence of necessity and contingency applies to both. The chief importance of interdependence is to ensure metaphysical stability. An alternative way of achieving this same goal is to postulate a fundamental strain of metaphysical necessity underlying the universe. In theistic traditions, that metaphysical necessity is vested in an eternal or everlasting actuality. However, as we have seen, if God were wholly necessary, God would have no contingent experience, nor any experience dependent upon contingent actualities. What other experience is there? To save divine experience, we might be tempted to hold that God already knows all there is to know.[13] Then, the future would have to be already determinate in order to be knowable and could not be the outcome of free determinations.

Even if foreknowledge were possible, it would be knowledge of a contingent world and would be itself contingent to that extent.

Without contingency, God would be excessively abstract, both in the sense of being merely a principle and in the sense of being less than actual. Both Plato and Whitehead agree, as over against Aristotle, that there can be no nontemporal subjectivity.[14] To be truly subjective, an actuality must be able to respond to novelty, and that novelty can only be exhibited contingently. What is necessary is always present, and, hence, can never be new. Without contingency, God cannot be subjective.[15]

Nevertheless, there is an important sense in which God is primarily necessary, and actual occasions are primarily contingent. God is the ultimate source of the metaphysical principles, so the occasions depend on God for metaphysical necessity. God, in turn, is dependent on the occasions for all the contingency God acquires. In this sense, God and the world require each other. The interdependence of necessity and contingency in each could not obtain unless they were dependent on each other.

Metaphysical necessity by itself ensures a basic underlying everlasting stability to the universe, but interdependence does this and more, by incorporating the contingent (and with the contingent finite freedom, radical plurality, and novelty) within this stability. Otherwise, these features remain adventitious and precarious. If sociality is merely interpreted in terms of relatedness, even between conscious persons, then true interdependence can be avoided. That is just what happens with the social interpretation of the trinity. Because the Father, Son, and Spirit experience a full and rich life among themselves, there is no need for the world to further enrich the divine life, so it is argued.

God without the world, just as the world without God, however, would destroy their interdependence. Whitehead would regard this as an instance of incoherence: "Incoherence is the arbitrary disconnection of first principles" (*Process and Reality*, 6).[16] Ultimately, there is a conflict of ideals at stake. Traditionally, following the omnipotent despot model, God has been conceived to be absolute, wholly independent, everything else being dependent on God.[17] Interdependence radically conflicts with this model. Whitehead affirms interdependence primarily for metaphysical reasons. It is the surest guarantee there is for an inclusive metaphysical stability. If two things require each other, neither can exist alone. If the web of interdependence embraces everything, then things can continue in terms of their necessities. (This is balanced by contingent features, allowing for both freedom and novelty.) It is better to trust in interdependence than to trust in God's grace, love, or goodness for the continuation of the world, especially if that grace seems to run counter to metaphysical necessity.

THE TRINITY AS NECESSARY: SOME DIFFICULTIES

Basically, I claim that trinitarian formulations that apply to necessary metaphysical conditions cannot help but be too abstract to do justice to the concrete particularity of Christian affirmations concerning Jesus' life, death, and resurrection. Metaphysical conditions are universal, applying to all actualities whatsoever, whether simple or complex, organic or inorganic, terrestrial or extraterrestrial. They are bound to be so general as to encompass all conditions.

Given the radical contingency of history, it is quite possible that Jesus might never have lived, nor need there have been any incarnation. God could have chosen an entirely different means of salvation for those of us who are now Christians. However, the structure of any metaphysical trinity would remain the same, whether or not it had any significance or relevance to us.

And yet the significance of any trinitarian structure depends upon the Christ-event. Without it, this structure would have no meaning for us. Classical theism may be willing to live with that conclusion, since the Christ-event could only be rendered fully intelligible if there were some necessary structure that could become significant in terms of the Christ-event. However, if God has contingent features, these are the ones that can enhance the Christ-event. They are features that need not have existed, if Christ did not exist. They express the difference which the actualization of Christ makes to God.

If the significance for the trinity arises from the particular historical situation with which it is associated, the significance of purely metaphysical conceptions becomes quite tenuous. Typically, Jesus is identified with the Word incarnate. The Word is justified as the means whereby God creates. In process terms, this would be the primordial nature, the complete ordering of all eternal objects. So far so good. The problem comes in making sense out of the incarnation of the Word. Is this the actualization of all possibilities whatsoever, or of all creative potentialities within God? Hardly. Is it the actualization of only those divine possibilities intended for the person of Jesus? Yet, what has this to do with cosmic creation? Also, if no more is meant, then what about those primordial possibilities for other humans, let alone for all other creatures, terrestrial or extraterrestrial?

Suppose there is intelligent life on some planet circling the star Tau Ceti. What could the trinity possibly mean to them? That God has an essential threeness? If we generalize the second member as the primordial structure through which God acts, it might have some relevance, but this could be achieved without invoking any relation to Jesus. Such a conception of the trinity might well strike them as gratuitous or cumbersome; it might even offend their sense of the absolute unity of the ultimate. On the other hand, if it had any intrinsic relevance to Jesus, the trinity would be very foreign to them. How can what happened once upon the third planet circling the sun have any salvific significance for them? However, it must, if we must express the trinity in necessary and universal terms implicated in the work of Jesus as the Christ. Only if the trinitarian concept were expressed in contingent terms, could it be restricted solely to humanity.

Historically, the concrete reality of Jesus was quickly reduced to the generality of the Logos. Early Christians, seeking ways to express the high significance of Christ, seized upon the figure of Wisdom in the book of Proverbs: "The Lord created me at the beginning of his work, the first of his acts of long ago" (Prov. 8:22). God creates in an orderly fashion, with wisdom. Hence, God must first create wisdom, by means of which the world could be made. Identifying wisdom with the risen Christ, the writer to the Colossians could write: "He is the image of the invisible God, the firstborn of all creation, for in him all things in heaven and on earth were created . . ." (Col. 1:15–16). This effort to exalt Christ abstracts from the concrete realities upon which the Christian faith rests, such that Christ was crucified under Pontius Pilate, or that he rose and was exalted to the right hand of God. In Christ, God was reconciling the world to Godself, but that plays no role here, nor is it taken up into the ordinary trinitarian formulations.

The trinity is usually regarded as a revealed doctrine. This agrees with the consensus that it is no part of philosophical theology. Still, the traditional formulation of the trinity in necessary terms draws heavily upon philosophical concepts. By revelation we normally mean the manifestation of God as expressed in the contingencies of history, such as the exodus from Egypt. If revelation outruns reason, it should not be because theology proposes self-contradictory or inconsistent "truths." Rather, the concrete manifestations of revelation outrun the abstractions of philosophical necessity. If the trinity is a revealed doctrine, it is a very singular one. It was not directly revealed to the bishops assembled at Nicaea, but the problem they addressed was uniquely Christian, grounded in the contingent revelation of the risen Christ. Can a purely necessary conceptualization do justice to this concrete problematic? If the doctrine of the trinity is generalized to make it universally significant, it is robbed of the very particularity that makes it important to Christians and which generated the struggle with strict monotheism in the first place. On the other hand, if we seek to particularize the trinity, metaphysical categories, including process ones, are of no use to us. The religious life lives from contingent particularities, and necessary concepts cannot do justice to them.

It is not primarily the inner consistency, or consonance with philosophical excellence, or fidelity to received formulations, that is in question. Traditional as well as other process conceptions of the trinity have striven to meet these criteria. It is, rather, the adequacy, or perhaps better, the applicability of those concepts to the root experiences of the Christian faith that is criticized. They are applicable only insofar as they are significant for the Christian community and illuminate its central doctrines. The significance of the abstract derives from the concrete. What is objectionable is the assumption that it is permissible to abstract from, and thus methodically disregard, these concrete contingencies. The contingent is the reason for the particular, and the particular reasons are as significant in this context as the universal ones, if not more so.

Wolfhart Pannenberg argues that without the trinity expressed in terms of the intimate interaction between God the Father and Jesus, God's personal subjectivity could not be established. This is a very fruitful way of reconceiving the trinity, for it may be a necessary trinitarian conception rooted in the contingencies of Jesus' life. Moreover, we agree that a purely nontemporal divine subjectivity, apart from some other factor, is ultimately untenable.

The usual assumption of nontemporal subjectivity rests upon the synthesis of Greek timelessness with Biblical divine subjectivity. Whitehead discovered that he could not prove that God is personal as long as God was conceived as exclusively nontemporal.[18] Ultimately, he did propose a second temporal, contingent, consequent nature, on the basis of which God's subjectivity could be asserted. For the subject is inherently temporal as a dynamic and responsive center of value. Since God is temporal, we will not need Pannenberg's alternative to establish divine subjectivity.

Since traditional thinking assumed God to be wholly necessary, its purely metaphysical structures are understandable. Process theists, however, are without excuse. The truth of divine contingency ought to be used in order to enrich our grasp of the trinity, thereby connecting it more directly with the Christian witness to Jesus and his resurrection. If God enjoys contingency, it is not necessary that our conceptions of the trinity be so abstract. This is the wrong level of concern. The trinity should not be about the necessary nature of God, but about the way we are reconciled with God through Christ. It concerns the contingent strategy of reconciliation proposed by Christianity, in contrast to Judaism and Islam, not about the divine essence they share in common. Insistence upon the Triune God is an unnecessary act of theological imperialism.

To show that the trinity can be expressed in terms of contingent features, I offer the following example. It is only an example. The general principle, that process theism ought to embody at least some contingent *personae*, is far more important.

The Trinity as Necessary

Clark Williamson, in his discussion of the trinity in *A Guest in the House of Israel*,[19] has carefully formulated the issue from which the doctrine of the trinity arose. "the good news of God in Jesus Christ is that we are justified by God's free grace, by no work of our own, and that the God who justifies us is the One who covenantally interacts with all others empowering even their faithful response to God's free grace."[20] In opposition to Gnostic claims to worship a new and better God, orthodox Christians insisted that "the God who saves us through Jesus Christ is the God of Israel, maker and redeemer of heaven and earth, that this God is one, and that this God . . . is the one and only God".[21]

While affirming an essential role for Christ, these formulations are strictly monotheistic. The same strict monotheism is present in

Paul's expression: "God was in Christ, reconciling the world to himself."[22] How, then, do we get to those trinitarian formulations so suspect in non-Christian eyes?

Note that the pretrinitarian statements exhibit a relational structure between God at one pole and human creatures at the other. Christ, then, serves as the means whereby God's salvific activity is extended to the Gentiles: "The key insight is utterly biblical: that God is the author of our salvation . . . that *if* we are saved through Jesus Christ, *then* God must be salvifically operative in Jesus Christ."[23]

It seems to be the reformulation of this insight in terms implicitly assuming that God is immutable that utterly distorts things. First, the reference to contingent, temporal human creatures (or more precisely, the Gentiles) is dropped. That undercuts the relational character of these statements, because one pole of the relation is eliminated. Instead of being the mediating term of the relation, Christ is reconceived both in eternal contrast to God and as part of the divine unity.

Rather than being the *per+sona*, the means *through which* God's salvation is bestowed on mankind, as may still be present in the "economic trinity," Christ is primarily conceived as a member of the "immanent trinity," which is strictly immutable. Apart from a contingent humanity to be reconciled to the divine, the trinitarian persons lack any function of their own except as endowed with subjectivity to relate to one another.

Then, the nature of the Father, as truly God, becomes obscure, for it must be the trinity as a whole, and not just one person, that is truly God. The very insight from which the trinitarian quest arose is then lost: that the Father of our Lord Jesus Christ is the God of Israel, the one and only God, for only this God saves.

Immutabilist assumptions need to be abandoned in order to preserve the essential role of God in Christ reconciling human beings to the divine. Humans are contingent, so that which reconciles them only has its existence and relevance contingently. God's salvific activity makes no sense *apart from* human beings.

THE TRINITY AS CONTINGENT

Although God has been conceived as timelessly knowing all future contingents, this was not ancient Israel's experience. The

Lord repented having made humans (Gen. 6:6), and also changed
the length of King Hezekiah's life by fifteen years (I Kings 20).
These verses are dismissed as "anthropomorphisms" by those who
presume to know better, but they are consonant with the vision of
process theism.[24] After the exile, however, when prophecy ceased
in Israel, God was increasingly perceived as immutable. First,
there was an emphasis on the constancy and fidelity of God: "For
I the Lord do not change" (Mal: 3:6). In the New Testament, this
emphasis was extended to cover all features of God's being,
speaking of "the Father of lights with whom there is no variation
of shadow due to change" (James 1:17). In First Samuel, God
could be depicted as first choosing Saul to be king over Israel,
while later rejecting him, regretting the prior decision (I Sam.
15:35). Paul, on the other hand, true to immutabilist assumptions,
can understand divine election only in terms of foreknowledge
and predestination (Rom. 8:29f). When the author of Hebrews
quotes from the Psalms a passage suggesting God's temporal
response to Israel's disobedience in the wilderness, a disclaimer is
hastily added: "although his works were finished from the foundation of the world" (Heb. 4:3).

This shift in Israel's understanding of God from the exile to
New Testament times has been largely ignored by Biblical schol-
ars. To my knowledge, there has been no close study of this transformation. I would guess that the Greek ideal of perfect being,
transmitted by Alexander's conquest, was the decisive influence,
but this has not been adequately studied. In any case, the
immutability of God was not perceived by any Christian or Jewish
writer of the time as an alien intrusion of Greek philosophy, but as
an ideal they also embraced as a matter of course. This ideal of
perfect being remains to this day the mainstay of classical theology. As articulated by Thomas Aquinas, to be perfect, the divine
being must be simple (excluding all multiplicity), solitary, self-
sufficient, immutable, impassible, the sole creator of the world. In
this, I think he is largely correct, but I question the assumption that
God is perfect being.

If, as Whitehead finally came to see, becoming is more fundamental than being, then God must be the perfect instance of
becoming. If so, God must be active receptivity, continually being
further enriched from the world. Such a world cannot be solely
created by God, because then God would be receiving only what
was already given, and there would be no novelty or enrichment

received. Thus, perfect becoming requires a new conception of creation essentially involving the activity of the creatures. This Whitehead provides by the theory of concrescence, which is really an alternative conception of creation as the self-creation of the creature out of its past causal conditions by the inspiration of God's directing aim.[25]

Most process Christologies merely seek to translate the classical formulations concerning Christ without revising their immutabilist assumptions. Thus, the most impressive process Christology, John Cobb's *Christ in a Pluralistic Age*,[26] attempts to show how the Chalcedonian formula could be understood in Whiteheadian terms. In contrast, I mean to bypass both the classical formulations and their expression in terms of process concepts. Let us consider the primal experience that gave rise to the doctrines of Christ and the trinity, speculating on how they might have been formulated in the absence of the assumptions of classical theism.

My thesis is that the church basically experienced God as Christ, but immutabilist assumptions prevented it from recognizing this fact. Visions of Christ replaced visions of God. The heavenly Christ commissioned the apostles (I Cor. 9:1, 15:5–9) as the God of Israel had commissioned the prophets. The spirit of God was experienced as the spirit of Christ (Rom. 8:9–11). Where heretofore the Lord had been experienced as the savior of Israel, the Christians experienced Christ as the savior of the world. However, the prevailing preconception that God could not change prevented the Christians from identifying these two images with one another. Peter proclaimed at Pentecost: This Jesus, whom you crucified, God has raised up and made both Lord and Christ (Acts 2:32–36). Christ was depicted as the heavenly Son of Man, standing at the right hand of God (Acts 7:56). God and Christ were perceived to be distinct figures, side by side. Unless God were capable of change, transformation into Christ would be impossible, and the new experience of Christ could only be explained by his sudden appearance alongside God. Yet, while the Son of Man was originally conceived to be a heavenly creature, the logic of the Christian salvific experience finally drove the Church to acknowledge Christ as divine, embarrassing as this was in the light of its heritage of strict monotheism. The deification of Christ within a monotheistic tradition cannot be explained in terms of pagan parallels, but is rooted, I submit, in this primal experience of God as Christ, obscured as this was by preconceptions of divine immutability.

The logic of perfection for divine being had momentous consequence for early Christian speculation, for it must consider where this heavenly Son of Man comes from. In Jewish thought, the Son of Man would have to have been created, yet he would share with God immutability, insofar as it is possible for a creature to be immutable. Thus, Enoch declares that the Son of Man "has been chosen and hidden before God, before the creation of the world and for evermore" (48:6; cf. 62:7). God acted in and before the foundation of the world, so that the creation of the Son of Man and the election of the saints could date from then, thus preserving God's immutability for the entire duration of the world. This concept of what remains unchanged from the foundations of the world seems to be a Hebraic way of affirming as enduring what the Greeks conceived as timelessly eternal.[27] Such a creaturely understanding of Christ may underlie the conviction that he is "the first-born of all creation" (Col 1:15) and possibly even the hymn magnifying Jesus' humble obedience into a justification of His glorious exaltation (Phil. 2:5–11). If Christ be thereby pre-existent, then Jesus' life must be seen as its incarnation, thereby generating the insoluble problem as to how the earthly Jesus could be both God and man. Moreover, a pre-existent Christ distinct from God raises all the questions that ultimately led to Nicaea. If we simply accept the possibility that God could be temporally transformed and that Christ names this transformation for the church, many of these speculative issues could be avoided.

If the preexistence of Christ were set aside, the temptation to see divinity in the earthly Jesus (as in John's gospel) would not arise. If Christ were not distinct from God, but God as transformed, we would not need to look for the presence of Christ in the life of Jesus (as in the synoptics). Rather, we must consider the way in which Jesus' life, ministry, and death affected God. Jesus seems to have lived out of an intimate communion with God, sufficient for him to have addressed God as "Abba," his intimate Father. Jesus' filial obedience to God's will could easily have evoked a responsive intensification of divine purposing. We may even think of God entrusting the divine cause to Jesus. Perhaps they together planned to confront the Jewish authorities in Jerusalem with their concern for the lost sheep of the house of

Israel. The undertaking was extremely risky, yet deemed worthwhile, even of overriding importance.

Mark, with his immutabilist assumptions, depicts Jesus' death as scripturally predetermined, but we may question whether it was ever willed by God. Had that death not taken place, and this Roman execution blamed on the Jews, perhaps the schism between Jews and Christians might never have occurred, and I refuse to believe that this schism could ever have been willed by God. Rather, I think we should conceive of God being intimately involved with Jesus' undertaking. The intensification of divine purposing brought them ever closer together, yet this purposing was ultimately defeated at Golgotha.

Were Jesus not subsequently exalted as the heavenly Christ, his crucifixion would have been just another martyrdom. Christians have retrospectively read infinite meaning into that act by claiming that Christ died for our sins, an act whereby we obtain reconciliation with God. As long as God and Christ are experienced as two distinct realities, it is possible to theorize, as Anselm did, about an atonement brought about by an objective transaction between the two of them. If God could not change, God could not suffer; even the God-man could not suffer insofar as he was God. The atonement was something that Jesus, only insofar as he was man, could do on behalf of an impassive God. Otherwise we could not be saved from our sins. This transactional theory cannot be affirmed, yet its central intent can be: The Cross of Jesus decisively reveals to us the suffering of Christ because of the sins of the world, most particularly if Christ names God as transformed by the death of Jesus; for in perhaps its deepest sense, God is transformed by the experience of human evil. Whatever causes conflict is to that extent evil. While it may be possible to work through a conflict to achieve harmony, the conflict cannot be fully experienced except through suffering. God's involvement with Jesus and his cause leads to God's own defeat at the Cross. The Cross gives us a glimpse of God's suffering; here it is made most manifest.

Yet, divine suffering occurs wherever evil is encountered. Were this not so, we could not be justified. Paul's proclamation of justification by grace means that we are fully accepted into the divine life despite our own unacceptability. All of our being and actions are incorporated into the divine life, not just that fragment that meets God's standards. The evil is accepted as well as the good, and this necessarily causes suffering. In the Cross of Jesus, God as Christ suffering our evil is most fully manifest.[28] The transformation of God by experiencing Jesus, however great in degree, is not different in kind from the way in which God is affected by all creatures. Moreover, it would have been quite gradual, extending throughout Jesus' life. During his life, God's concern for Jesus would be primarily mediated to the disciples by Jesus himself. Jesus' death, however, was a sore disappointment to their expectations, shocking them into experiencing God in a radically new manner. The gradual transformation of God by experiencing Jesus was suddenly, dramatically, revealed to the disciples on the third day. The concerns, aims, and personality traits that had characterized their beloved Master were now experienced as characterizing the Living God. God had become Christ for the early Christians. God was primarily experienced as intimately related to them through their common concern, a concern fully shared by God, for the life, cause, and death of Jesus.

However, because the disciples found it impossible to anticipate any divine transformation, God and Christ were experienced as distinct figures, although in intimate association. Besides God, a second figure appeared, ultimately to be explained as "hidden from the foundations of the world." Jesus as the Christ was exalted to the heavenly places. Moreover, because the disciples fully expected the resurrection of the dead at the end of the age, this experience of the exalted Jesus would be naturally interpreted in terms of his own resurrection. We do not gainsay the importance and centrality of that basic experience for the church, but it can be understood in an entirely different way once we divest ourselves of the unnecessary assumption of immutability in terms of which the early church interpreted that event.

The church has always proclaimed that the Christ was intimately bound up with the life of Jesus. Thus, there have been all sorts of attempts to combine an eternal, immutable, divine nature with a temporal, mutable, human nature in the person of Jesus. Christ pertained to God only in respect to God the Son, that eternal capacity which could become the God-man in incarnation. Our proposal makes it possible to ascribe Christ to God unqualifiedly. Strict monotheism need not be compromised. At the same time, the intimate relation between Christ and Jesus is affirmed, for God could only become Christ through his transforming experience of Jesus. Without Jesus, God could not have become Christ.

On the other hand, without God, Jesus could not have become the Christ, for Jesus has become fully God insofar as it is possible for any creature to become God by being completely incorporated into the life of God such that his existence in God can be revelatory to others. Nevertheless, in his earthly life, apart from God's experience of him, Jesus is purely human. The earthly Jesus is not yet the Christ. On analogy with a Boddhisattva, we may appropriately designate him as the Christ to be. It is first in the event proclaimed as His resurrection that Jesus is exalted into the Godhead. Thus, we can fully affirm with conservative Christianity that the heavenly Christ is truly God without the embarrassment liberals have felt with the notion of the earthly Jesus being at once both God and man.

THE FATHER AND THE SON AS CONTINGENT

Thus far, my argument has been largely addressed to fellow Christians. What has been primarily transformed is our image of God, the way God has been experienced and worshipped by the church. If Christ is "the visible image of the invisible God" (Col 1:15), however, so is God the Father. As John Courtney Murray observes, in Christianity "God still remains the one God of the Old Testament. Only now, the name God has a new supposition, in the technical sense. It stands for the Father. He is not *the* God. Everywhere in St. Paul and St. John that one encounters the word God, one should read, as its sense and as the direction of its address, 'the Father.' This is now God's proper name. He is 'the Father of our Lord Jesus Christ' in whose manifestation as Son the Name of God was now revealed."[29] Whatever the meaning of "God the Father" in later trinitarian speculation, it signified in New Testament usage the God of Israel, the God who rescued Israel out of the house of bondage. It also signified the relationship that existed between these two visible images of God. The Father had existed before Christ in the antecedent history of Israel, and Christ is furthermore derived from the visible God of Israel.

Traditional immutabilist preconceptions have radically covered over this original understanding of the relation of the Father to the Son. From the creed, we learn that the Son is begotten of the Father "before all worlds" and that phrase is customarily understood to mean nontemporal generation, not too different from the eternal procession of Nous from the One in neo-Platonic thought. The historical contingencies of Israel's life and Jesus' life and death are then undercut by nontemporal necessity, and the richness of God's relation with Israel is lost. However, the language of the trinity corrects an erroneous supposition that the language of God's transformation by Jesus suggests; namely, that Christ as the image of God for the Church somehow supersedes the image of the God of Israel. For while these images of God arise in different historical circumstances, the Father and the Son co-exist in the trinity as equally valid means of access to God.

The deepest meaning of the trinity, thus, concerns the relationship between the Christian and Jewish communities. In particular, it concerns how their different perceptions of God are to be correlated. Here it is clearly not enough to say that both worship the same God. Of course they do, but insofar as God is the same for all religions, God is merely abstractly considered. The Enlightenment's disdain for the particularities of revealed religion in the quest for common consensus thereby ignores the salvific power these particular traditions have fostered. The problem is how to affirm the salvific power in another tradition without undermining one's own.[30] Christians tend to forget that Christianity is by and large an extension of Judaism to the Gentiles. Paul was quite aware of this: "Theirs is the adoption as sons; theirs the divine glory, the covenants, the receiving of the law, the temple worship and the promises" (Rom. 9:4). These spiritual riches can only belong to those who are born or become Jews. Salvation becomes possible for Gentiles through the Cross of Christ, whereby God's suffering acceptance of our unrighteousness is revealed, but the essential core of God's salvation of Israel is not abrogated thereby. It still remains accessible to the original covenant people.

As Christians, we are drawn to God through Christ in the specific terms of later trinitarian speculation, but that becomes possible for us by conceiving the *Personae* as the various images of the invisible God. The derivation of the Son from the Father, then, expresses the truth that the Christ comes forth from the expectations and traditions of Israel. Thus, in the Exodus, God became the Lord and Savior of Israel, while through the events the church celebrates as the resurrection of Christ, God became the savior of the world, the savior of Gentiles as well as the savior of the Jews. God is still the savior of both. Immutabilist conceptions allowed the church to believe that if Christ were now the savior of the world, he must always have been, and that this is the only acceptable mode of salvation. Christ then supersedes Israel. But this means, as we have seen, that Christ would supersede God the Father, if God the Father is to be identified with the God and Savior of Israel. Exclusivistic claims based on such passages as "no one comes to the Father, except by me" (John 14:6) must mean a form of parricide, if they deprive God the Father of any independent salvific power. If Christ were now the sole means of salvation, then those who cling to the original covenant would be excluded from God's favor. On the contrary, the continued vitality of Israel as the people of God is necessary as a witness to God's original grace, a grace now extended to Gentiles through God's transformation as Christ.

I do not intend to revive the ancient heresy of Sabellius, who held that God is not at one and the same time Father, Son, and Spirit, but has been active in three consecutive manifestations or energies—first in the *persona* of the Father as creator and lawgiver, then in the *persona* of the Son as Redeemer, and last in the *persona* of the Spirit as the giver of life. The continued co-existence of the Father and Son marks a crucial difference. Here we may think of religious traditions, particularly those which stand in a direct relationship of derivation, on the analogy of parent and child. The parent's continued existence is not essential for the life of the child, even though the child could not have come into existence without the parent. But the existence of the child is no reason for the replacement of the parent. On the contrary, the continued existence of the parent nurtures the child. Both can co-exist; both can respect one another; both can be enriched by the continued existence of the other. With reference to the divine persons, Sabellius taught that the Father was merely one of the manifestations of the one God. He put the Father formally in a position of complete equality with the other persons, thus preparing the way for Augustine's doctrine of the trinity. Instead of the subordinationism of Paul's formula, God, Christ, Spirit, we have the coordination of the three persons, Father, Son, and Spirit. If we view the persons as images of God, this is as it should be, for just as Christ does not displace the God of Israel, neither is Christ subordinate to the God of Israel. Both are equally salvific images for their respective communities.

Given the prevailing immutabilist assumptions, Sabellianism could be easily dismissed as heretical. If God could not possibly change, how could there be three temporal modalities, particularly if these were to be regarded as more than merely apparent? Immutability entails impassibility, and Sabellianism could be easily rejected because it would require God, in the form of the Son, to suffer. Or, as they understood the charge, God the Father would suffer. Such patripassionism was roundly condemned. These charges lose their power once we reject the underlying assumption of immutability.

If we forgo this assumption, the eternality of the trinitarian persons need no longer be claimed. This has several advantages. As we have seen, the rootage of trinitarian thinking in the relationship between Israel and the church now becomes evident. Difficulties in supposing how trinitarian considerations could be relevant to God's relation to intelligent life elsewhere in the universe disappear. We need to learn that trinitarian concerns have no place in God apart from the way we Christians are intimately related to God, and how we conceive other salvific communities to be related to God. Trinitarian thinking concerns contingencies essential to our salvation, not to some eternal threeness of the abstract divine nature.

Summing up, we have seen how it is possible for both God and Jesus to become Christ, if Christ names this transformed reality having both God and Jesus as necessary constituents. God can become Christ only by experiencing Jesus, and Jesus can only become Christ by being taken up into the life of God. This the disciples proclaimed as the resurrection. This primal event is the very foundation of Christianity, which achieves its finest expression in the doctrine of the trinity. I have simply found a rather different conceptuality by which to understand this formula, permitting the *persona* of the risen Christ to be understood in contingent terms.[31]

NOTES

1.   Chapter 7 of *The Lure of God* (Philadelphia: Fortress Press, 1978), 99–112.

2.   "John Cobb's Trinity: Implications for the University," in *Theology and the University: Essays in Honor of John B. Cobb, Jr.*, ed. David Ray Griffin and Joseph C. Hough, Jr. (Albany: State University of New York Press, 1991), 148–165.

3. Cyril C. Richardson, *The Doctrine of the Trinity* (Nashville, TN: Abingdon Press, 1958).

4. *Ibid.*, 8f.

5. Charles Hartshorne, *The Divine Relativity* (New Haven, CT: Yale University Press, 1948), chapter 2.

6. It would be more appropriate to reverse the clauses in these two antitheses.

7. Note that Whitehead's two natures for God are formally distinct in this sense. To maintain clarity, I use *Persona* nonsubjectively, so that it can function as one aspect of the divine actuality, or as a way the one divine subjectivity is made manifest, reserving the term "Person" to mean what is itself a subjectivity.

8. Although nontemporal "begetting" can be expressed in terms of Whitehead's own philosophy, it is no longer available to me, because I have come to deny the uncreated character of eternal objects: "The Creation of 'Eternal' Objects," *The Modern Schoolman* 71(3) (March 1994), 191–222. If all "eternal" objects are temporally emergent, then none is available for a nontemporal envisagement. If so, the primordial nature dissolves into the consequent concrescence, except for the metaphysical principles, which must be exemplified by all occasions.

9. For this reason, Whitehead refers to "the perishing occasions in the life of each temporal Creature" (*Process and Reality*, 351). The temporal Creature is a living person, that is, a personally ordered series, not simply a single occasion.

10. *Whitehead's Metaphysics of Extension and Solidarity* (Albany: State University of New York Press, 1986), 50–58, *et passim*. While I agree that creativity is co-extensive with the present and future, I do not see how creativity can pertain to the past, a perfectly good domain of the extensive continuum.

11. *Trinity and Process: A Critical Evaluation and Reconstruction of Hartshorne's Di-Polar Theism Towards a Trinitarian Metaphysics* (New York: Peter Lang, 1992). See my review in *The Modern Schoolman* 71(4) (May 1994), 322–25.

12. Interdependence is usually thematized by Whitehead in terms of coherence, one of the criteria for metaphysical theory. " 'Coherence' . . . means that the fundamental ideas . . . presuppose each other so that in isolation they are meaningless. . . . It is the ideal of speculative philosophy that its fundamental notions shall not seem capable of abstraction from each other" (*Process and Reality*, 3). We may

illustrate this principle by the contrast between existence and characterization. Eternal objects have existence only as ingredient
within actual entities, while actual entities have characterization
only by means of the eternal objects.

13. This is somewhat akin to Leibniz's pre-established harmony. To
    avoid making each monad causally contingent upon others, God
    creates its inner principle such that it appears to be synchronized
    with all others. Although each finite monad only gradually learns
    how it relates to others, all the pertinent information is already
    stored up in its inner principle.

14. Otherwise the gods and souls, being subjectivities, would be on par
    with the Forms. The atemporal Forms, however, are superior to that
    which is subjective, therefore implicitly taken to be temporal. In the
    Sophist, Plato does speak of the soul as having life and motion.

15. The problem is compounded for three necessary subjectivities.
    After an eternity of social interaction, what possible novelties could
    the trinitarian persons have for each other?

16. Whitehead had a particular understanding of coherence, which is
    more rigorous than the usual understanding: Coherence "is the
    ideal of speculative philosophy that its fundamental notions shall
    not seem capable of abstraction from each other" (*Process and
    Reality*, 3). This is so if those notions are interdependent.

17. In recent years, many theologies have become willing to affirm
    divine suffering, yet few would go so far as process theism. They
    are unwilling to break with the claim that God is absolutely inde-
    pendent of everything else.

18. Chapter four of *Religion in the Making* appears to be an exception
    to this statement. In the first two levels of *Process and Reality*, how-
    ever, the affirmation of divine personality is conspicuously missing.
    (See "The Riddle of *Religion in the Making*," *Process Studies* 22(1)
    (Spring 1993), 42–50.) Since in the later book, Whitehead was
    attempting a rigorous natural theology in accordance with the direc-
    tive of the Gifford lectureship, we can infer that Whitehead did not
    then have a satisfactory argument for divine personality. Hence,
    chapter four is hypothetical, sketching what God would be like on
    his principles, if God were personal.

19. Clark Williamson, *A Guest in the House of Israel: Post-Holocaust
    Church Theology*. (Louisville, KY: Westminster/John Knox Press,
    1993), 225–32.

20. *Ibid.*, 228.

21. *Ibid.*, 230.

22. 2 Corinthians 5:19.

23. Williamson, 230.

24. I have explored these passages extensively in *The Lure of God: A Biblical Background for Process Theism* (Philadelphia: Fortress Press, 1978).

25. "An Alternative to *Creation Ex Nihilo*," *Religious Studies* 19(2) (June 1983), 205–13.

26. John Cobb, *Christ in a Pluralistic Age*, Philadelphia: Westminster, 1975.

27. More precisely, the New Testament writers may have exempted God's original creative activity from the principle of complete immutability, identifying immutability with divine rest. Thus, after writing that "his works were finished at the foundation of the world," the writer comments "For in one place it speaks about the seventh day as follows, 'And God rested on the seventh day from all his works' " (Heb. 4:4).

28. This need not mean that God cannot ultimately overcome this suffering, transforming the evil into tragic beauty. See my essay, "Divine Persuasion and the Triumph of Good," in *Process Philosophy and Christian Thought*, ed. Delwin Brown, Ralph E. James, and Gene Reeves (Indianapolis: Bobbs-Merrill, 1971), 287–304.

29. *The Problem of God* (New Haven: Yale University Press, 1964), 27.

30. Here Paul Van Buren's reflection on the trinity is most instructive: "It is one thing for the Jews to call upon God as Father and to know him immediately and always as their God. That is their right and their duty because of their election, because they are called to precisely that immediate relationship by God himself: I will take you for my people, and I will be your God (Exod. 6:7). For Gentiles to call upon this God is another thing, a strange thing, which can only happen because God has made toward them a further movement and has drawn them to Himself in a further way. Just this way in which God is Himself in reaching out to us Gentiles and drawing us into the Way in which we know and worship Him, just this reality of God—and so our apprehension of Him directly in this His reality—is what we express with the doctrine of the Trinity. With those words—One God, Father, Son and Spirit—we express our apprehension in the one God, the God of Israel, who by His Spirit and through His Son has drawn us to Himself. It is the only adequate

way for the Gentile church to confess the God of Israel." *Discerning the Way* (New York: Seabury Press, 1980), 69f.

31. Those who are familiar with the argument of *The Lure of God* will appreciate the extensive reconception of the resurrection of Christ this essay entails. Yet, there are important continuities. Both stress the role of the risen Christ as the key to New Testament thought. Both appreciate the importance of temporal transformation. Both seek to get behind the reported visions of the risen Christ to the imperceptible reality these refer to. But I did not then recognize that this event could be understood in terms of a particular transformation of God, a clear possibility entailed by process theism. *The Lure of God* conceives of the experience interpreted as Jesus's resurrection solely in terms of creaturely transformation. The risen Christ was there understood to be the inner subjectivity, the dynamic coordinating agency of the Body of Christ, a new evolutionary emergence of which Christians constitute its members. The Arian nature of this solution was recognized (p. 95), but its difficulties were underestimated. It makes God and Christ into two distinct subjectivities, entailing a departure from strict monotheism insofar as Christ is worshipped. Moreover, such a Christ is neither divine nor human, but rather a transhuman creature.

Basic to this understanding, however, was the notion of Christ as temporal emergence brought about by the life and death of Jesus. If we are to correct the Arian solution there proposed by merging the two subjectivities of God and Christ into one, we need to account for the temporal emergence of Christ as the mutual transformation of both God and Jesus.

The Trinity and Modified Whiteheadian Metaphysics

Emphasis on God as Tripersonal

Gregory A. Boyd

The Self-Sufficient Sociality of God:
A Trinitarian Revision of Hartshorne's Metaphysics

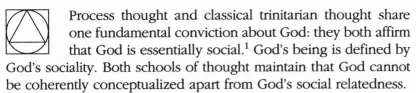 Process thought and classical trinitarian thought share one fundamental conviction about God: they both affirm that God is essentially social.[1] God's being is defined by God's sociality. Both schools of thought maintain that God cannot be coherently conceptualized apart from God's social relatedness.

The ways process thought and trinitarian thought conceptualize this sociality, however, differ greatly. Chief among these differences is that for classical trinitarian thought, God's essential sociality is defined within Godself. The only metaphysically necessary relationship God has is within the Trinity of divine Persons. The relationship God has with the world is wholly contingent, a matter of divine choice. For process thought, in contrast, God's essential sociality is defined by relationship with the world, a relationship that lies "beyond the accident of God's will."[2] The notion that God could exist apart from the world is, within process thought, an unintelligible notion. Process thought, thus, holds to a necessary God–world relationship, trinitarian thought holds to a necessary God–God relationship. Another way of saying this is that process thought holds that God's sociality is *world-dependent*; whereas, classical trinitarian thought holds that God's sociality is *self-sufficient*.

From the classical trinitarian perspective from which I write, it is hard to overemphasize the significance of this difference, because, as a number of trinitarian thinkers have argued, a great deal of what is distinctive in orthodox Christianity is adversely affected when the self-sufficient sociality of God is abandoned.[3]

Among other things, it is difficult to coherently maintain the Christian view of creation and salvation by grace, the incarnation, the ability of God to answer prayer and supernaturally intervene in history, and God's final victory over evil if God's sociality with the world is a matter of metaphysical necessity. It is chiefly for this reason that most orthodox trinitarians to date have rejected process thought, although they may otherwise be attracted to it as a plausible metaphysical system.

The question I address in this essay is this: Is it possible to overcome this impasse? Is there a way of affirming the essential insights of process thought while not abandoning the self-sufficient sociality of God? Is it possible to arrive at a position that enjoys the metaphysical explanatory power of process thought but also affirms that God does not need to be related to a nondivine order? In this essay, I attempt to answer this question in the affirmative. Indeed, my argument goes one step further and suggests that process thought, when purged of certain mistaken notions, actually *requires* a view of God as self-sufficient in sociality.

Because I find his articulation of process thought to be the most persuasive, in this essay, I restrict my discussion to the writings of Charles Hartshorne, although most of my critique could be applied with equal force to process thought in general. After providing a brief exposition of what Hartshorne understands metaphysics to be about, I seek to locate three features of Hartshorne's thought that lead him to posit a necessary God–world relationship. In doing this, I offer a critique of each of these features with the result that a necessary God–world relationship is avoided, while a God–God relationship is required. My goal is to arrive at a position that retains the explanatory force of Hartshorne's metaphysical system but that requires, rather than rules out, a view of God as self-sufficient in sociality.

AN OUTLINE OF HARTSHORNE'S THOUGHT

A statement is a metaphysical truth, according to Hartshorne, if it is necessarily and categorically true.[4] As necessary, a metaphysical truth must be true by definition. Its denial must result in contradiction. And as categorical, a metaphysical statement must be true in every conceivable state of affairs. Hence, metaphysical truths are logical truths without being tautologous and experiential without being empirical. Metaphysics, in a word, is the search for a priori truths about existence.[5]

Among the assertions that constitute metaphysical truths, according to Hartshorne, are the statements "something exists," "experience occurs," "experience is socially related to other experiences," "experience is constituted by a felt aesthetic value," and "God exists as the unsurpassable instance of experienced sociality and aesthetic value." Hartshorne maintains, correctly I believe, that in no conceivable state of affairs, could these truths fail to be exemplified. For the purpose of this present essay, we assume Hartshorne is, thus far, correct.[6] In any event, these assertions represent views shared by all "orthodox" Whiteheadians, although the way Hartshorne arrives at them and articulates them is distinctive.

The question this present essay concerns itself with is this: Assuming Hartshorne is correct in his analysis of these four statements as a priori truths, why does he deem it necessary to postulate a necessary God–world relationship rather than a necessary God–God relationship? Why cannot the experiential, social, and aesthetically defined necessary features of being be fulfilled within the one necessary being, God? To this question we now turn.

1. Experience as Creative Synthesis

The Asymmetrical Nature of Concrete Relations. The first reason why the affirmation of the above mentioned a priori truths leads Hartshorne to construe God's sociality as being world-dependent rather than self-sufficient has to do with the way he works through the a priori truth that "experience occurs." According to Hartshorne, experience "cannot generate its own content" and cannot have itself as its own datum.[7] He writes:

> Experience has to have a content; it is experience of something. Philosophers have argued about the proposition, "Perhaps all we directly experience is our own mental state at the time." But mental states are just experiences over again, so that the proposition means, "Perhaps our experiences are of nothing except themselves." We must reject the absurd idea that any experience can thus furnish its own sole datum. A mere awareness of the same awareness is nonsense.[8]

Herein lies the necessary sociality of experience: it must have something *outside of itself* as its content. And what is the necessary content of experience? As is well known, Hartshorne, following

Whitehead, maintains that the answer is found principally in memory.[9] In memory, we find that a multiplicity of past objects are
experienced in a new unified way.[10] The present "prehends" the
past; the objective content of the past, plus the new synthesis of
this content, constitutes the "being" of any present experience. For
process thought, our understanding of the ultimate nature of
things, of "actual occasions," of causation, time, and the social
structure of reality, is to be founded in this asymmetrical understanding of the present prehending the past in novel ways in the
same way that our memory re-experiences the past. All concrete
relations, therefore, are of the present prehending the past. There
are, at the level of concrete reality, no contemporary relations.

It is, I believe, this asymmetrical understanding of the sociality of experience *as a necessary condition of being* that requires
Hartshorne, and process thought in general, to postulate a necessary God–world relationship. If God is defined concretely as an
unsurpassable experience, and if experience cannot have itself as
its own datum, and if experience must be constituted as a creative
synthesis of an antecedent multiplicity of objectified data, then, it
seems, God must eternally be related to a past multifarious reality for the concrete content of God's own self-defining experience. The experience that defines God as God, in other words,
must be constituted by a moment-by-moment synthesis of the
just-past world.

If this analysis of experience is metaphysically sound, then I
do not see how the abandonment of the self-sufficient sociality of
God can be avoided. However, I do not believe this analysis is
correct. It is, I contend, based on an arbitrary metaphysical prejudice and reductionistic assumption that leads Hartshorne mistakenly to identify contingent features of experience as necessary.

Locating a Metaphysical Prejudice. We must first ask why our
experience of memory is invested with the authority of providing
the analogical key to understanding the necessary features of all
concrete reality. It is true that memory is constituted as a present
experience of the past, but it is also true that we experience contemporary phenomena as contemporary. We experience ourselves
as being related to our world in a contemporary mutually defining
way. Indeed, starting with the concrete reality of phenomenological experience, some philosophers, such as Martin Buber, have
argued that the "most concrete" experience humans have is the

prereflective experience of *"das Zwischen."* Buber argues that there is, at a prereflective level, a "mutual givenness of subject and object," a "primary togetherness which antedates their separation."[11] Sharing insights with Merleau-Ponty, Buber argues that the present consists most fundamentally in the preconscious self/world unity in which each must be seen as a polar constituent of a fundamental singular symmetrical relation.[12] This primal symmetry is attained at a conscious level only when we cease making "the other" an "it" and abandon ourselves to it as a "thou."

The question is, why is this phenomenological experience of the self/world unity, of the self and the world as contemporaneous, symmetrically related, and mutually defining, passed over in favor of memory as Hartshorne searches for the key to understanding the a priori features of all experience? The answer is that Hartshorne considers this mutually defining encounter with "the other" at a phenomenological level to be abstract.[13] What is "really" going on in an "I–Thou" encounter, according to Hartshorne, is that one society of actual occasions synthesizes the other just-past society, and this other society of actual occasions in turn synthesizes the now-past society of occasions that had just experienced it. According to Hartshorne, our conscious awareness is too dull to pick up this moment-by-moment asymmetrical exchange, and thus the relation *seems* to be symmetrical and contemporary. However, "in reality" this symmetricality represents only the abstract features of the truly concrete asymmetrical relation, and to mistake the abstract for the concrete is to commit "the fallacy of misplaced concreteness."[14]

This line of reasoning strikes me as circular. If it is assumed that memory holds the analogical key to understanding the a priori conditions of concrete experience, then, of course, our phenomenological experience of contemporaneity must be judged as being abstract, because it does not conform to these conditions. However, why grant memory this preferred ontological status in the first place? Indeed, even if it is granted that memory provides the key to understanding actual occasions, it is not clear why what happens at the level of actual occasions is designated as being "more real" than what happens at the level of the phenomenological wholes of which these actual occasions are constituents. Is there any metaphysical justification for the assumption that the smallest analyzable units of an entity are what is "most real" about that entity? Is there, in short, any justification for the process doctrine that actual occasions are alone "real"?[15]

Justus Buchler brings out this charge of arbitrary reductionism forcefully when he writes concerning Whitehead's *Process and Reality*:

> If we ask why . . . any kind of unity or oneness is "more of a unity," a truer oneness than any other; why individuals are "more real" than societies, why they "make up the sole reality of the universe," when non-individual actualities [*nexūs*] have been discriminated just as decisively; what it means to be a "completely real thing"—we find no answer.[16]

As Buchler, Ross, and others have effectively argued, whether something is analyzed as concrete or abstract, determinate or indeterminate, actual or possible, is perspectivally contingent. Moreover, the integrity of any given perspective cannot be undermined by an arbitrary preference for another.[17] It is an unwarranted assumption to assume that what physics or metaphysics says is true about the smallest constituents of what we experience at a phenomenological level is "truer," "more real," or "more concrete" than what we actually experience at a phenomenological level.[18]

If metaphysics is concerned with the a priori features of concreteness as such, it must take into account the perspectival relativity of its categories. However, this, I suspect, is precisely what Hartshorne fails to do. And this omission leads him mistakenly to judge the contingent features of our experience of memory as being necessary and categorical features of concreteness as such. For a variety of reasons, I affirm Hartshorne's view that to be is to be an experience of something. However, his understanding of what this "something" must be is mistaken, owing to his nonperspectival understanding of what it is to be concrete.

The very fact that our phenomenological experience is concrete, contemporary, and symmetrical, as Buber shows, demonstrates this. For, if asymmetrical relationality were truly a priori, its alternative would constitute a self-contradiction.[19] Moreover, the fact that the asymmetrical relationality of the present to the past is dependent upon the speed of light also demonstrates that it is not an a priori truth, unless we want to maintain the prima facia implausible position that the speed of light is a logical, not empirical, limitation on being.[20]

God's Self-Defining Triune Experience. If our case against Hartshorne's analysis of the a priori content of experience is correct, then there are no longer any grounds for maintaining that

God needs an antecedent, nondivine world to provide the content of God's concrete experience. And if God is necessary, as Hartshorne argues, and the world is not,[21] and if experience is necessarily social, as Hartshorne further argues, then the only thing metaphysics requires us to say is that God, the one necessary Being, must exist as a social experience *of God's own Self.*

This is not to say that God's necessary self-defining experience "generates its own content," a notion Hartshorne rightly maintains is absurd. It simply implies that God must eternally exist as distinct socially related centers of experience. Nor does this necessary sociality within God imply that everything about God's self-defining sociality must be necessary, a grave mistake classical theism made with its doctrine of God as *actus purus.* There are ways of coherently maintaining the self-sufficient, necessary and, therefore, eternal sociality of God's self-experience without ruling out contingency within God, although it is beyond the scope of this present essay to spell these out. Suffice it for the present to note that no contradiction is committed in maintaining the *fact* that God is self-related, is necessary and eternal, even as one, while also maintaining that the *way* God is eternally self-related is contingent.[22]

2.   Divergent Multiplicity and the Intensity of Aesthetic Satisfaction

The Nature of Aesthetic Satisfaction.   A second reason Hartshorne is led to construe the sociality of God as being world-dependent rather than self-sufficient is found in the way he works through the a prior truth that "experience is constituted by a felt aesthetic value." I am, for a variety of reasons, convinced that this standard Whiteheadian doctrine is correct.[23] However, the way it is analyzed in Hartshorne's thought, and in process thought in general, is misconstrued. And it is this misconstrued aspect of that a priori truth that leads Hartshorne and other process theologians to believe that it can only be exemplified in a God–world relationship rather than in a God–God relationship.

Hartshorne's analysis of aesthetic value renders the world necessary to God, because he, following Whitehead, holds that the intensity of an aesthetic experience "depends upon contrast, the amount of diversity integrated into an experience."[24] "Beauty of all kinds," Hartshorne writes, "is unity in variety, and the greater the variety, the greater the value of the unity."[25] God's aesthetic experience in any given moment is unsurpassably intense only because God, in contrast to other actual occasions, prehends the entire world. And because the possible number of contrasting relationships within the nondivine order is infinite, and because each divine prehension of a just-past world is synthesized in God's mind with the infinite complexity of the previously experienced worlds, God's aesthetic experience is being forever enriched and, thus, is forever intensifying. There can, in short, be no "maximal instance" of aesthetic satisfaction, not even for God.[26]

If this analysis of aesthetic valuation is correct, then it seems, once again, that the self-sufficient sociality of God must be abandoned. God's aesthetic experience would not be unsurpassable if there were no world, for a higher intensity of aesthetic value would be conceivable; namely, an experience of an ever-increasing complex world. But God is, by definition, "that than which none greater can be conceived."[27] Hence, God, by definition, must forever be experiencing a nondivine world.

According to Hartshorne, the necessity of God's experience of the world remains, even if God is conceived of as triune. He writes:

> Even the trinity gives no sufficient . . . contrast. What is required is maximal contrast, not only on one level, as between the persons of the Trinity, but between levels within the unity of God—for instance, between the contingent and changing and the necessary and immutable.[28]

The intensity of aesthetic satisfaction depends upon the "maximal contrast" of what is experienced, and this, Hartshorne argues, God could not have if only the sociality of divine persons were experienced. Thus, God needs a contrasting nondivine world to experience if the divine self-defining experience of beauty is to be unsurpassable. At the very least, it would be "wrong or foolish [of God] not to create," for this would be choosing a lesser good over a greater good. But God, by metaphysical necessity, "cannot do wrong or be foolish." Hence, Hartshorne concludes, "if there is necessity in God, there is necessity in the world."[29]

Such a conclusion is unavoidable if Hartshorne is correct in maintaining that the intensity of an aesthetic satisfaction is contingent upon the scope and depth of contrasting relationships experienced and that there can, therefore, be no maximal instance of aesthetic satisfaction. It is my conviction, however, that both aspects of this analysis are mistaken. Anything like a full discussion of the nature of aesthetic experience, of course, would lead us far astray from the purpose of this essay. It will suffice for our purposes simply to call in question the a priori status of Hartshorne's own aesthetic theory.

The Unnecessary Correlation of the Scope and Intensity of Aesthetic Experience. It is undeniable that any aesthetic experience involves an experience of relationship. I agree with Hartshorne that it is true a priori that no unrelated simple entity could even exist, let alone be beautiful (because to be is to be an experience of aesthetic value). And I concur, to a point, that it is generally true in our experience that the intensity of our aesthetic satisfaction is correlated with the scope and depth of the relationships we experience. However, the supposition that this correlation is itself an a priori feature of aesthetic satisfaction goes too far, in my estimation.

Since a priori truths must be universally exemplified, we must ask: Is Hartshorne's correlation of the intensity of aesthetic satisfaction with the scope and depth of what is experienced exemplified in all our experience, especially those we would identify specifically as aesthetic in nature? Do we find that the intensity of our experiences is universally proportioned to the breadth of our experience? Is it really the scope and depth of contrasting relationships that most fundamentally renders one's aesthetic enjoyment of (say) a sunset intense? Is it this that provides Botticelli's *Birth of Venus* or Rembrandt's *Supper at Emmaus* with their satisfying quality? Does the "massiveness" (to use Whitehead's phrase) of relations have anything to do with the ability of Wordsworth's or Goethe's poems to move us deeply? And is the power of Beethoven's or Debussy's music centered on, or even related to, the quantity of contrasting chords they contain? I cannot see that it is.

Indeed, is it not frequently the case, as minimalists have maintained, that the intensity of aesthetic satisfaction is often correlated with the simplicity of what is experienced? How can the playing of a single oboe sometimes move us more profoundly than an entire orchestra? And why are scientific theories and mathematical formulas, like some dances, poems, scenes from nature, and paintings, experienced as more beautiful precisely because of their *lack* of complexity? It is, of course, very difficult to specify exactly what it is about such experiences that renders them intensely satisfying, as the history of aesthetic theory from Plato to the present demonstrates. However, it seems counterintuitive to follow Hartshorne and Whitehead in supposing that the quantity of what is experienced is essential to it. As one aesthetician writes:

> . . . aesthetic values are not ordered by their scope. If one cloud gives as much pleasure in contemplation as the whole sunset, then the whole sunset adds nothing, although it is larger. If one chord gives as much pleasure as the whole composition, then the rest of the composition is superfluous . . . The poem of a few lines may be as beautiful as the poem of great length, and the novel of great scope is not a finer work of art merely because of its inclusiveness.[30]

Thus, while I grant that the intensity of an aesthetic experience is many times connected with the scope and depth of the contrasting relations that constitute it, this seems to be a contingent, not a priori, feature of such experiences. At the very least, I hope my critique has shown that scope and depth of contrast are not built into the *very meaning* of "aesthetic intensity," which is what would have to be the case if Hartshorne were correct.

If metaphysics can say anything beyond the simple truth that the concept of aesthetic experience, as the concept of existence itself, involves experiential sociality, my proposal would be that the intensity of an experience is correlated with the degree to which one's experience is penetrated by, or defined by, what we experience. To experience intensely means to experience deeply, not necessarily broadly, and this entails that our concrete being at that moment is significantly defined by what we are experiencing.[31] Just *why* a particular experience is felt intensely is caused by many variables and, thus, is contingent. The scope and depth of the relationships experienced may be among these variables, but this is a contingent matter. Moreover, it is Hartshorne's misidentification of this contingent feature of aesthetic experience as a necessary feature that leads him to postulate that God without the world could not enjoy as much aesthetic satisfaction as would God with the world.

Can There Be a Maximal Aesthetic Satisfaction? It is, I believe, also this mistake that leads Hartshorne to suppose that there can be no maximal instance of aesthetic satisfaction. If the intensity of an aesthetic satisfaction is necessarily dependent upon the scope and depth of relations experienced, and if there is no upper limit to the scope and depth of relations the nondivine world can achieve, then while God's experience of the total world at any given moment will be unsurpassable at that moment, it will, nevertheless, be forever intensifying as new world relationships are synthesized with already past world relationships. No end to this improvement is conceivable.

Once we reject Hartshorne's quantitative analysis of the intensity of aesthetic experience, however, there remain no grounds for holding this view. Indeed, there are at least two further arguments that can be made against it. First, it seems that an acme of aesthetic experience *is* conceivable. Do we not sometimes experience what we might call "peak experiences," rare delectable momentary experiences in which our enjoyment and appreciation of an aesthetic experience reach a zenith? In rare, profoundly penetrating experiences of nature, art, worship, or sexual intimacy, does our experience not sometimes attain a pinnacle beyond which we cannot imagine going? Indeed, in light of the fact that our experience always has an "upper ceiling" on it, is it not Hartshorne's concept of an eternally increasing intensity of aesthetic satisfaction that is unintelligible rather than the concept of a maximal instance of aesthetic satisfaction? Is not the notion of an eternally intensifying pleasure as inconceivable as the notion of an eternally intensifying pain? In any event, if an acme of satisfaction (or pain) is conceivable, this is, I believe, enough to show that Hartshorne is mistaken in thinking that it is a priori that there can be no acme of aesthetic satisfaction.

Second, if the concept of a maximal instance of goodness, power, wisdom, and love is intelligible when applied to the greatest conceivable being, as Hartshorne admits, why is the concept of a maximal instance of aesthetic satisfaction unintelligible when applied to this being? It is only Hartshorne's quantitative analysis of aesthetic satisfaction that requires that he say this. Relatedly, we are able to speak meaningfully of God's unsurpassable goodness, power, wisdom, and love by analogically referencing God's unsurpassable possession of these qualities with our own limited experience of these qualities. But what provides the analogical reference for meaningfully speaking about God's eternally self-surpassing aesthetic satisfaction? As we have already argued, nothing in our own experience corresponds to this. We can analogically speak about an aesthetic satisfaction that is "greater than which none other can be conceived," in just the same way we speak about God's other "greatest conceivable" attributes. However, for just this reason, I maintain, we cannot conceive of

God's aesthetic experience getting forever greater, any more than we can conceive of his power or goodness getting greater.[32]

God's Unsurpassable Truine Aesthetic Experience. If our case against Hartshorne's analysis of the nature of aesthetic satisfaction is correct, then there is no longer any reason for maintaining that God needs an antecedent nondivine world to provide the content of his unsurpassably intense aesthetic satisfaction. Rather, the metaphysical conditions for sociality and aesthetic satisfaction are satisfied within the one necessary divine reality of Godself. In this view, the necessary content of God's aesthetic experience is God's own sociality, and the unsurpassable intensity of this aesthetic satisfaction is the unsurpassable degree to which each person within God's sociality surrenders to, is penetrated by, and thus is defined by the others. This is, in classic trinitarian terminology, the *perichoresis* of the three persons of the trinity. In orthodox trinitarian terms, it is equivalent to saying that God is love (1 Jn 4:8).

From this perspective, in contrast to the standard process perspective, God is as beautiful without the world as with it. God does not need the world to be unsurpassably beautiful. This view does not imply, as Hartshorne supposes, that the world holds no value for God.[33] It only implies that the aesthetic value the world has for God is in *expressing*, not *constituting*, the aesthetic value God eternally finds within Godself. And far from undermining the value of the world for God, this view, I argue, *increases* its value before God—precisely because now God does not need it to be God. The world, thereby, takes on the beauty of grace and free love that is greater than the beauty any necessary relationship could express.[34]

3. The Principle of Contrast

The Necessity of Contrasting Terms. There is one final aspect of Hartshorne's philosophy that leads him to construe God's sociality as being world-dependent rather than self-sufficient. This final feature has to do with the way he works out a general principle of his philosophy rather than the way he works through the various statements he regards to be candidates for metaphysical truths. In a word, it concerns the way he works through his "principle of contrast."[35]

The principle of contrast states that the meaning of any proposition is contingent upon the meaningfulness of its contrast.

For Hartshorne, this entails that all talk about the divine presupposes the reality of the nondivine. To talk meaningfully about the unsurpassable instance of love or power presupposes the reality of surpassable instances of love or power. Hence, if the divine is metaphysically necessary, as Hartshorne holds it to be, then the nondivine must likewise be necessary.[36]

If Hartshorne's analysis of the principle of contrast is correct, then we must, by logical necessity, abandon the concept of the self-sufficient sociality of God. The concept of God existing independent of the world must here be judged as being strictly incoherent. I do not, however, believe Hartshorne's analysis is correct.

Confusing Logic and Ontology.   Although I affirm the principle of contrast itself, I must ask: On what basis can it be argued that both terms of the contrast must have the same metaphysical status? Doesn't this represent a confusion of logic and ontology? True, a term has meaning only if its contrast has meaning. But doesn't this hold true whether one, both, or neither term of the contrast represents an *actual* or *merely possible* state of affairs? The principle of contrast, in other words, is a logical and linguistic principle. It is perfectly abstract and, hence, is indifferent to the ontological status of what is being contrasted. It specifies that the *meaning* of one term is contingent upon the meaning of its contrast, but cannot specify that the *actuality* of one thing is dependent upon the *actuality* of its contrast. Thus, I agree with Hartshorne in holding that the divine existence must contrast with nondivine existence, but I deny that this in and of itself requires that the nondivine existence must be actualized.

In this light, it would be possible to speak meaningfully of God existing as a supremely powerful and good Being throughout eternity alone. God would be supremely powerful and good in contrast to all other *possible* nonsupreme examples of power and goodness, but not necessarily in contrast to any *actual* instances of nondivine power and goodness. Whether nondivine realities exist is, on this score, a contingent matter. This requires, of course, that one aspect of what is necessary is the *possibility* of creating contingent nondivine actualities, and hence the sum total of what is necessary in God is, as Hartshorne argues, contingent. However, whether this possibility is ever actualized is part of what is contingent, not what is necessary.[37]

Rendering Abstract Necessity Intelligible.   Maintaining this position avoids the paradox that is created in Hartshorne's own system when he affirms, on the one hand, that the nondivine world is exclusively com- posed of contingent realities, while denying, on the other hand, that the totality of the nondivine world is contingent. This is paradoxical, because the actuality of the nondivine world is nothing over and above the totality of the actual contingent events that constitute it. Hence, it seems, there is nothing for the supposed necessity of the nondivine world to attach itself to. In short, necessary existence is inconceivable apart from a necessary existent. Because the nondivine world, by defi- nition, has no necessary existence, it cannot itself necessarily exist. Or, to state it otherwise, the concept of "a necessary, but wholly contin- gent, world" constitutes a self-contradiction.

Hartshorne could respond to this criticism by maintaining that the necessity of the contingent world is an a priori abstract meta- physical requirement, and, thus, it is not necessary to render it intelligible by attaching it to a concrete necessary reality (which, by definition, could not exist in a world of contingencies.) However, this response does not succeed, because the point is that the exhaustive contingency of the world undermines the intel- ligibility of any supposed abstract necessity to it. Abstractions are, in Hartshorne's own thought, abstractions from the concrete.[38] But how can we arrive at an abstraction that specifies a necessary exis- tence from a reality that is exclusively contingent? The abstraction, in this instance, outruns the concrete reality from which it arises.

God's Actuality as the Only Metaphysical Necessity.   We might point out that Hartshorne faces this very same problem in rela- tionship to God's abstract nature, because, in his view, it is only the abstract nature of God that is necessary. On a concrete level (God's Consequent Nature), God is wholly contingent. But how is the abstract necessity of God to be rendered intelligible if every- thing concrete about God is contingent, while abstractions are held to be derivative from concreteness? How can an abstraction from the concrete possess a quality (viz., necessity) which the concrete it abstracts from altogether lacks? What, in other words, renders intelligible the necessity of God if God's actuality is alto- gether contingent?

I certainly agree with Hartshorne's arguments concerning the necessity of God, but for just this reason, I maintain that God must be essentially constituted by a *necessary* actuality.[39] The abstract necessity of God, I argue, is not rendered intelligible if God's actuality is wholly contingent. Once we locate the necessary experiential, social, and aesthetic features of being within the one necessary being, however, this problem is solved. For what is abstractly necessary is, in God, also concretely necessary.

If my case against Hartshorne's analysis of the principle of contrast is correct, then there are, again, no longer any grounds for maintaining that the supreme Being must eternally contrast with an actual nonsupreme world. Indeed, there are, we have seen, good metaphysical grounds to deny that God *must* do so. The nature of metaphysical necessity is intelligible only as applied to a necessary actuality and, hence, not as applied to a world of contingencies.

Finally, to bring this essay full circle, what I have been arguing is that the nature of this sole necessary actuality is intelligible only on the supposition that God satisfies within Godself all the a priori conditions of being; namely, as being self-sufficient and unsurpassable in sociality and aesthetic satisfaction. By metaphysical necessity, then, God must exist as a plurality of experiential centers, socially related in an unsurpassably intense aesthetic satisfaction by virtue of the unsurpassable openness and availability each center has toward the others. Among all the available theistic options, I submit, only the classical trinitarian understanding of God articulates this conception unambiguously.

CONCLUSION

It is my conviction that nothing essential to process metaphysics is compromised in the revision of Hartshorne's thought I have been proposing. Although a number of modifications within process thought can (and, I think, need to) be made on the basis of what has been said here, the only *necessary* modification is that the process analysis of actual occasions being constituted as an aesthetic experience derived from a creative synthesis of an antecedent multiplicity of objectified data must be seen as being a description of a *contingent* state of affairs rather than as an a priori feature of being as such. The generality of the process view of reality, in other words, must be seen as an empirical, not metaphysical, generality.

Indeed, far from compromising anything essential in process metaphysics, it is my conviction that this revision of Hartshorne's thought actually improves the explanatory power of process thought, although I cannot presently defend this thesis any further than I already have. Suffice it to say that, among other things, my proposed revision avoids the difficulties that surround the process view of the abstract necessity of the wholly contingent actuality of the world and of God. The supposition of a self-sufficient social God who satisfies the a priori requirements of being within Godself and who is alone necessary provides the metaphysical foundation for a coherent understanding of the contingent social process that constitutes the contingent world. Moreover, it does so in a way that philosophically expresses the best and most important insight of the church's trinitarian faith.

NOTES

1. I am defining here "classical trinitarian" as that view of God, reflected in the Nicene and Athanasian creeds, which affirms that God is triune not only in God's activity, but in God's eternal essence. This, I take it, is the essence of trinitarian orthodoxy. I do not, however, intend to import any of the other aspects of what has come to be labeled "classical theism" into my definition of "classical trinitarianism." The distinctive feature of "classical theism" is the view of God as *actus purus*, a view that process thought has rightly criticized. For a succinct discussion on "classical theism" from a process perspective, see David Griffin, *God, Power and Evil: A Process Theodicy* (Philadelphia: Westminster Press, 1976), 16ff., 73ff.

2. Charles Hartshorne, *Whitehead's Philosophy: Selected Essays, 1935–70)*, 17. See also Alfred N. Whitehead, *Process and Reality: An Essay on Cosmology*, ed. D. Griffin and D. Sherburne (New York: Free Press, corrected ed. 1978), 95–96, 348; Charles Hartshorne, *Man's Vision of God and the Logic of Theism* (New York: Willett, Clark & Co.; New York: Harper and Brothers, 1964), 233; idem, *Reality as Social Process: Studies in Metaphysics and Religion* (Glencoe, IL: Free Press, 1953; Hafner, 1971) 139ff.; idem, *Creative Synthesis and Philosophic Method* (Peru, IL: Open Court, 1970. Lanham, MD: University Press of America, 1983) 12; and idem, *Omnipotence and Other Theological Mistakes* (Albany, NY: State University of New York, 1984), 75.

3. See Robert Solokowski, *The God of Faith and Reason* (Notre Dame, IN: University of Notre Dame, 1982), 19 and Norris Clarke, *The Philosophical Approach To God* (NC: Wake Forest University, 1979),

71. I argue this point extensively in *Trinity and Process: A Critical Evaluation and Reconstruction of Hartshorne's Di-Polar Theism Towards a Trinitarian Metaphysics* (New York: Peter Lang, 1992), especially 271–95 and 328–37.

4. See Charles Hartshorne, *Logic of Perfection (Peru, IL: Open Court, 1962)*, 285; Hartshorne, *Whitehead's Philosophy*, 9; and Hartshorne, *Creative Synthesis*, 19.

5. For a full discussion of Hartshorne's understanding of metaphysics as the search for a priori truths about existence, see the author's *Trinity and Process*, 23–26.

6. For a full explication and defense of Hartshorne's position, *Trinity and Process*, chs. 1–3.

7. Hartshorne, *Creative Synthesis*, 114.

8. Hartshorne, *Logic of Perfection*, 227. See also Charles Hartshorne, *Beyond Humanism: Essays in the New Philosophy of Nature* (Chicago: Willet & Clarke, 1937; New York: Bason Book, 1968), 182–83); Hartshorne, *Creative Synthesis*, 7, as well as the author's *Trinity and Process*, 43ff.

9. See Charles Hartshorne, "Religion in Process Philosophy," in *Religion in Philosophical and Cultural Perspectives*, ed. J Clayton Feaver and William Horosz (New York: Van Nostrand Rhinehold, 1967), 252–53. See also Hartshorne, *Whitehead's Philosophy*, 75, 137; Charles Hartshorne *Divine Relativity: A Social Conception of God* (New Haven, CT: Yale University Press, 1948), 101–104; Hartshorne, *Reality as Social Process*, 74–77; Charles Hartshorne, *Whitehead's View of Reality* (New York: Pilgrim Press, 1981), 8–9; Charles Hartshorne, *Creativity and American Philosophy* (Albany: State University of New York, 1984), 161, 172; *Logic of Perfection*, 227.

10. Hartshorne, again following Whitehead, also holds that perception illustrates this principle of the past being re-experienced in the present, although the temporal structure of experience is more ambiguous here than in memory. See *Whitehead's View*, 8; and Hartshorne, *Creative Synthesis*, 91–97, 217–18.

11. Martin Buber, *I and Thou*, trans. Walter Kaufman (New York: Charles Scribners Sons, 1970), 55.

12. "In the beginning," Buber writes, "is the relation." Ibid., 69. So too, "The world and I include each other reciprocally." 141. See also 78.

13. See Hartshorne, *Creative Synthesis*, 78–79, 105, 193–94, 235; *Logic of Perfection*, 78, 245f., 288.

14. According to Hartshorne, "Mistakes in metaphysics can all be viewed as cases of 'the fallacy of misplaced concreteness,' the confusion between concreteness as such and less basic abstractions whose instances are themselves abstract." *Creative Synthesis*, 22. The metaphysician is, thus, described as "a critic of abstraction." *Creative Synthesis*, 57. See also Whitehead, *Process and Reality*, 7–8, 18. Not surprisingly, Hartshorne criticizes such phenomenologists as Husserl and Merleau-Ponty of committing this fallacy. See Charles Hartshorne, *Insights and Oversight of Great Thinkers: An Evaluation of Western Philosophy* (Albany: State University of New York, 1983), 271ff., 374.

15. "Actual entities," Whitehead writes, "are the final real things of which the world is made of." *Process and Reality*, 18. See Hartshorne, *Whitehead's Philosophy*, 119–20.

16. Justus Buchler, "On a Strain of Arbitrariness in Whitehead's System," *Journal of Philosophy*, 66 (2) (1969): 592.

17. The whole of S.D. Ross, *Perspective in Whitehead's Metaphysics* (Albany: State University of New York Press, 1983), and E. Lazlo, *The Systems View of the World* (New York: George Braziller, 1972), are relevant here, as is David Braninskil, *"Metaphysical Generality and the Principle of Ontological Parity: An Examination of the Ontology of Justus Buchler in Comparison With The Cosmology of Alred North Whithead"* (Ph.D. diss., State University of New York, 1976).

18. Solokowski's point is well taken: "The partial truth of science [is] taken as the truth of the whole." "The Question of Being," *Review of Metaphysics* 43 (1990): 712.

19. Hartshorne holds that the concept of symmetrical relationality is meaningful when applied at the level of abstraction, but not at the level of concreteness. See Boyd, *Trinity and Process*, 35–37. My point here is that our phenomenological experience of symmetrical relations *is* concrete, and, thus, the notion of concrete symmetrical relationality is meaningful, proving that asymmetrical relationality is not an a priori feature of concreteness. Only Hartshorne's reductionistic, nonperspectival understanding of concreteness prevents him from affirming this.

20. Recent empirical experiments that carry through Bell's theorem of the Einstein, Podolsky, and Rosen thought experiment—most notably those of Alain Aspect—suggest that it may be possible for causality to be symmetrically efficacious in a contemporary instant, sometimes referred to as "quantum nonlocality." See J. Cushing and

E. McMullin, *Philosophical Consequences of Quantum Theory: Reflections on Bell's Theorem* (Notre Dame, IN: University of Notre Dame, 1989), 27ff. and passim. Whether or not we accept these empirical investigations as compelling, the very fact that an empirical discovery *could* refute the supposed exclusivity of the temporal asymmetrical relationship between actual occasions (namely, the concept of supraluminal causality involves no logical contradiction) is enough to show that asymmetrical relationality is not an a priori feature of concreteness.

21. I have thus far only ruled out one of the three main reasons why Hartshorne holds the necessity of the nondivine world. I attempt to refute the other two in the subsequent two sections of this essay.

22. For a fuller discussion, see the author's *Trinity and Process*, 208–33, 374–401.

23. *Ibid.*, 81–88, 168–176.

24. Hartshorne, *Creative Synthesis*, 303. The whole of Hartshorne's essay, "The Aesthetic Matrix of Value," ch. 16 of *Creative Synthesis*, is instructive here. This is what Whitehead called the "massiveness" that "intensity proper is finally dependent upon." Alfred N. Whitehead, *Adventures in Ideas* (New York: Macmillan, 1933; New York: Free Press 1961), 253. See also Hartshorne, *Creative Synthesis*, 248, 262.

25. Charles Hartshorne, *Anselm's Discovery: A Re-Examination of the Ontological Argument* (Peru, IL: Open Court, 1965), 28.

26. See Hartshorne, *Omnipotence and Other Theological Mistakes*, 10 and *Creative Synthesis*, 116, 303.

27. Hartshorne modifies and defends this Anselmian definition of God (as well as his ontological argument) throughout his book, *Anselm's Discovery*.

28. Hartshorne, *Man's Vision of God and the Logic of Theism* (Willet, Clark & Co: New York, 1941; New York: Harper and Brothers, 1964), 218, 36–37.

29. Hartshorne, *Creative Synthesis*, 265–65. See also *Creative Synthesis*, 293 and Hartshorne's comments in *Existence and Actuality: Conversations With Charles Hartshorne*, ed. John Cobb Jr. and Franklin Gamwell (Chicago: University of Chicago Press, Chicago, 1984) 101.

30. Harold Lee, *Perception and Aesthetic Value* (New York: Prentice-Hall, Inc., 1938), 83–84. Hartshorne nowhere explicitly addresses

this objection to his aesthetic theory. Indeed, throughout his writings, Hartshorne tends to take his correlation of aesthetic intensity with the scope and depth of what is experienced as being self-evident (which is understandable, if, in fact, his correlation is an a priori truth). For example, Hartshorne writes, "There is good reason to think multiplicity does contribute to value. A complex beauty is superior to an ultra-simple one, a symphony to a chord." *Creative Synthesis*, 248. This is, of course, generally true in our experience. But the question remains: Is the breadth or scope of an experience *necessarily* proportioned to the intensity and, hence, aesthetic value of that experience? This is nowhere proved, but it needs to be. It is *not* self-evident. The very fact that the history of aesthetic theory has exhibited so many differing theories on what constitutes beauty itself calls into question the self-evident (hence, a priori) nature of Hartshorne's theory. In my estimation, the classical view of Plato, Plotinus, Augustine, Aquinas, and many others up to the present, the view that holds that beauty (viz., that which produces aesthetic experience) is a transcendental reality, an irreducible metaphysical surd, and is, as such, undefinable in terms outside of itself, warrants far more consideration as an alternative to Hartshorne's view than he gives it. For some twentieth-century defenders of various versions of the classical view, see C. E. M. Joad, *Matter, Life and Value*, (London: Oxford University Press, 1929), 266–83, reprinted in E. Vivas and M. Krieger, eds., *Problems in Aesthetics*, (New York: Rinehart, 1953), 463–79); A. C. Rainer, "The Field of Aesthetics," *Mind*, XXXVIII (1929): 160–183); T. E. Jessop "The Definition of Beauty," *PAS*, XXXIII (1933): 159–72; and T. M. Greene, "Beauty and the Cognitive Significance of Art," *Journal of Philosophy*, XXXV (1938): 365–81. For representative selections and discussions on the diversity of aesthetic theories in the western tradition, see M. C. Beardsley, *Aesthetics: Problems in the Philosophy of Criticism* 2nd ed. (Indianapolis: Hackett Publishing Co., 1981); H. Osborne, *Theory of Beauty* (London: Routledge and Kegan Paul, 1952), E. Vivas, M. Kriedger, eds. *Problems in Aesthetics* (New York: Rinehart, 1953); Samuel Alexander, *Beauty and Other Forms of Value* (London: Macmillan, 1933); and Arthur Danto, *The Transfiguration of the Commonplace* (Cambridge, MA: Harvard University Press, 1981)

31. The central feature of our human experience of aesthetic value that should be generalized to a metaphysical level would be what certain German aestheticians have referred to as *Einfuhlung*, the act of "feeling oneself into an object," sometimes called "aesthetic sympathy." See H. Lee, *Perception and Aesthetic Value*, ch. 3.; J. K. Feibleman, *Aesthetics* (New York: Humanities Press, 1968), 148ff.. What is a priori in aesthetic experience is that the subject must be

open to the experienced object and the object available to the subject, and the more this is so, the more intensely the experience is felt. This poses a difficulty for process categories, for it presupposes that there is something to a present subject prior to its experience of "the other," something process thought denies. I have elsewhere argued that a concept of an "enduring subject" can be affirmed, without falling back into Greek substantialist thought, by conceptualizing the ground of the experiencing self (whether of a phenomenological whole or of an actual occasion) as an *ontological disposition*. See the author's *Trinity and Process*, 105–16, 383–401.

32. One could argue this in the other direction: the fact that we *can* always conceive of more novel relations added to previous relations: whereas, we *cannot* conceive of an eternally increasing intensity of aesthetic satisfaction, itself proves that the intensity of an aesthetic satisfaction is not necessarily contingent upon the "massiveness" of what is experienced.

33. See Hartshorne, *Omnipotence and Other Theological Mistakes*, 8, and Hartshorne, *Existence and Actuality*, 101.

34. For more on the beauty of God and its relationship to the beauty of the world as it relates to process thought and the trinitarianism of Jonathan Edwards, see the author's *Trinity and Process*, 374–401.

35. See Hartshorne, *Creative Synthesis*, 32, 89–90, 99ff., 139ff., 166, 245. For a fuller discussion of this central principle of Hartshorne's thought, see the author's *Trinity and Process*, 34f.

36. Hartshorne writes, for example, "The necessarily existent abstraction 'something' divides a priori into two correlative abstractions, divine or unsurpassable something and non-divine or surpassable something , creator and creature. Both sides are equally abstract. If, then, abstractness implies necessity, 'God' and 'not God' must both be necessary." *Creative Synthesis*, 250–51.

37. That is, the decision of God to create or not to create is contingent, and hence there is contingency in God, even if God refrains from creating a world. I agree with Hartshorne's critique of classical theism on this score. Contingency is one of God's eternal perfections, not a defect. See Hartshorne, *Logic of Perfection*, 37–38; Hartshorne, *Anselm's Discovery*, 123. We could further maintain that it is conceivable that the way God is eternally self-related involves contingency, while maintaining that the fact that God is triune is itself necessary. God's self-relationship must be eternally unsurpassable, but there are an infinite number of ways this metaphysically abstract truth could be actualized. Creating a nondivine world is, in

this view, *one* of the ways God's contingency constitutes this necessary self-relationship.

38. "Abstract reality is derivative." Hartshorne, *Creative Synthesis*, 22; see also 57–67.

39. This would mean that at the point of what is necessary in God, God's abstract nature and concrete existence would be synonymous. Thus, I affirm, with significant modifications, Aquinas's maxim that "God's essence is his existence." This only leads to the classical understanding of God as *actus purus* if God's actuality is defined substantially, which I deny. Following the lead of Jonathan Edwards, I rather conceptualize God's eternal self-related essence in dispositional, hence dynamic, terms. See ibid, 215–28, 384ff.

Joseph A. Bracken, S.J.
Panentheism from a Process Perspective

Panentheism is certainly a key word in the vocabulary of process-relational metaphysics, aptly describing the God–world relationship that most disciples of Alfred North Whitehead wish to espouse. Although God and the world are strictly interdependent, the full reality of God is still more than the current reality of the world.[1] In my judgment, however, the notion of panentheism is easier stated than worked out in logical rigour. For, as I see it, one group of Whiteheadians under the leadership of Charles Hartshorne tend implicitly to collapse the reality of the world here and now into the enduring reality of God; whereas, another group under the tutelage of Bernard Meland and Bernard Loomer tend to collapse the reality of God here and now into the enduring reality of the world.

Following the lead of Charles Hartshorne, for example, Whiteheadian "rationalists" claim that the world is the "body" of God. Thus, just as the soul is a society of personally ordered actual occasions that gives coherence and unity to the various societies of living and nonliving actual occasions within the human body, so God as a transcendent society of actual occasions gives coherence and unity to the myriad number of societies of occasions making up the world.[2] There is, however, a key difference between the body–soul relationship and the God–world relationship that Hartshorne and his followers seem to have overlooked. Whereas in Hartshorne's psychology, the human soul likewise perishes with the death of the body, in his understanding of the God–world relationship, God does not perish with the demise of any given world. At least in principle, God simply acquires a new "body," a new world with which to be related. Furthermore, from moment to moment the present world of finite occasions never has the same constituents; only patterns of interrelation survive from one generation of actual occasions to the next so as to provide a sense of continuity in the history of the universe. Hence, when one asks where previous moments in world history have gone, the answer can only be that they have been incorporated into the ongoing life of God. They likewise exist, to be sure, within the self-constitution of contemporary actual occasions. However, they are at best partially incorporated into the becoming of new occasions; only in God are they retained in their full objective reality.[3]

Whiteheadian "empiricists," on the other hand, under the tutelage of such individuals like Bernard Meland and Bernard Loomer tend to collapse the reality of God here and now into the enduring reality of the world. Meland, for example, in *Fallible Forms and Symbols* identifies the empirical reality of God with "Creative Passage" or "the Ultimate Efficacy within relationships."[4] Even if one were to think of it with Meland as "a work of judgment and grace, a primordial and provident goodness",[5] the net effect of Meland's thinking is to collapse the reality of God here and now as "Ultimate Efficacy" into the enduring reality of the world as an ongoing process. Similarly, in his controversial essay "The Size of God," Bernard Loomer identifies God and the world process in the following manner:

> The World is God because it is the source and preserver of meaning; because the creative advance of the world in its adventure is the supreme cause to be served; because even in our desecration of our space and time within it, the world is holy ground; and because it contains and yet enshrouds the ultimate mystery inherent within existence itself.[6]

Presumably something more than the world as a concrete actuality here and now is being mediated to Loomer through such an experience of the world. However, insofar as "God" is thus so intimately involved with the world as an ongoing process, it seems fair to say that, for Loomer as well as for Meland, the reality of God here and now is effectively absorbed into the enduring reality of the world.

Still other process-oriented "empiricists" (e.g., William James, John Dewey, and Henry Nelson Wieman) could be cited in favor of this same approach to the God–world relationship. However, rather than enter into an extensive survey of material already available elsewhere,[7] I now set forth my own position, which, as I see it, mediates between that of the "rationalists" and that of the "empiricists" spoken of above. That is, I will propose with the "rationalists" that the reality of God does indeed "contain" the reality of the world; the world as a very large but still finite cosmic society is participant in the all-comprehensive society proper to the three divine persons of Christian belief in Their dynamic relationship to one another. But in line with the "empiricists," I also argue that human beings do not experience their participation in the community of the three divine Persons except in the terms described by Meland, Loomer, and the other "empiricist" thinkers noted above; namely, as a principle of creative transformation operative within the matrix or field of activity proper to this world.

As I hope to make clear later in the paper, human beings, thus, directly experience only the underlying *nature* of God, that by which the three divine persons are themselves sustained in their dynamic interrelations. They come to experience the *entitative* reality of God as three persons only in and through the medium of their personal faith. That is, through reflection and prayer, they learn to identify the activities of the three divine persons in their lives as belonging precisely to those persons and not simply to an impersonal principle of creative transformation. But, even here, they do not experience the persons as fixed entities but rather as the subjects of ongoing activities in their lives. The divine persons, in other words, are *subsistent relations*;[8] that is, subsistent acts of relating to one another and to all their creatures. Consistent with a process-relational orientation, their being is their ongoing process of becoming.[9]

Evidently, then, I will be setting forth an understanding of the God–world relationship, which is grounded as much in traditional Christian theology as in the contemporary process-relational metaphysics of Whitehead. Furthermore, in setting forth this proposal, I assume that the Whiteheadian category of society requires much more elaboration than Whitehead himself gave it in *Process and Reality (PR)* and other works. For, Whitehead's own writings do not clarify the ontological basis for the agency of societies. As corporate entities with enduring characteristics, they require clear differentiation from purely momentary aggregates of actual occasions. Charles Hartshorne has, to the present, provided the standard Whiteheadian solution to this problem by suggesting that the agency of a more complex ("structured") society is generally provided by the agency of the current actual occasion within a key subsociety or "soul"; its agency at any given moment is then communicated to all the other actual occasions constitutive of the structured society in the following moment.[10] Although this certainly makes sense in terms of human beings and other animal organisms endowed with a central nervous system, it makes far less sense with respect to atoms, molecules, and cells, which likewise exhibit some limited degree of individuality and agency but which do not seem to possess "souls."

Hartshorne, to be sure, distinguishes between "compound individuals," which clearly act as a unitary reality and such "composite individuals" as lower-level animal organisms and plants, which "are individuals only in a slight degree." Yet, it would seem that a measure of ontological agency is required for even these composite individuals to retain enduring physical characteristics over an extended period of time. Similarly, although it may well be true that there is more real individuality in atoms than in their inorganic composites (e.g., stones and other mineral formations);[11] nevertheless, the latter do retain a minimal cohesiveness over time, for which Hartshorne, in my judgment, has no satisfactory explanation. For, although each of the constituent occasions of a given society retains a "genetic identity" with all its predecessors in the same society, it has no link with its contemporaries beyond its own somewhat individualized "prehension" of one and the same "complex eternal object" (*PR*, 51–52). Accordingly, it is, at least theoretically, possible that a Whiteheadian society could instantaneously cease to be or in any event dramatically change character if its constituent occasions unexpectedly failed to reproduce that complex eternal object within their individual self-constitutions in basically the same way.[12]

As I see it, a much simpler explanation for the continuity of Whiteheadian societies is to propose that all societies, without exception, exercise a type of collective agency—derivative from the interrelated agencies of their constituent actual occasions— which is necessary to sustain in existence the complex eternal object or structural pattern spoken of above and, thus, to maintain the unity of the society as a whole. Agency in the proper sense, therefore, belongs solely to actual occasions, as Whitehead himself maintained (*PR*, 46). But there is a derivative agency proper to societies that varies in intensity, depending upon the type of ontological totality involved.

In stones and other inanimate compounds, it is the minimal agency required to sustain a certain pattern or configuration of its constituent occasions vis-à-vis one another over time. In plants and lower-level organisms, it is the agency required to sustain a democratically organized structured society where no part is dominant over the other parts. Finally, in higher-level animal organisms where a "soul" is operative, it is the conjoint activity of all the member societies (the societies of inanimate occasions and the nexuses of living occasions as well as the "personally ordered" or enduring subsociety of living occasions constituting the soul) that produces the unity and the agency proper to the organism as a whole. Hartshorne did not err, accordingly, in attributing agency for the entire organism to the dominant subsociety, but he did err, in my judgment, in not sufficiently recognizing that this dominant agency has to be coordinated with all the other subordinate agencies within the organism so as to achieve the unity and collective agency of the whole.

Perhaps one reason why Whiteheadians have tended to follow Hartshorne on this point is, in my judgment, that with Hartshorne, they seem to imagine societies as layered, hierarchically structured aggregates of mini-entities (actual entities) rather than as environments or structured fields of activity for the psychic events (actual occasions) taking place within them.[13] In *Process and Reality*, for example, Whitehead notes that a society is "an environment with some element of order in it, persisting by reason of the genetic relations between its own members" (138). Then a few lines later, he adds:

> The causal laws which dominate a social environment are the product of the defining characteristic of that society. But the society is only efficient through its individual members. Thus in a society, the members can only exist by reason of the laws which dominate the society, and the laws only come into being by reason of the analogous characters of the members of the society. (*PR,* 139)

The picture that seems to emerge from this description of the reciprocal relationship between a society and its constituent actual occasions is that of a structured field of activity for successive generations of occasions. The initial set of occasions set up the pattern of interaction for subsequent generations of occasions. But it is the field that sustains the pattern from one generation to the next. In this sense, the field is the enduring reality; the occasions as psychic energy-events come and go.

Moreover, as the quotation from *Process and Reality* makes clear, there are laws resident in the field that intrinsically affect the self-constitution of successive generations of actual occasions. The laws, to be sure, came into existence through the "decisions" of the first set of occasions and have subsequently been modified by the "decisions" of subsequent generations of occasions. In that respect, the field makes no decisions, because it is not itself a subject of experience. However, as noted above, it exercises a collective agency in and through the interrelated agencies of its constituent occasions, which determine the laws for subsequent generations of occasions. Furthermore, if the field contains a dominant subsociety of personally ordered living occasions or "soul," the field equivalently becomes conscious in and through that subsociety. The field proper to the subsociety is then coterminous with the field proper to the organism as a whole. A human being, for example, is a structured field of activity for all the myriad subsocieties of occasions operative within the body. But the human being exercises conscious control over the body with its innumerable subsocieties of occasions, both living and nonliving, in and through its "soul" or dominant subsociety of personally ordered living occasions.

In any event, in using this imagery of a Whiteheadian society as a structured field of activity, I can now set forth a new understanding of the God–world relationship. As noted above, I work with the traditional Christian understanding of God as triune rather than unipersonal. I argue, first of all, that each of the three divine persons is an enduring or personally ordered society of fully living, conscious actual occasions whose range of experience is infinite in depth and comprehension. Thus, each of the persons presides over an intentional field of activity that is co-extensive with all that is and can be. Moreover, because, by definition, there can be only one such infinite or strictly unlimited field of activity, the three divine persons necessarily occupy the same field of activity. Each of them, to be sure, has a different *subjective* focus in intentionally grasping or "prehending" the field; but it is one and the same *objective* field that they all prehend. Unlike human beings, therefore, whose intentional fields of activity are never completely the same, the three divine persons have no sphere of activity proper to themselves simply as individuals. All that they are is common to all three persons. Hence, they are one God, because all of them together preside over one and the same all-comprehensive divine field of activity.[14]

Yet, as noted above, they represent three different subjective foci or centers of activity within the field. Thus, they are three separate "personalities," exercising interrelated but still different functions within one and the same field of activity. How is this to be understood in Whiteheadian terms? First of all, I argue that all three divine persons participate in the divine primordial nature, the divine consequent nature, and the superjective nature of God, albeit in different ways. That is, while all three persons survey the vast realm of possibilities existent within their common field of activity at any given moment, the "Father"[15] alone "decides" which possibility is appropriate for that moment of their common history. Second, while all three share in the divine consequent nature, the "Son" alone "decides" to actualize the possibility chosen by the "Father" for their common life together. Finally, while all three share in the divine superjective nature, the "Spirit" alone "decides" to use this principle of activity to sustain the ongoing conversion of potentiality into actuality and thus to perpetuate their life together as a community of divine persons. Each divine person, accordingly, has an indispensable role in the maintenance of their common life.

Admittedly, this is only a speculative model for the innertrinitarian life, not a privileged picture of the way things actually are. But, as I indicate below, it does serve to make clear how this world of ours can be participant within the communitarian life of the three divine persons and yet retain its separate ontological identity in line with the doctrine of panentheism. For, as I see it, by virtue of the role that the "Father" plays within the divine life, the "Father" can be said to be the subsistent principle of potentiality for the world of creation. That is, the "Father" offers not just to the divine "Son" but likewise to all newly concrescing finite occasions at every moment what Whitehead calls an "initial aim" (PR, 244); namely, a possibility of existence, to which the "Son" and all finite occasions must in some measure respond in order to exist. The "Son," on the other hand, by virtue of the "Son's" role within the divine life is the subsistent principle of provisional or current actuality for the world of creation. That is, the "Son" together with these finite occasions, in thus responding to the initial aim of the "Father" at every moment, actualizes what was merely potential in terms of the "Father's" offer. Finally, the "Spirit" by virtue of the role the "Spirit" plays within the divine life is the subsistent principle of ultimate actuality within creation. That is, the "Spirit," in anticipation of the fullness of the divine life and the further perfection of the created universe, keeps prompting the "Father" to offer and the "Son" together with all finite occasions of the moment to respond, so that the joint process of the divine life and of all creation will be sustained.

In brief, then, the doctrine of panentheism is vindicated, because the three divine persons and all their creatures share a common life. That is, all the myriad subsocieties of actual occasions within this world together help to structure the field of activity proper to the cosmos as a whole. However, this enormous but still finite field of activity is itself incorporated into a still more comprehensive field of activity proper to the three divine persons in their dynamic interrelations. Thus, the world is structured according to the trinitarian pattern of life for the three divine persons. But, as noted earlier, human beings normally do not recognize this trinitarian pattern of existence except through prayer and reflection on the Christian Scriptures. For, as Aristotle made clear in his definition of movement in the *Physics* (movement is "the fulfillment of a potentiality insofar as it remains a potentiality" [201a10]), any process involves a principle of potentiality, a principle of provisional or current actuality, and an entelechy or principle of ultimate actuality. But to associate these principles with the activities of the three divine persons within the world is to move beyond the empirical evidence provided by the experience of movement within oneself and the surrounding world and to enter the realm of faith where empirical realities are given a higher value or further significance. It is a step that not everyone takes, if only because it is not necessary for the practical understanding of life in this world. However, for those who have faith in this vision of things, it has the power to transform their entire existence.

The activities of the divine persons in the world, to be sure, are not simply interchangeable with the principles of potentiality, provisional actuality, and ultimate actuality for the world process. Otherwise, the experience of God would be completely indistinguishable from the experience of the world. Rather, the experience of the activity of the three divine persons in a person's life should be felt as a further specification of the way in which that person experiences potentiality, provisional actuality, and ultimate actuality within the individual's personal life and within the world process as a whole. The "Father's" initial aim for each moment of consciousness, for example, includes all relevant possibilities for oneself but is designed to realize an optimal set of possiblities both for oneself and for the world in which one lives at any given moment. Hence, the "Father's" presence is felt in the "lure" toward the achievement of higher ethical and religious values in our lives at any given moment. Similarly, the "Son" is, indeed, the principle of provisional actuality for ourselves and for the world process as a whole, in that all finite occasions are, sometimes consciously but more often unconsciously, united with the "Son" in the latter's ongoing response to the "Father." But what the "Son," each individual self, and the world as a whole together are right now is only instrumental to the achievement of further goals and values in the light of the "Spirit," the principle of ultimate actuality for the world process and, thereby, the long-term goal of the "Father's" initial aims for each occasion at every moment. Without controlling the events taking place in this world, therefore, the three divine persons provide constant stimulus to Their creatures for further growth and development. Furthermore, as I see it, human beings can, over a period of time, recognize this ongoing direction from the divine persons and incorporate it into the patterns of their own lives through prayer and reflection on the Scriptures.[16]

At the beginning of this essay, I proposed that the nature of God, that is, the ontological ground or condition for the existence and activity of the three divine persons, is a principle of creative transformation operative within an all-encompassing matrix or field of activity. At this point, it should be clear what this matrix or field of activity, in point of fact, is. It is the intentional field of activity constituted in the first place by the divine persons in their dynamic relations to one another, but also further structured by the presence and activity of innumerable finite actual occasions from time immemorial. Thus understood, it can be readily assimilated to what Whitehead calls the extensive continuum, that is, the all-encompassing "relational complex," which "underlies the whole world past, present, and future" (*PR*, 103). As Whitehead further notes, this field of activity or relational complex is real "because it expresses a fact derived from the actual world and concerning the contemporary actual world" (*PR*, 103). But it is not itself an actuality, because it is that in which actualities; namely, actual occasions, continuously emerge and are related to one another. It is, accordingly, part of the nature of God, and indeed part of the nature of every finite occasion as well, because it is an indispensable condition for the existence and activity of every actual occasion, finite and infinite alike.[17]

Now it is time to examine the other component of the divine nature that, likewise, enters into the nature or process of self-constitution for all finite occasions. As noted above, this is a principle of creative transformation, that whereby the three divine persons and all finite occasions continuously come into existence. Elsewhere I have argued that this principle of creative transformation is, in fact, Whiteheadian creativity.[18] Whitehead himself, to be sure, does not say that creativity is the principle of the divine nature or, for that matter, that it is the nature or essence of all finite occasions. For him, it is simply a metaphysical given: "that ultimate principle by which the many, which are the universe disjunctively, become the one actual occasion, which is the universe conjunctively" (*PR*, 31). But, upon reflection, because creativity exists only in its instantiations, with God as its primordial instantiation and all finite occasions as its derivative instantiations (*PR*, 47; 344), logically it has to be part of the underlying nature of God and part of the underlying nature of all finite occasions. For, as noted above, it is that *by which* God and all finite occasions continuously come into existence.

In his book *Whitehead's Metaphysics of Extension and Solidarity*, Jorge Luis Nobo claims that within Whitehead's system "creativity and extension [i.e., the extensive continuum] are indissoluble aspects of one ultimate reality—a reality underlying the becoming, the being and the solidarity of all actual entities," including God as the primordial actual entity.[19] Nobo, to be sure, does not identify this "ultimate ground of the organic universe" with the divine nature or the ground of the divine being. But God, too, like finite actual occasions, is at any given moment a "creature" or product of the action of creativity (*PR*, 135). Likewise, God, too, as the ever-concrescing infinite actual entity, exists within the extensive continuum. Otherwise, God could not be in solidarity with finite occasions and, thus, both affect, and be affected by, those same occasions (*PR*, 101–4). Hence, creativity and the extensive continuum are the ontological ground of the divine being as well as the ontological ground of all finite beings. But, as noted above, because neither creativity nor the extensive continuum exist in themselves as ontological actualities but only in the actual entities in which they are instantiated, then, logically, they must primordially exist in their primordial instantiation; namely, God. They together constitute, accordingly, in the first place the ground of the divine Being and then only in the second place the ground of creation.

Within Whitehead's own scheme, to be sure, it is more difficult to picture creativity as "located" in God as the ground of the divine being and then from that "location" serving as the ontological ground for the existence and activity of all finite actual occasions. For, in *Process and Reality*, Whitehead seems to picture creativity as mediating between God and the world (*PR*, 528). But, if this is really what Whitehead meant, then, as Ivor Leclerc notes, he was inadvertently guilty of a category mistake.[20] For, as noted above, he elsewhere expressly says that creativity exists only in its instantiations. Because God is its primordial instantiation, creativity must exist first and foremost within God and be structured by its operation within God so as intrinsically to affect its operation within finite actual occasions (*PR*, 344). Hence, contrary to what Whitehead himself seems to imply, creativity is in the first place the ontological ground of the divine being and activity, and only in the second place, the ground of the being and activity of all finite occasions.

Within the trinitarian understanding of God I sketched above, however, it is quite easy to think of creativity as the principle of the divine being, which in turn, becomes the principle for the existence and activity of all creatures. In fact, as I have argued elsewhere,[21] creativity within a trinitarian context is best understood as a principle of *intersubjectivity* by virtue of which actual occasions, both finite and infinite, come into existence and are related to one another in terms of various societal configurations. That is, whereas, for Whitehead and most Whiteheadians, creativity is seen exclusively as the ontological principle for the self-constitution of individual actual occasions, I propose that creativity is, likewise, the principle whereby those same occasions in and through their processes of self-constitution also co-constitute the various societies to which they belong. In empowering individual actual occasions to become themselves, creativity also empowers them to be related to one another according to various societal configurations up to and including the universe as a whole.[22]

All this, as I see it, is simply the logical consequence of shifting the emphasis in process-relational metaphysics from the subjective unity of the individual actual occasion (as in Whitehead's

thought) to the objective unity of the society (societies) to which
it belongs. Within this neo-Whiteheadian scheme, God, too, is a
society, not, however, in Hartshorne's sense of a cosmic "soul" or
personally ordered society of conscious actual occasions, but
rather in the sense of a structured society, a more complex society
of coexisting subsocieties (the divine persons). Likewise, this
modest reordering of Whitehead's vision allows for the incorporation of the world as likewise a structured society, a society of subsocieties, into the already existing societal reality of God.

The net effect, then, is a much stronger emphasis on the
social character of reality than either Whitehead or Hartshorne
presumably ever envisioned. For both of them, the intrinsically
social character of reality is guaranteed by the fact that every
actual occasion both influences and is influenced by every other
actual occasion in the world process (*PR,* 104–5).[23] Within the present scheme, however, the focus is not on the individual actual
occasion and its relation to all other occasions, past, present and
future, but rather on the objective order of things, the cosmic society, which the individual occasion and its contemporaries here
and now coconstitute and which will survive their passing away.
New attention is, thus, given to the reality of the social whole over
and above the contribution of the individual parts or members.[24]

In the remainder of this article, I try to show the pertinence of
this neo-Whiteheadian reinterpretation of the God–world relationship for Meland, Loomer, and others in the tradition of empirical
theology. My basic point in the paper has been that creativity and
the extensive continuum as the ground of the divine being are likewise the ground of the created universe and all finite entities within
it. Hence, in experiencing the ontological ground of their own existence and activity, human beings are simultaneously experiencing
God: not, to be sure, God in an entitative sense as either unipersonal or tripersonal, but rather God in terms of the divine nature.
The nature of God, in other words, is the indispensable condition
for God to be God and for all finite entities to be themselves. It is,
therefore, divine and, thus, worthy of human worship even though
it is not personal but rather an impersonal or, better said, a
transpersonal reality, the foundation of the intersubjective existence
of the divine persons and all their creatures with one another.

Hence, when Meland speaks of the Ultimate Efficacy within
relationships, he is, indeed, correct to think of it as an experience
of God, or in any case, as an experience of the divine nature.

Moreover, when he describes Ultimate Efficacy as "a work of judgment and grace, a primordial and provident goodness",[25] it is clear that he is not simply describing a strictly impersonal principle of creative transformation within the world process but rather the activity of a personal being (as I see it, the Holy Spirit of traditional Christian theology) Who is operative in the world of creation through the divine nature, the Whiteheadian principle of creativity.

Similarly, when Loomer at the end of "The Size of God" describes the world as "an interconnected web endeavouring to become a vast socialized unit of experience with its own processive subjectivity,"[26] he, too, is experiencing God in terms of the divine nature. The world understood as an impersonal process does not, after all, "endeavour" to become anything, because it lacks a subjectivity proper to itself. But the field of activity constituted by the three divine persons and all finite actual occasions is such "a vast socialized unit of experience with its own processive subjectivity" or, better said, intersubjectivity. For, it exists only by virtue of the fact that all these momentary subjects of experience, finite and infinite alike, continuously come into existence and are interrelated with one another within its boundaries. The divine nature is, thus, the ontological foundation for an all-embracing cosmic society with an ever-growing corporate subjectivity represented in the first place by the three divine persons but likewise including all enduring personally ordered societies of finite actual occasions.[27]

Henry Nelson Wieman, who as a process-oriented thinker at the University of Chicago Divinity School from 1927 to 1947 exerted considerable influence on the thinking of both Meland and Loomer, argues along similar lines that God is "what operates in human life to transform man as he cannot transform himself to save him from evil and lead him to the best that human life can ever attain."[28] God, in other words, is empirically experienced as a principle of creative transformation that functions within and among human beings to promote an increase rather than a decrease in shared human goodness and value.[29] However, this principle of creative transformation, taken by itself, is quite vague and seems ill-defined to qualify as a definition of God or, indeed, of any other isolable reality within human experience.[30] Hence, contrary to what Wieman himself ambitioned, it might be better, first, to concede that we are dealing here strictly with an empirical knowledge of God, that which can be gained simply from ordinary human experience, and then to leave open the possibility of a further knowledge of God, which can be gained from prayer and reflection both on the Christian Scriptures and on the special character of these creative or transformative events in our lives.

We might be led, in other words, to associate the principles of potentiality, provisional actuality, and ultimate actuality, which are invariably operative within such transformative events with the activities of the "Father," the "Son," and the "Holy Spirit" within our lives. On the other hand, because this is only an option for interpretation, not a necessary inference from our experience, we might well prefer not to make this association with the persons of the Trinity. Nor can this judgment be logically contested by the Christian "believer." Because all that the "believer" and "nonbeliever" alike experience is an *activity*; its attribution to one of the divine persons or to God in a unipersonal sense is a matter of interpretation. God as an empirically verifiable *entity* is simply not available to experience.

Many contemporary theologians in the empirical and historicist tradition likewise could be cited here. Gordon Kaufman, for example, in line with his earlier work on "constructing" the concept of God,[31] has argued persuasively in recent years that the term "God" does not represent a transcendent personal being but rather is the symbol for "the complex of physical, biological and historico-cultural conditions which have made human existence possible, which continue to sustain it, and which may draw it out to a fuller humanity and humaneness."[32] At the same time, he talks about "a hidden creativity at work in the historico-cultural process" and "an ultimate tendency or power, which is working itself out" in nature and human history so as to produce the reality of spirit.[33] In line with my own neo-Whiteheadian scheme outlined above, I would agree with Kaufman that "the complex of physical, biological and historico-cultural conditions" that first created and subsequently sustained human life on this earth is certainly to be identified with the activity of God in the world. For, these conditions are grounded in the divine nature as the ontological source for the existence and activity both of the divine persons and of all finite actual occasions. However, in line with Kaufman's further remarks about "a hidden creativity" at work in the world, I would further urge that these same processes are no substitute for the full entitative reality of God as the latter can be discerned through prayer and reflection on the text of Scripture. At least for me and other "believers," the hidden creativity at work in the world through these processes points to God as a tripersonal Being who gives direction and order to these creative processes without, at the same time, controlling them rigidly.

However, as noted above, in matters of interpretation, we should always have the freedom to make that choice which is most nourishing to our own faith, religious or secular. As Michael Polanyi made clear in his celebrated book *Personal Knowledge* years ago, all claims to objective knowledge are at the same time personal to the speaker or writer, because they are grounded in a fiduciary framework (a set of personal convictions about the nature of reality), which cannot itself be fully verified.[34] Hence, even in empirically oriented theology, rival faith-claims are implicitly operative, and human reason is employed as an instrument to explain and justify what we are already inclined to believe on the basis of personal experience.

The brunt of this article has simply been to justify the faith-claim of those Christians who claim that they experience the presence and activity of the three divine persons in this world. Reason or philosophical reflection has been employed, first, to rethink the Whiteheadian category of society as an environment or field for successive generations of actual occasions and then to apply this hypothesis to the God–world relationship in terms of interpenetrating fields of activity. The field of activity proper to creation is, thus, seen as a semiautonomous reality governed by its own empirical laws of development even as it is included within the all-comprehensive field of activity proper to the divine being. The three divine persons, accordingly, can be at work in creation to achieve their own designs without interfering with the freedom of their rational creatures or with the laws governing the evolution of the cosmos. Only in this way, as I see it, can we consistently espouse a process-oriented doctrine of panentheism without inadvertently collapsing the world into God or God into the world.[35]

NOTES

1. Cf. Charles Hartshorne, *The Divine Relativity. A Social Conception of God* (New Haven, CT: Yale University Press, 1964), 89.

2. Cf. Charles Hartshorne, *Man's Vision of God and the Logic of Theism* (Hamden, CT: Archon Books, 1964), 174–211.

3. Basically the same comments could be made about Whitehead's concept of God as the sole transcendent actual entity that keeps incorporating into its "consequent nature" successive generations of finite actual occasions. The "world" always exists as the counterpart of God, but at every moment it is a different world, constituted by a new set of finite occasions. Thus, in the end, for Whitehead as for Hartshorne, the world is continuously absorbed into God.

4. Bernard Meland, *Fallible Forms and Symbols: Discourses of Method in a Theology of Culture* (Philadelphia: Fortress Press, 1976), 151–52.

5. *Ibid.*, 152.

6. Bernard Loomer, *"The Size of God," The Size of God: The Theology of Bernard Loomer in Context* (Macon, GA: Mercer University Press, 1987), 42.

7. Cf., e.g., Nancy Frankenberry, *Religion and Radical Empiricism* (Albany, NY: State University of New York Press, 1987), 83–129; also William Dean, *History Making History: The New Historicism in American Religious Thought* (Albany, NY: State University of New York Press, 1988), 99–182.

8. Cf. Thomas Aquinas, *Summa Theologiae* (Madrid, Spain: Biblioteca de Autores Cristianos, 1951): I, Q. 29, a. 4 resp.

9. Cf. here Joseph A. Bracken, "Subsistent Relation: Mediating Concept for a New Synthesis?," *Journal of Religion* 64 (1984): 188–204.

10. Charles Hartshorne, "The Compound Individual," in *Philosophical Essays for Alfred North Whitehead* (New York, NY: Russell & Russell, 1936), 212–17.

11. *Ibid.*, 215.

12. Cf. on this point Hartshorne, *Man's Vision of God*, 206: "A group of persons in an elevator has as a group a unique pattern, but there is no reason for thinking of this pattern as an agent which acts on its parts, and upon other things. The pattern is the way in which the parts act on each other, and upon the outside environment, it does not itself act. But a genuine primary individual, an organism, does itself act; it is not merely the way its parts act." On the one hand, a group of people in an elevator are clearly nothing more than an aggregate that will break up or at least change shape as soon as the elevator doors are opened at the next floor. On the other hand, because a stone does not break up or change shape quite so readily, it would seem to be much more than a simple aggregate. Here

I would argue that what Hartshorne describes as the "parts" acting on one another so as to produce an objective pattern is, in fact, a separate type of agency proper to societies, a collective agency derivative from the interrelated individual agencies of the "parts" (constituent occasions), as I explain below.

13. Cf. here Joseph A. Bracken, "Energy-Events and Fields," *Process Studies* 18 (1989): 153–165.

14. Cf. on this point Wolfhart Pannenberg, *Systematic Theology*, vol. 1, trans. Geoffrey Bromiley (Grand Rapids, MI.: William B. Eerdmans, 1991), 382–84. In discussing the nature or essence common to the three divine persons, Pannenberg comes to the same conclusion as I do, albeit for different reasons; namely, that the nature or essence of God is an unbounded field of activity constituted by the three divine persons in dynamic interrelation.

15. The traditional divine names are placed within quotation marks in this article to indicate their purely metaphorical, nonsexist intent. But, even more fundamentally, by interpreting the reality of "Father," "Son," and "Spirit" in Whiteheadian terms as interrelated personally ordered societies of living actual occasions, I have effectively removed all traces of gender from these traditional names for the divine persons. For, actual occasions have no gender, and the societies to which they belong possess gender only by reason of contingent circumstances, not necessarily.

16. Cf. Joseph A. Bracken, *The Triune Symbol: Persons, Process and Community* (Lanham, MD: University Press of America, 1985), 62–69.

17. Cf. on this point William A. Christian, *An Interpretation of Whitehead's Metaphysics* (New Haven: Yale University Press, 1959), 395–96. However, Christian also contends that there are good reasons in support of the opposite position; namely, that God not be considered in space and time, therefore, not be part of the extensive continuum. For example, God has no spatial or temporal boundaries like finite actual occasions existing in space and time. If, however, by Whitehead's own admission each finite actual entity "is everywhere throughout the continuum" (*PR*, 67), this particular objection seems to lose much of its force. Furthermore, the mere fact that Whitehead did not explicitly make God's "region" within the extensive continuum co-extensive with the continuum as a whole (Christian, *An Interpretation*, 394) does not seem to forbid my extension of his thought on this point.

18. Joseph A. Bracken, S.J., *Society and Spirit: A Trinitarian Cosmology* (Cranbury, NJ: Associated University Presses, 1991), 127–28,

131–33; also *The Divine Matrix: Creativity as Link between East and West* (Maryknoll, NY: Orbis Books, 1995), 56–62.

19. Jorge Luis Nobo, *Whitehead's Metaphysics of Extension and Solidarity* (Albany, NY: State University of New York Press, 1986), 255.

20. Ivor Leclerc, *Whitehead's Metaphysics* (London: George Allen & Unwin, 1958), 53–54.

21. Bracken, *The Triune Symbol*, 46.

22. *Ibid.*, 45–46.

23. Cf. also Hartshorne, *The Divine Relativity*, 25–30.

24. Cf. on this point Hartshorne, *Man's Vision of God*, 207, where he pictures reality as "a system of individuals on many levels and of many kinds," presided over by God as the supreme individual. In contrast, I imagine reality as a cosmic society in which the created universe with all its myriad subsocieties is incorporated into the communitarian life of the three divine Persons.

25. Meland, *Fallible Forms and Symbols*, 152.

26. Loomer, "The Size of God," 51.

27. Cf. here Marjorie Suchocki, "Radical Empiricism: Radical Enough?," *American Journal of Theology and Philosophy* 13 (1992): 180: "what Loomer means by 'processive subjectivity' might be better described by 'processive intersubjectivity.' The 'unit of experience' resulting from the interconnected endeavor of the world might be communal rather than singular, so that the resultant God is more akin to a society than to an actual entity." Likewise implicit in my own understanding of the God–world relationship is the further proposal that finite actual occasions do not lose subjectivity upon completion of their process of self-constitution in the temporal order, but rather retain subjective immediacy, albeit in a transformed condition, upon incorporation into the divine communitarian life. Cf. on this point *Society and Spirit*, 140–52.

28. Henry Nelson Wieman, "Knowledge, Religious and Otherwise," *Journal of Religion* 38 (1958): 20.

29. Henry Nelson Wieman, *The Source of Human Good* (Carbondale, IL: Southern Illinois University Press, 1946), 54–83, esp. 58–69.

30. Cf., e.g., Frankenberry, *Religion and Radical Empiricism*, 122–26; likewise, Robert Mesle, "Added on Like Dome and Spire: Wieman's Later Critique of Whitehead," *Process Studies* 20 (1991): 41.

31. Gordon Kaufman, *The Theological Imagination; Constructing the Concept of God* (Philadelphia: Westminster Press, 1981), 263–79.

32. Gordon Kaufman, *Theology for a Nuclear Age* (Philadelphia: Westminster Press, 1985), 42.

33. *Ibid.*, 41, 43.

34. Michael Polanyi, *Personal Knowledge: Towards a Post-Critical Philosophy* (New York: Harper Torchbook, 1964), 249–68, esp. 266–67.

35. Donald Gelpi likewise offers a process-oriented Trinitarian understanding of the God–world relationship (cf. Donald L. Gelpi, S.J., *The Divine Mother: A Trinitarian Theology of the Holy Spirit* [Lanham, MD: University Press of America, 1984], 90–100). Elsewhere I have given my reasons for not fully endorsing his approach (Bracken, "Panentheism from a Trinitarian Perspective," *Horizons* 22 [1995]: 18–19, esp. 32–33).

Emphasis on God as One

Philip Clayton
Pluralism, Idealism, Romanticism:
Untapped Resources for a Trinity
in Process

> Religion is the translation of general ideas into particular thoughts,
> particular emotions, and particular purposes; it is directed to the
> end of stretching individual interest beyond its self-federating par-
> ticularity. Philosophy finds religion, and modifies it; and conversely
> religion is among the data of experience which philosophy must
> weave into its own scheme (*Process and Reality*, 15f.).

1. TRINITIES PHILOSOPHICAL AND THEOLOGICAL, NECESSARY AND CONTINGENT

Neither philosophers nor theologians have ever really been satisfied with the division of labor on the God-question. Theologians at
their best have held to the goal of conceptual rigor; still, they have
often felt shackled by the foreign demands of the discipline of philosophy, which were often perceived as conflicting with beliefs
from the very tradition with whose preservation they were charged.
Philosophers, by contrast, have expressed impatience with the (to
them inexplicable) concern of theology to preserve the merely contingent beliefs of a religious tradition that seemed hopelessly arbitrary and dogmatic. Standard criteria for turf separation; e.g.,
systematic theology is characterized by particularity, philosophical
theology by generality[1]—generally fail to satisfy either side.

No area of this discussion has been more disputed than that
of the doctrine of the trinity. Is it a necessary result of reason, an

arbitrary, even contradictory belief left over from doctrinal squab-
bles nearly two millennia ago, a faith-insight allowing for philosophical explication but not proof, or a model useful in different
ways within theology and metaphysics? Because of the centrality
of the questions it raises, the debate surrounding the trinity offers
a particularly effective test case for establishing the lines between
philosophy and theology. Moreover, because of its associations
with Scholastic metaphysics, and particularly with the thought of
Thomas Aquinas, it becomes a crucial locus in the dialogue
between "classical" and process metaphysics. At the same time,
the dispute is so laden with past misunderstandings and conceptual confusions that one wonders initially whether perhaps no
progress whatsoever can be made here.

In the following pages, I defend a version of process trinitarianism that attempts to mediate between the usual positions in
classical and process metaphysics. If the argument is successful, it
will cast doubts on the widespread assumption that these two
schools of thought are intrinsically opposed. The key element of
my proposal is a distinction between the *necessity* of a three-fold
division within God on the one hand (if God is to fulfill the religious and metaphysical functions attributed to the divine, and if
God's subjectivity is to be conceived in any way analogous to
ours) and, on the other, the *contingency* of God's free self-revelation, including God's revelation as Father, Son, and Holy Spirit.
Under this view, the particular trinitarian form that God's self-revelation has taken in the Christian tradition[3] is a result of God's
response to free human decisions and to the (nondetermined)

Process thought stemming from Whitehead can play a particularly important role in this discussion. This is partly because
Whiteheadians have subjected substance-based metaphysics, and
in particular the static categories of medieval, perfection-based
language about God, to keen critical scrutiny. But it is also
because of the specific dilemma with which Whitehead struggled:
Is God nontemporal and nonpersonal, a category of the ultimate
but not in fact an actual entity; or is God personal and temporal?[2]
This dilemma, I argue, represents one of the most basic, if not *the*
most basic conceptual issue in the history of the metaphysics of
God. Whether or not we side with Whitehead's own attempt at a
rapprochement, and with the concepts of entity and person on
which it rests, we dare not fall beneath his level of understanding
of the problem.

development of the world. Nonetheless, the trinity that God has been revealed to be is at the same time an expression of a structure or potentiality that was present in God's nature from the start.

2. "Neoprocess Thought" and the Demise of Whiteheadian Orthodoxy

In Whitehead's own day, the key issues in the debate with Christian theologians concerned matters such as orthodoxy, submission to the Pope, and faithfulness to the creeds.[4] These are not (obviously) the burning loci of controversy in the confrontation between Christianity and the Academy today. Through a series of steps that we can only mention here, science and epistemology since Whitehead's day have discarded most of the vestiges of positivistic empiricism; noncreedal Christianity has gained significant ground, and even conservative theologians speak increasingly of multiple models of God.

As a result, the once sharp dichotomies have become fuzzy. Attempts such as William Christian's famous effort to keep metaphysics and Christianity separate—because, as he thought, they were a danger to each other—are no longer necessary. Prof. Christian thought it necessary to limit metaphysics to the study of *kinds* of being and to "the structural relations between things of these sorts"; conversely, Christianity could only address the question, "What is it that is of central and ultimate significance for human life?"[5] But the changes in the intellectual climate just alluded to have made such sharp divisions no longer necessary. It's not clear that even the quote with which I opened still represents a fundamental dividing line between philosophy and theology.

If theologians' claims have become epistemically more humble, so also have those of metaphysicians in many cases (and in the remainder should have!). Lewis Ford only follows a long tradition when he equates the realm of the metaphysical with the realm of the necessary. But it's no longer obvious that this line of demarcation can make good on its own epistemic claims. With the failure of Kant's twelve categories (and those of his competitors) to live up to their alleged necessary status, and with their transformation at the hands of twentieth-century philosophers into multiple conceptual schemes and "ways of worldmaking,"[6] the delineation of the realm of the metaphysical by means of the distinction necessary/non-necessary has become unworkable. In its place, we need to turn again to Whitehead's own insistence on pluralism and on the preliminary nature of all knowledge: There are a variety of ways of cutting the world—and the God–world relationship. This fact points toward a "pluralistic metaphysics," which implies (*inter alia*) multiple "models of God."[7] What is interesting for our purposes is that this shift does not make an appeal to Christian content irrelevant; quite the contrary. For now the source of beliefs is less important; what counts first and foremost is their fruitfulness as models in various explanatory and theoretical contexts. If we take the opening quotation to this article seriously, then we can attend closely to the data of Christianity without leaving the domain of metaphysics; indeed, close attention of this sort will be a precondition for an adequate metaphysics.

Along with changes in the stance of Christianity and the epistemic status of metaphysics, a third transformation should be mentioned (even if it cannot be fully argued here): the demise of Whiteheadian orthodoxy. By this I mean both that major difficulties have been discovered in Whitehead's doctrine of God (among other difficulties), and that there has been a gradual shift in Whitehead scholarship from interpretation toward fundamental rethinking on a number of points. This descriptive claim is also a normative one: "process trinitarianism" only becomes a live option once the strictures of orthodoxy in interpretation are removed.

Moreover, it is right that they be removed. I agree with Neville that Whitehead's doctrine of God "cannot be sustained in critical scrutiny."[8] This is why trinitarian thinkers—and not only they!—should be encouraged to rethink Whitehead, to propose modifications in key Whiteheadian concepts, to explore alternative process conceptualities. The mark of a process thinker has never been orthodoxy; given Whitehead's own views, "orthodox Whiteheadianism" is probably an oxymoron. Thus, the term *Neo*process Thought in my heading, which connotes and encourages a movement beyond the stage where consistency with (even the basic tenets of) Whitehead's thought served as the criterion of adequacy. Indeed, one might well argue that there never was such a stage, that from the very beginning Whitehead's readers and followers were rethinking fundamental points. Although the full case can't be made here, I suggest that surveying the work of contemporary thinkers who have been significantly influenced by Whitehead would show that there is scarcely a key premise of his thought that hasn't been modified or rejected. This move beyond Whiteheadian orthodoxy is what has made the project of a (neo)process trinitarianism viable and exciting today; it will be presupposed in what follows.

If we were not working now in the context of neoprocess thought, one key assumption of my argument would probably seem unpalatable: the tenet that atomism is not finally adequate as a theory of individuality. Of course, Whitehead was never merely an atomist; there are a number of aspects of his thought that go beyond strict atomism, although it remains the dominant paradigm in his thought. He clearly holds, for example, that the whole of the actual occasion is more than the sum of its parts.[9] Likewise, the objective immortality of all past occasions in God is more than the "objective" content of these occasions themselves, because God also values them in the divine appropriation. Thus, Joseph Bracken is in one sense extending a Whiteheadian principle when he argues that we have to ascribe to societies a nonreductive reality, a reality that is not reduced to the parts of which they consist. He speaks of the "key point on which I differ, if not from Whitehead, at least from some Whiteheadians. That key point is that communities (or, in Whiteheadian language, structured societies of a particular complexity) exercise an agency which is not simply reducible to the agency of their constituent actual entities. The whole, in other words, is more than the sum of its parts . . ."[10] A similar point has been argued repeatedly in the biological sciences and the philosophy of science under the heading of the doctrine of *emergent properties*.[11] I mention it now, because the proposal that follows belongs in this sense to neoprocess thought. If a structured society cannot exercise agency, then God as three-in-one will probably be unthinkable from the start.

3. GOD FOR US, GOD WITH US

Neville's starting point is "everything determinate needs determination."[12] Before this point, there is no God, nothing determinate whatsoever, but only sheer indeterminacy (which is indistinguishable from sheer nothingness). No specific metaphysical conclusions, and much less a concrete doctrine of God, can be developed until the primordial selection of basic metaphysical principles has taken place *ex nihilo*.

I wish to proceed "backward," as it might at first appear, i.e., from the opposite end from which Neville (and Hegel, with his pure undifferentiated Being) begin. Where does the trinitarian doctrine begin, and what is its immanent "logic"? The chief interest of the classical theological doctrine of the trinity was to think of God's real involvement with humanity. If God is eternally Father, Son, and Spirit, then it will be possible to speak of a divine life, a divine community, analogous to our own. From all eternity, God will have included within Godself a (self)-giving and receiving, a choosing and being chosen, a begetting and a being begotten—and some process of mediation between these two poles. According to the classical view, the eternal Son is identical with an individual human being, Jesus, at least in one nature (because Jesus' human nature is not taken into Trinity itself). God's involvement with humankind in the form of the incarnation of the second person reduces the gap between God and God's creation. Human history can now be understood only in conjunction with, or as a part of, *Heilsgeschichte*.

Notice how this closeness between God and humanity raises the possibility of a reduction of God *to* humanity. The danger is twofold. A full reduction would make the very existence of God a projection of human wishes, human aspirations, or the happenstances of human reason. The other danger of projection transpires through an illicit transposition of human categories onto the divine. The divine "otherness" may be lost when we characterize it too fully with human predicates, construing the trinitarian God as a group of persons on the model of a human society. God would then exist *only pro nobis*, reducing the divine nature to the product of God's interactions with us and nothing more.

The need, then, was to correct for an overly anthropomorphized understanding of God. So the starting point; namely, attempting to think "God with us, God for us," was supplemented conceptually with the notion of "God in and of Godself." That is, the classical doctrine of the trinity avoided reductionist tendencies by insisting on an eternal nature in God (especially in the nature of the Father) that remained unaffected by interaction with humans; alternatively, the entire trinitarian structure itself was understood to precede all interactions with the world.

However, can an approach that begins with thinking of the self-revealing God use that very same framework to theorize about God apart from all revelation? Can the "trinity of revelation" be projected backward to a trio of divine persons before the foundation of the world? Or must we *change* the underlying basis if we wish to speak of "God in and of Godself," appealing no longer to "the manner in which God reveals Godself" but rather to purely conceptual considerations? It is my argument that success in specifying the transcendent divine nature is not best guaranteed by an immanent trinity of Father, Son, and Holy Spirit, understood as the mirror image of the economic trinity, although now extrapolated into God's essence apart from any interaction with the world. Where, then, *are* we to start the effort to think about the "hidden" side of God? And why conclude that the resulting structure will still be trinitarian?

4. A MEDITATION ON THE INFINITE

The most effective entré and guideline for conceiving this otherness of God is, I argue, the finite–infinite distinction. This might seem a questionable starting point for a Whiteheadian, given Whitehead's insistence that "it belongs to the nature of physical experience that it is finite" (*Process and Reality* [PR] 345). He speaks here of God's consequent nature as being "determined, incomplete, consequent, 'everlasting,' fully actual, and conscious," but never actually calls it infinite. Still, Whitehead's position is too ambiguous, as Lewis Ford has shown,[13] and his flirtation with the concept of the infinite too great for us to rule out all connection between process thought and the theory of the infinite. What is it, then, about the concept of the infinite that makes it ineliminable for an adequate theism? A brief meditation, inspired by Descartes, may help convey the role that this concept has to play; the rest of the paper wrestles with its significance for process theism.

"When I turn my mind's eye upon myself," writes Descartes in Meditation 3, "I understand that I am a thing which is incomplete and dependent on another and which aspires without limit to ever greater and better things" (VII, 51).[14] This is the Cartesian original intuition: I am finite. We know our finitude immediately through our dependence on an "other" or others outside ourselves. This starting point can be expressed philosophically, psychologically, biologically, existentially. In its various guises, it has been called a fundamental intuition, a logical truth, as well as conceptual, analytic, and a priori. What these various labels have

in common is the insight that no additional evidence needs to be
called in on its behalf. The intuition of finitude is, I suggest, the
first and the basis for all subsequent reflection on God and on
ourselves.

Now for the second step. I am finite; I am *not infinite*. Insofar
as it occurs without argument and *appears* to rely on negation
alone, the transition from intuiting finitude to an intuition of the
infinite has a good claim to immediacy. The original intuition—I
am finite—gives rise immediately to the idea of *something without
limits*. To be aware of finitude is to have, however implicitly, the
idea of the infinite. The two are equiprimordial—if, indeed, the
idea of the unlimited is not actually the more primitive of the two.
Insofar as I can only intuitlimits against the (assumed) backdrop of
an unlimited whole, perhaps my sense of dependence already
implies the prior idea of something that is independent. *How* to
think this is a matter for later reflection; for now I suggest only that
the idea of the infinite arises as the natural and inevitable counterpart to the intuitive awareness that we as finite beings have of
our finitude.

Like the original intuition, this idea also has an immediate link
with our being in the world; we could deepen it by developing a
philosophical anthropology or phenomenology based on types of
the experience of the unlimited.[15] Because the idea of the unlimited arises directly out of our immediate intuition that we are finite,
it already suggests a religious side to human existence—as long as
"religious" is taken in a broad sense and as neutral (at this point)
on the question of the existence of a divine being or beings. The
reciprocal relationship between human finitude and the idea of
the infinite helps to define human existence, even before full theoretical explication. "Finite being," with its implicit contrast to
infinity, thus becomes a general term for our ontological status as
beings with limits.

It is easier to grant the intuition of the infinite when we
acknowledge what it does *not* prove. If (as I think) the ontological proof is not rationally compelling, the idea of an infinite being
does not entail its actual existence. Neither does it entail an actual
comprehension of this infinite.[16] Focusing on the original emergence of the idea of the infinite gives us reason to assert an ontological link between finitude and infinitude, even if no clear
content for the idea of an infinite God can yet be formed.[17]
However rich the intuition of the infinite may be as an intuition,

then, it will underdetermine philosophical debate. Still, if the intuition is admissible in the sense presented, it can help to sort out the conceptual frameworks that attempt to think the nature of God "in and of Godself." Further, without being a "proof" of theism, it does help to foster our understanding of theistic beliefs, and may even provide a source of *prima facie* evidence as we consider signs of "God with us" that point in the direction of an infinite being.

Once the ideas of the finite and infinite are given, certain implications follow with greater or lesser immediacy. For example, if the idea of an infinite is granted, then by its nature it will be prior to the idea of the finite.[18] If this argument is valid, it will reverse the order of presentation above; the infinite will be prior to the finite in everything except the order of discovery. Infinity is not understood by negating a boundary or limit; i.e. negating the finite; instead, all limitation first implies a negation of the infinite. Furthermore, it could perhaps be shown that the infinite is the condition of the possibility of the existence of finite things. This would give it a type of transcendental status, reminiscent of Kant's regulative ideas; it would be in part an a priori idea, rather than just the product of experience.[19] But enough has been said to suggest how the progression from intuition to philosophy proper might proceed. Let us, therefore, break off the meditation here; in a moment it will be clear what role this originary intuition has to play in the search for a process trinitarianism.

5. THINKING WITH WHITEHEAD BEYOND WHITEHEAD

So suppose we identify the infinite with God in some way. Wouldn't this raise insuperable problems? An individual being, it seems, cannot be infinite, for to be *a* being is to exist alongside other beings and to be limited by them. However, God can fulfill the functions of primordial envisagement and concrescence, responding to the world at all moments, it seems, only if God is understood as (in some sense) an actual occasion like others. How then could we think about a dimension in God that is not in itself a feature of a personal being?

And yet this is precisely the modification of Whitehead that recent process thought has been pursuing as the most profitable. As Cobb puts it: "My own judgment, informed by Marjorie

Suchocki, is that we need to reflect more radically on the unde-veloped insights of Whitehead about the profound difference between the one nontemporal actual entity which originates con-ceptually and the many temporal actual occasions which originate physically." More concretely, "in *some* respects the everlasting concrescence of God must resemble temporal succession as well as genetic succession, and in some respects it must be profoundly different from both."[20]

This suggestion of Suchocki and Cobb is the one I wish to pursue in the remaining pages. But first, we should pause for a moment and survey the lay of the land. What are the major alter-natives that are open to process thinkers? The range of available options looks something like this:

(1) *Dipolar theism.* The unchanging or eternal (antecedent) nature of God is supplemented by a responsive (consequent) side. The one represents the essential nature of God, the other the responsive nature. The responsive pole could be conceived as a single, eternally concrescing actual entity (Whitehead) or, because it must evidence a high level of continuity, as a personally ordered society of actual occasions (Hartshorne).[21]

(2) *Classical theism.* Although God may have both essential and responsive sides, the more important is his essential nature. The responsive side may either be subordinated to the essential, or (in more extreme views) even dismissed as not actually a part of God's nature at all. Traditional theists are worried that trying to make room for God's becoming in history may marginalize or eliminate God's essential properties and perfection.

(3) *All metaphysically significant divine properties are neces-sary.* Whatever emerges on the responsive side could be treated as merely contingent. According to this view, we are free to draw conclusions and to theorize about God as revealed in interaction with humans. However, everything that we say remains under the aegis of God's contingent pattern of self-reve-lation; therefore, the theoretical conclusions tell us little or noth-ing about the nature of God internally or metaphysically; that is the task of a priori metaphysics. Gregory Boyd, for example, who writes primarily vis-à-vis Hartshorne, holds a view of God "as internally social, as alone actually necessary, and as actually infi-nite while nevertheless being open to contingent expressions of this antecedent necessity," a view that, he tells us, "fulfills all a

priori requirements and retains the advantageous elements of both the classical and neoclassical views of God, while avoiding the difficulties of both."[22]

(4) *God as power of the future.* The eternal pole, by contrast, might be dropped from the picture completely. This would make God fully responsive. If Whitehead was wrong in separating God and Creativity, and the two are to be identified instead, then this responsive God would have to be located entirely in the future (Lewis Ford).[23]

(5) *God as society of persons.* God could be understood as a collection of occasions of some sort. Clearly, it is not very satisfactory to treat God as a mere aggregate, yet it may also raise insoluble problems to think of God (or one pole of God) as personal. In *The Triune Symbol*, Joseph Bracken drew a distinction between the three divine persons as "personally ordered societies of occasions" and the one God as a structured society (or society of subsocieties) in Whitehead's sense.[24] In his more recent *Society and Spirit*, he generalizes the concept, thinking of Whitehead's societies as "structured fields of activity for their constituent actual occasions."[25] A field has a certain unity in itself, and yet it is able to encompass other fields or occasions within it. This notion allows for the sort of inclusion relation that is conceptually necessary for a trinitarian metaphysics. In particular, it can serve as the conceptual basis for *panentheism*, the inclusion of the world within God: "while all finite entities exist in God and through the power of God, they are ontologically distinct from God in terms of both their being and activity" (ibid., 123). We return to these themes below.

(6) *God is not a being.* The very idea of God being "a being" at all could be cast into question. This would involve some fundamental rethinking, obviously, because the belief that God is a being has been a leading assumption through most of the tradition and is the position taken by Whitehead at many points in *Process and Reality*. (God as the "power of the future," in Ford's sense, would also not be a being at all.) If we pursue this possibility, it will be necessary for us to say *what* God is insofar as God is not a being, e.g., being itself (following Ivor Leclerc), the good, ground, or the infinite per se. This route may be a difficult and rocky one; yet it is the one on which I believe we are propelled when the question of God is formulated in the manner so far explored.

6. Toward a Schellingian Process Theology

It is at this point that we can profitably supplement Whitehead's reflection with the work of the nineteenth-century thinker whose philosophy may stand the closest to Whitehead's: F. W. J. von Schelling. There are resources in the German Idealist thinkers that are, I believe, crucial for a successful process trinitarianism. True, the texts in question are difficult, sometimes murky ones, and in crucial aspects they require updating in light of twentieth-century developments. However, the difficulties do not justify the prejudices, many traceable to the analytic philosophical tradition, that have blocked serious study of these thinkers in recent years. In the rich tradition from Kant to Hegel, as I've argued elsewhere,[26] the work of Schelling's middle period stands out as a philosophical basis for trinitarian thought. What contributions can this thinker make to the contemporary debate?

A helpful list of the significant parallels between Whitehead and Schelling is already available.[27] As Braeckman notes, first, Schelling defines the imagination as "the activity whereby the infinite is unified into the finite, or as the act through which the many become one." Yet this is exactly how Whitehead understands Creativity. For both, nature itself is creative activity, *natura naturans*, and things are identified through their own creative advance. Second, in both, there is creative advance. Nature is an agency that "by developing itself, constitutes an evolution toward ever more complex instances, i.e., toward human consciousness in the end." Third, in both, this process functions by means of "internal causation." Each actual entity becomes itself through its own process of concrescence. Likewise, Schelling holds that the organism produces or "constitutes" itself.

However, instead of developing further links, let us turn immediately to the major difference. Both philosophers center their metaphysics on a mental principle, one of activity, feeling, and valuation. However, "In Schelling the paradigm of this basic structure is given by the *self-conscious* Ego, whereas Whitehead's paradigm is an *unconscious* experience."[28] In other words, Schelling's idealist theory of consciousness would seem at first to rule out any final rapprochement of their positions. Is not the core of Whitehead's view that the primary units are atomistic moments of self-consciousness or awareness, actual occasions that synthesize their predecessors and pass immediately into a state of objec-

tive existence (objects for other awarenesses) as soon as their subjective moment of concrescence has passed?

Much could be said about the mistakes and misinterpretations
in Whitehead's famous chapter on "The Subjectivist Principle."
Whitehead was not enough of a scholar of Idealism (as
Braeckman shows, he admits to only secondary knowledge of the
literature) to differentiate between Hegel's overly metaphysical
and absolutistic theories and the more cautious claims of
Schelling's writings on divine freedom and potency. Thus, he was
unable to appreciate how the subjective inclusion relations of
Schelling's dipolar theism could avoid the heavy-handed laws
attributed to the rational development of *Geist* by Hegel.
However, these resources supplement Whitehead's own thought
at what may be its weakest points. Basically, I suggest, Whitehead
never found an adequate principle to account for the continuing
identity of awareness and valuation of conscious beings through
time. Moreover, God remained an exception to Whitehead's own
principles. Something like Hartshorne's early correction of
Whitehead—viewing God as a personally ordered society of
actual occasions—was necessary to overcome the difficulties. Yet
by the time we make the necessary corrections, be they
Hartshorne's or others, we have already moved beyond an atomistic theory of consciousness and, hence, beyond the conceptual
limits of a (strictly speaking) Whiteheadian metaphysics.

The differences notwithstanding, it is fair to say that what
Hartshorne calls a personally ordered society and Bracken a structured field of activity, Schelling calls a center of self-consciousness. The main difference is that, for process thinkers, there is a
level *beneath* self-consciousness, which is taken to be in some
sense fundamental. Thus, Bracken argues against Hegel that
objective spirit is present at all levels of nature, even where self-
consciousness is missing.[29] At the same time, using the concept of
field, he also uses Hegel against Whitehead to argue that societies
of occasions have a real identity as individuals; *the construction of
identity is not just "from below" in an atomistic sense.* The later
chapters of his *Society and Spirit* offer a trinitarian view of God
according to which each of the divine Persons is understood "as a
succession of actual occasions" which form an "objective unity as
one God" in the form of a "structured society."[30]

The starting point, then, for the rapprochement between
process and idealist thought is, as Bracken has seen, thinking of

societies of actual occasions as fields (or something like fields), which have their own reality. They are not ontologically derivative, in the sense of being reducible to the actual occasions they include, but are characterized instead by a reality that can only be described from the perspective of the whole. What happens to the theory of actual occasions when the emphasis is shifted from part to whole?

7. Is God a Subject?

This move brings us to the transitional question in our analysis: Is God then subjective *an sich*, apart from or prior to any relationship with the world?

Schelling argues that God is *potentially subjective*; that is, must be thought of as possessing the structure of subjectivity. However, God is not actually subjective, in a sense analogous to existing human subjects, until God interacts with an other. From the standpoint of philosophical reflection, then, before the foundation of the world it makes sense to speak only of a structural potentiality for subjectivity.[31] To have such a potential, it must be a complex stucture, one with multiple elements or "moments." From the standpoint of theology, of course, something else happens: additional considerations are introduced via the concept of revelation, which incline us to view the structure as enough like human consciousness that we can and must speak of it as subjectivity. Now, such a move can be made only by appealing to the four dimensions or facets of subjectivity: life, movement, consciousness, and responsiveness. The task in the following section, therefore, will be to evaluate the structure that we examine in this one, in order to decide whether it has the components necessary for speaking of a divine subjectivity independent of the world. Does it make sense to speak of an actual divine community prior to the creation of the world of finite occasions?

As we have seen, Whitehead translated the "eternal will of God" as used within Christianity into the Consequent Nature of God, in order to conceptualize it metaphysically.[32] But, as has often been pointed out, he was inconsistent on this matter. Whitehead often treats God generically, as "the principle of limitation" or concretion *(Religion in the Making* [*RM*] 78, 80; *Science and the Modern World* [*SMW*] 221f., *PR*, 345). At other points, however, he does not include God among his lists of categories and principles at all, but treats God as a single individual. Even where God *is* understood as a being, it is clear that in many ways God must be an exception to the nature of other beings (in contradiction to the principles at; e.g., *PR*, 319, 205f.).

The traditional way of construing the problem is first to treat God as *a* being, then to specify ways in which God is *different* from other beings, and finally to introduce some sort of principle of analogy to draw the two together. I find this approach philosophically problematic, thanks in part (to mention only one factor) to the difficulties with specifying the analogy relation in a way that does not reduce to equivocity. But what can be offered in its place? Let us begin more radically, dismissing the notion of God as *a* being completely (at least at the start) and trying to specify what might remain. At the end, I believe, we will discover similarities strong enough to justify reintroducing talk of God as a being; but first we must wrestle with the *other* dimension of the God-question. For the idea of infinite being examined above stands in tension with the idea of *a* being (in contradistinction to, and hence limited by, other beings). Recall that Plato treated God as the *arche*, the source, the good itself,[33] a doctrine that Plotinus appropriated in his own way when he made the One the center of his metaphysics of ascension and participation. Aquinas likewise saw that God would have to be "being itself" (*ipsum esse*). What was it that these thinkers saw and that Schelling elevated to the center of his doctrine of God?

8.   God as Ground and the "God Above God"

For a philosophical theology motivated by Schelling there will be three moments in God:

1. *Infinite Creative Ground.*   I suggest that we first construe the One or being itself as Infinite Creative Ground. The notion of *infinity* expresses the absolute lack of limitation and, by implication, the nonexistence of any other being or thing that might do the limiting. The idea of *Ground* hints at the connection with the finite things that we (as finite beings) know to exist; that is, in some way this infinite dimension must serve as the ground of what exists. Ground is preferable to "cause" in order not to confuse the

notion of finite causes with this ultimate ground. (As Kant argued, our ordinary category of cause depends on the context of empirical experience.) As Ground of the finite, as we saw above, the infinite precedes the finite and serves as the condition of the possibility for the existence of anything finite whatsoever.

Finally, we speak of it as *Creative*, because it grounds the many and makes them one; through it the many become one. It is what makes the universe a *uni*verse not a multiverse. Whitehead speaks of creativity as the "ultimate which is actual in virtue of its accidents" and can be characterized only through them: "In the philosophy of organism this ultimate is termed 'creativity'; and God is its primordial, non-temporal accident" (*PR*, 7). Creativity in Whitehead, like the infinite in much of the Western tradition, is indeterminate and as such unknowable. It is the potential for creative development, not the dictator of the outcome of this process.[34]

Now where, conceptually speaking, is this Ground to be located? There are three possibilities: There is a Ground outside of God, which is God's foundation; this Ground is within God in some sense; or the Ground is identical to God. The first seems impossible: a god would not be God, in the sense that the tradition has maintained, if dependent on an external Reason. Nor can the consequent nature of God simply *be* the Ground, since it itself is the result of interactions with the world. Hence, I suggest, we should speak of a Ground *within* God. And this obviously entails that we must work with a multiple, as opposed to monistic, picture of God.

The inclusion of Ground within God may at first seem easier to accept than that Creativity would be a principle included within divinity (in the broadest sense of the word). At any rate, process thought has tended to separate Creativity and God.[35] But this is a mistake. It misses the fundamental and apparently unavoidable tension between God as ultimate principle and God as *a* personal being. The reason to think that the tension may be unavoidable is that the history of Western philosophy seems to represent (as Ivor Leclerc has argued) a profound and long-lasting vacillation between these two approaches to the term "God."[36] "Simply choose one or the other," we are tempted to say; yet it appears that any theistic metaphysic will be flawed precisely in its dismissal of the one side or the other.

The logic is inescapable: as long as we wish to advocate both God as ultimate principle and God as a personal being, we must incorporate both ideas within our conception of God. As Schelling (see Note 31) writes,

> As there is nothing before or outside of God he must contain within himself the ground of his existence. All philosophies say this, but they speak of this ground as a mere concept without making it something real and actual. This ground of his existence, which God contains [within himself], is not God viewed as absolute, that is insofar as he exists. For it is only the basis of his existence, it is *nature*—in God, inseparable from him, to be sure, but nevertheless distinguishable from him." (Schelling, *Werke* 7:358f.)

Divinity must include the ground of being as well as the highest personal being. The two cannot be posited as separate: the ground of being cannot exclude the highest being, nor can a being be God without including the ground of being within itself. However, because God as ultimate principle and God as person stand (in certain respects) in opposition to one another, they cannot simply be asserted simultaneously side by side—*unless* we think of them as in some way mediated by a third. The two must be conceived as combined, yet they cannot be identical. Here we have, I submit, the central challenge in theistic metaphysics. As philosophical theologians, we are trinitarian because *both* of these ideas are essential to an adequate theory of God, and because both can be predicated of God simultaneously only through the mediation of some third principle.

2. *Consequent.* Because we know ourselves to be finite, we know that finite things exist; thus, we know that the infinite Creative Ground has a consequent. Like the notion of cause and effect, the relationship Ground/Consequent is a reciprocal one: consequent requires ground, and ground is unthinkable without consequent. As finite, the world both requires God and cannot be identical to God.

Note that by "Consequent" Schelling does not first mean the consequent nature of *God*, but the world, the "other" to God, that results from God as Ground. Schelling also insists that the world results through a free divine creative act, but we will not be able to explore the strengths and the obvious difficulties of this notion here (e.g., how can a Ground carry out a free act, if God is only personal as actually self-conscious?). The important point is that the finite world represents a genuine other to its infinite ground.

3. *Mediation.* Shall we remain satisfied with this dualism, or must we, as I suggested above, think it as a threefold structure? Can the Ground and its Consequent be thought of together? Schelling writes:

> Here at last we reach the highest point of the whole inquiry. The question has long been heard: What is to be gained by that [sc. Schelling's] initial distinction between being insofar as it is basis (*Grund*), and being insofar as it exists? For either there is no common ground for the two—in which case we must declare outselves in favor of absolute dualism; or there is such common ground—and in that case, in the last analysis, the two coincide again. (Schelling, *Werke* 7:406)

As is well known, Schelling's answer is the responsive (self-conscious) nature of God, the God who encompasses both the divine Ground and the world of finite beings that results from it. God encompasses the world without becoming identical to it or swallowing up its genuine otherness.

The relationship between Schelling and Whitehead on this question remains remarkably close. On the one side, if there is at present something finite "within" God that did not always exist, then God must be in a sense different from before; and if this finite dimension is in a state of becoming, then God also *is* (in this particular sense) as becoming or process. Conversely, the "other" side of God—the absolute in its limitlessness, or as the ground of being—remains always self-identical. This pair of terms (ground and consequent or result) best expresses the two sides of divinity: the sameness and difference, God's position "above" creation and yet God's intimate involvement with it. Schelling labels the union of these two moments the divine self-consciousness; it is the result of God's experience of the world. Similarly, if less clearly, Whitehead saw that the consequent nature could be analogous to the human experience of creativity and valuation, and still guarantee objective immortality to past actual occasions.

Thus, Schelling became a trinitarian philosopher, arguing for a unification of Ground and Consequent in the divine self-consciousness, which is the appropriation of both without overcoming their difference. "All existence must be conditioned in order that it may be actual, that is, personal, existence. God's existence, too, could not be personal if it were not conditioned, except that he has the conditioning factor *within* himself and not outside him-

self" (Schelling, *Werke* 7:399). Division, Schelling adds, is the condition of God's own existence *qua* personal (Ibid. 7:403).

I suggest that the philosophical question on which this unification turns is one's position concerning the nature of divine
experience. There is a way to think divine self-consciousness (and
in a related sense, human self-consciousness) that avoids
Whitehead's worries about subjectivity. If the divine is conscious,
then it is conscious in a threefold way: of itself as Ground, of its
product, and of the relationship between self and product. God as
conscious of the world clearly incorporates the world without
abolishing God's distinction from it.

The position just sketched is called *panentheism*. This position is apparently foreign to Whitehead.[37] The reason perhaps
has to do more with Whitehead's lack of familiarity with the tradition of German Idealism than with any inherent incompatibil-
ity between idealism and process thought. In my framework,
panentheism emerges out of the dialectic between the infinity
and the finiteness of God. We have already discovered a dialectical relation between the absolute as ground and the personal
God as consequent. A similar relationship of difference-in-same-
ness characterizes God's relation to the world, which is construed neither as external to God (for what could be external to
infinity?) nor as identical to God (because the predicates of the
absolute certainly cannot be predicated of us as individuals).
According to Schelling, *if an ultimate principle is to be (adequately) thought* at all, it must be thought out of the unity of the
finite and infinite: "Until our doctrine acknowledges such a
power in God, or until it grasps the absolute identity of the infinite and finite" (Schelling, *Werke* 8:74), there is no place to speak
of the personality of God. Schelling's insight is to see that *freedom* provides the best means for thinking through the relationship of infinite and finite. "Freedom," he argues in *The Ages of
the World*, "is the affirmative concept of unconditioned eternity"
(Ibid. 8:235).

There is much more to be said about panentheism as a framework position for theistic metaphysics, one that is capable of han-
dling the transition to systematic theology as well. As we saw in
discussing Bracken's *Society and Spirit*, detailed defenses of it are
already available. It seems to me that this metaphysical framework
best allows for an inclusion of individuals within God in a way
that their own subjective immediacy does not disappear. As

Marjorie Suchocki has written of the God–world relationship, the key is that "the occasion can become itself and more than itself in God. The occasion is linked into the concrescence of God, even while remaining itself. Thus the peculiarity obtains that the occasion is *both* itself *and* God: it is apotheosized. As a participant in the divine concrescence, it will feel its own immediacy, and God's feeling of its immediacy as well."[38]

9. THE TRANSITION TO SYSTEMATIC THEOLOGY

We have been able to establish a trinitarian structure within the context of a fundamentally philosophical argument. This view allows us to say that there is process and development within God, although the whole of God is not conscious.[39] God is clearly not a single actual entity like any other, and yet important analogies remain between human and divine development and experience. The first step was to leave behind a strict atomism, which takes all larger groupings as mere societies or aggregates, in favor of an ontology based on the principle that there must be wholes that are greater than the sum of their parts (under atomism there *could* be no greater whole that included its parts). The chief share of the work was then performed by the notion of infinity and Ground as developed in the philosophy of Schelling. Along the way, we have noted the ways in which this view requires a modification of Whitehead's thought and have suggested why such changes represent an advance.

The argument to this point has sought to satisfy philosophical theologians (at least to satisfy them that I am addressing the relevant questions!). What we say in closing must satisfy systematic theologians, whose concerns are not automatically addressed by a viable philosophical theology alone. Even if the three moments sketched above survive the scrutiny of philosophers, it does not yet follow that they will correspond one-to-one with Father, Son, and Spirit. The Ground within God is not conscious; furthermore, the consequent is the world as a whole, not just the Son, and it contains *many* consciousnesses. Finally, unlike the theological trinity, divine consciousness seems to pertain only to the third moment.

The point of contact between the two turns on the question of the transition from philosophical to systematic theology and the relationship between them. Like the systematic theologians, I have maintained, against absolute monism, that God is multiple.

Furthermore, I have tried to show that a dualistic theory of God is insufficient, that some third moment is required in order to mediate between infinite and finite, ground and consequent. The position is, thus, clearly trinitarian in at least this minimal sense. (Incidentally, we need not worry about larger numbers: beyond three, God would just be a society; hence, an aggregate).

Nonetheless, I have not claimed that a line of metaphysical reflection will lead all the way to the threefold God of the Christian tradition. A gap remains. To this extent, Thomas Aquinas was right: there is no question of a complete transition from the philosophical to the theological trinity. A switch in perspectives remains necessary—the switch that Barth and Jüngel (and now even Pannenberg!) have labeled that from *von unten* to *von oben*. It must rely upon an observation drawn from salvation history: God has revealed Godself as Trinity; God has acted in a trinitarian manner. Only the actual history of salvation, and not a priori metaphysical speculation, can supply knowledge of what God's free self-revelation encompasses, if it is to be truly free.[40] Indeed, only a brief reflection on the historical dimension of the Christian religion is needed to see the inevitability of breaking with and moving beyond metaphysical argumentation. Even if, as I have argued above, a "moment" of God's being encompasses humanity, and even if it could be shown that this relationship requires God's incarnation in a single human being,[41] it would take historical and not metaphysical arguments to make the case that Jesus represents the best candidate for this honor. Thus, no more should be expected from metaphysics than a general indication of God's relationship to the world and humanity; the rest is contingent on free divine choices and the happenstances of human history.

Still, my claim is somewhat stronger than that made by Boyd and discussed above. Necessarily, God would reveal Godself as trinity. However, how can this be because I have already argued that Father, Son, and Spirit are not necessary? What is necessary about the threefoldness of systematic theology, and why is it not, as Lewis Ford argues, purely a matter of contingency?

The answer lies, again, in panentheism. *The panentheistic structure is inherently trinitarian.* Here we return to the theological reflection in section 3. Our first premise there was "God for us"; this I shall not argue for here (that would be apologetics) but shall presuppose. However, to think the presence of God metaphysically *means* to think of God in God's identification with the world; and this identification is what we call the second person of the trinity. Yet, if God were totally absorbed in the world, God would lose all separation from the world. In becoming purely immanent, God would become finite. Recall that we found the infinity of God to be a necessary part of God's nature; to become purely immanent would, therefore, mean to cease to be God. What is it, then, that remains separate or "beyond" the world? Clearly, God, and yet a different part or aspect of God: God in (and as) the first person.

Finally, although this may be somewhat harder to see, there must be God in and as the relationship between first and second person, God as the power that relates these two persons and unifies them; and this we call the third Person. It may be that we will not be successful at describing the nature *and the necessity* of the Spirit's mediating work in the detail with which contemporary systematic theologians (especially Pannenberg, Moltmann, and Jüngel) have attempted it.[42] But, even as a philosophical theologian, I can see that the *type* of mediation will be one that people in my field have too often avoided: one of love. Even if we cannot follow all the details of Schelling's position, we can espouse the basic insight of his trinitarian philosophy: the division that we have encountered is there so that the two

> should become one through love; that is, it divides itself only that there may be life and love and personal existence. For there is love neither in indifference nor where antitheses are combined which require the combination in order to be; but rather . . . this is the secret of love, that it unites such beings as could each exist in itself, and nonetheless neither is nor can be without the other. Therefore, as duality comes to be in the groundless, there also comes to be love, which combines the existent (ideal) with the basis of existence (Schelling, *Werke* 7:408).

But the structure just described is not the same as the actuality of it. Or: the economic does not equal the immanent trinity. It had to *happen* to be real. And Hegel, notwithstanding, it had to happen through the free reaction of God to the world. This is the reason that metaphysical reason could never derive the persons of the Trinity a priori, despite the fact that their Ground lies in a metaphysical doctrine: panentheism.

Is the immanent or the economic trinity prior? It depends upon which question we ask. If you mean philosophically; i.e., you raise the question of logical priority, then the immanent trinity is prior. If you mean salvifically, then the economic trinity is. I am tempted to put this conclusion somewhat more radically: there *is* no immanent trinity. The extrapolation from *deus pro nobis* to *deus in esse*, God *an sich*, is always arbitrary. Beyond God's actions in history, there is only the *potential structure* that we explored above, the sort of structure accessible to pure reason.

10. CONCLUSION

Whitehead says at one point, in contrasting the philosophy of organism with philosophies of the absolute, "One side makes process ultimate; the other side makes fact ultimate" (*PR*, 7). At too many crucial points in *Process and Reality*, his philosophy remains dualistic: "In our cosmological construction we are, therefore, left with the final opposites, joy and sorrow, good and evil, disjunction and conjunction—that is to say, the many in one—flux and permanence, greatness and triviality, freedom and necessity, God and the World" (*PR*, 341).

I have argued, in effect, that for a process system to be trinitarian, it must make both fact *and* process ultimate, both primordial envisagement and resulting actuality, both ground and consequent. However, these pairs are incompatibles; they can only both be ultimate if they are mediated in some way. It is this that makes an adequate metaphysics trinitarian: that it includes the step of mediation in the very essence of the position. I avoid the word "dialectical" because of Hegel's overblown claims on its behalf. Nonetheless, we find in the third moment—philosophically speaking, God's panentheistic appropriation of the world as God's other; theologically speaking, God's salvific and self-sacrificial love for the world—the core and completing moment of our understanding of God.

NOTES

1. See Joseph M. Hallman, "How Is Process Theology Theological?" *PS* 17(2) (1988): 112–17, following Edward Farley, *Ecclesial Man: A Social Phenomenology of Faith and Reality* (Philadelphia: Fortress, 1975). Hallman speaks of the "principle of positivity": "Tracy suggests . . . that we distinguish between philosophical theology, with

its universal concerns, and systematics, which is hermeneutical and particular. Farley's answer is itself philosophical: one begins reflection with the particular, trying to capture the unique features of that to which one attends." More convincing is Hallman's attempt to do justice to both the provincial and the "generic" or general features of religion. In this sense he quotes Farley, "[In provincial hermeneutics,] the essential features and 'truth' of the historical faith are identified with one of its specific historical expressions" (58).

2. See Lewis Ford, "When Did Whitehead Conceive God to be Personal?" *Anglican Theological Review* 72(3) (1990): 280–91.

3. I do not argue here for the truth of Christian revelation claims (though I do hold such arguments to be important). Our goal, instead, is to establish the relationship between what Christians claim and the conclusions of the best metaphysical reflection on the nature of God.

4. The debate about Whitehead's Christianity is nicely summarized in Victor Lowe's "A.N.W.: A Biographical Perspective," *Process Studies* 12(3) (1982): 137–47 and Paul G. Kuntz, "Can Whitehead Be Made a Christian Philosopher?" *Process Studies* 12(4) (1982): 232–42, esp. biographical note 6.

5. William Christian, in the *Christian Scholar* 50 (Fall 1967): 306f.

6. Nelson Goodman, *Ways of Worldmaking* (Indianapolis, IN: Hackett, 1978).

7. See my *Das Gottesproblem. Gott und Unendlichkeit in der neuzeitlichen Philosophie* (Paderborn, Germany: F. Schöningh Verlag, 1996) and *Toward a Pluralistic Metaphysics: Models of God in Early Modern Philosophy* (forthcoming), along with the works by Sallie McFague: *Metaphorical Theology: Models of God in Religious Language* (Philadelphia: Fortress Press, 1982), and *Models of God: Theology for an Ecological, Nuclear Age* (Philadelphia: Fortress, 1987).

8. Robert C. Neville, *Creativity and God: A Challenge to Process Theology* (New York: Seabury, 1980), 146.

9. This is one of the points of similarity with Aristotle that Rorty emphasizes in his article "Event and Form," in *Explorations in Whitehead's Philosophy*, ed. Lewis Ford and George L. Kline (New York: Fordham University Press, 1983).

10. Joseph A. Bracken, S.J., "Process Philosophy and Trinitarian Theology," *Process Studies* 8(4) (1978): 217–30, quote 220. Bracken adds, ". . . so that the whole exercises an agency which transcends the specific interaction of individual parts with one another."

11. David H. Jones, "Emergent Properties, Persons, and the Mind–Body Problem," *Southern Journal of Philosophy* 10 (1972): 423–33; Charles A, Krecz, "Reduction and the Part/Whole Relation," *Philosophy of Science* (1988): 71–87; Gerhard Roth, "Self-Organization, Emergent Properties and the Unity of the World," *Philosophica* (1990): 45–64; Eileen Barker, "Apes and Angels: Reductionism, Selection, and Emergence in the Study of Man (Some Recent Books)," *Inquiry* 19 (1976): 367–87; Roger Wolcott Sperry, *Science and Moral Priority: Merging Mind, Brain, and Human Values* (New York: Columbia University Press, 1983); Mario Augusto Bunge, *The Mind–Body Problem: A Psychobiological Approach* (Oxford: Pergamon Press, 1980); Bunge, *Scientific Materialism* (Dordrecht: D. Reidel, 1981).

12. Robert C. Neville, *A Theology Primer* (Albany: State University of New York Press, 1991), chap. 3.

13. Lewis Ford, "In What Sense is God Infinite? A Process Perspective," *Thomist* 42 (1978): 1–13; "The Infinite God of Process Theism," *Proceedings of the American Catholic Philosophical Association* 55 (1981): 84–90. As is well known, Ford himself eventually settled for the position that God could be infinite only if *fully* future.

14. Roman numeral references are to C. Adam and P. Tannery, eds., *Oeuvres de Descartes*, 12 vols., revised edition (Paris: Vrin/CNRS, 1964–76). The English translation (*The Philosophical Writings of Descartes*, 3 vols., trans. John Cottingham, Robert Stoothoff, Dugald Murdoch., [Cambridge: Cambridge University Press, 1985ff.]) includes marginal references to the *Oeuvres*.

15. Arguably, this is the central project or goal of Wolfhart Pannenberg's *Anthropology in Theological Perspective*, trans. Matthew J. O'Connell (Philadelphia: Westminster Press, 1985). Such a project might appeal to our experience of (apparently) unlimited size or power or duration; e.g., the size of the universe or its possibly unlimited duration; to the experience of the sublime (as analyzed in Kant's *Critique of Judgment*); to the physical mathematical realms of the infinitely large and infinitely small and the infinite infinities of Cantorian set-theory; and to philosophical concepts such as the infinite or Absolute.

16. Descartes also grasped this limitation: "My point is that, on the contrary, if I can grasp something, it would be a total contradiction for that which I grasp to be infinite. For the idea of the infinite, if it is to be a true idea, cannot be grasped at all, since the impossibility of being grasped is contained in the formal definition of the infinite" (Fifth Resp., VII, 368).

17. Here Marion is right: "Si l'infini doit se percevoir par idée, ce sera
     non par l'impossible représentation d'un objet, mais par la présence
     de l'infini même, manifeste par le jeu contrasté de l'ego avec Dieu."
     See Jean-Luc Marion, *Sur la théologie blanche de Descartes.*
     Analogie, création des vérités éternelles et fondement (Paris: Presses
     Universitaires de France, 1981), 404. Marion adds elsewhere that
     "noncomprehension does not signify nonawareness": "one can (and
     must) know God as infinite without the clarity of a methodical
     object" ("The Essential Incoherence of Descartes' Definition of
     Divinity," in *Essays on Descartes's Meditations*, ed. Amélie Rorty
     [Berkeley: Univ. of California Press, 1986], 297–338, quote 335n.56).
     On the same subject, see also his *Sur le prisme métaphysique de*
     Descartes. Constitution et limites de l'onto-théo-logie dans la pensée
     cartésienne (Paris: Presses universitaires de France, 1986), chap. 4.

18. Descartes already realized this point with particular clarity: "I see
     manifestly that there is more reality in infinite substance than in
     finite substance, and yet that I have in some way in me a notion of
     the infinite that is prior to my notion of the finite—that is, the notion
     of God is prior to the notion of myself. For how would it be possi-
     ble that I can know that I doubt and that I desire—that is, that I lack
     something and that I am not perfect—unless I had in me an idea of
     a being more perfect than me, by comparison to which I might
     know the defects of my own nature" (Descartes, Meditation 3,
     French ed., IX, 36).

19. I develop this idea in detail in *Toward a Pluralistic Metaphysics*,
     chap. 5.

20. John Cobb, Jr., "Response to Neville," *Process Studies* 10(4) (1980): 98.

21. This was also the response of John Cobb, Jr., *A Christian Natural*
     Theology (Philadelphia: Westminster, 1965).

22. Gregory Boyd, *Trinity and Process: A Critical Evaluation and*
     Reconstruction of Hartshorne's Di-Polar Theism Towards a
     Trinitarian Metaphysics (New York: Peter Lang, 1992), 402.

23. On the first notion see Ford, "Temporality and Transcendence," in
     Hartshorne, Process Philosophy, and Theology, ed. Robert Kane and
     Stephen H. Phillips (Albany: State University of New York Press,
     1989), 151–167. On the latter notion, in addition to Ford's *The Lure*
     of God: A Biblical Background for Process Theism (Philadelphia:
     Fortress Press, 1978) see especially his articles "The Divine Activity
     of the Future," *Process Studies* 11 (1981): 169–79; and "Creativity in
     a Future Key," in *New Essays in Metaphysics*, ed. Robert C. Neville
     (Albany: State University of New York Press, 1987), 179–98.

24. Joseph A. Bracken, *The Triune Symbol: Persons, Process and Community* (Lanham, MD: University Press of America, 1985). More recently, see his *The Divine Matrix: Creativity as Link between East and West* (Maryknoll, NY: Orbis Books, 1995). See also his "Process Philosophy and Trinitarian Theology," Parts I and II, *Process Studies* 8(4) (1978): 217–30 and *Process Studies* 11(2) (1981): 83–96; and "Energy-Events and Fields," *Process Studies* 18(3) (1989): 153–65.

25. Joseph Bracken, *Society and Spirit: A Trinitarian Cosmology* (London and Toronto: Associated University Presses, 1991), 129.

26. *Toward a Pluralistic Metaphysics: Models of God*, esp. chaps. 7–9.

27. See Antoon Braeckman, "Whitehead and German Idealism: A Poetic Heritage," *Process Studies* 14(4) (1985): 265–86. The following citations are taken from 278ff. There are certainly other important parallels, such as those between Schelling's "potencies" in *Ages of the World* and Whitehead's primordial envisagement, and the stress on the movement from potential to actual. Incidentally, I do not agree with Braeckman's reading of Schelling in exclusively Kantian (transcendental) terms. His interpretation runs into some difficulties already with objective idealism; it is untenable after the Bruno dialogue of 1803 and certainly by the time of the 1809 essay *On Human Freedom*.

28. Braeckman, "Whitehead and German Idealism," 279.

29. Bracken, "Subjective Spirit: The Power of Radical Self-Determination," in *Society and Spirit: A Trinitarian Cosmology,* chap. 4

30. Bracken, *Society and Spirit,* 129. Bracken is perhaps the only process thinker who has been able to appropriate the insights of Schelling. See also his discussion and use of the anthropological suggestions of Wolfhart Pannenberg on pp. 101ff. Chap. 5 attempts to mediate between Hegel and Whitehead.

31. According to Schelling, God was always the (potentially) self-manifesting God, and hence the Creator God, although there was a phase (metaphorically, a time) when God was not manifest in anything outside of Himself. The advantage of this framework is that it allows us to say that the questions of how divinity can be (in itself) and how it can become manifest are two ways of formulating the same question (cf. 8:255f.). Nonetheless, there remains a real difference (probably stronger than Aristotle's metaphysics grants) between the not-yet-manifest and the now-manifest, between the "time" before and after there was a world. There may be a natural movement to the next potency, as Schelling thinks (8:275), and nature may

(indeed must) be spoken of as a potentiality vis-à-vis the godhead (8:280f.), which may (but not must!) develop eventually to something godlike; but God is only *actually* conscious, and thus actually the Being whom he has become, when the actual process of creation and its subsequent development has taken place (cf. 8:262).

Unless otherwise indicated, citations refer to *Friedrich Wilhelm Joseph von Schellings sämtliche Werke*, 14 vols. in two divisions, ed. K. F. A. Schelling (Stuttgart and Augsburg: J. G. Cotta'scher Verlag, 1856–1861). I indicate the four volumes of the 2nd division as vols. 11–14 respectively. Page references to English translations are not given, because they invariably include marginal numbers keyed to the German critical edition. Major English translations of Schelling include (from vol. 7) *Schelling: Of Human Freedom*, trans. James Gutmann (Chicago: Open Court, 1936) and (from vol. 8) *The Ages of the World*, trans. Frederick de Wolfe Bolman, Jr. (New York: AMS Press, 1942, 1967).

32. See Nathaniel Lawrence, "The Vision of Beauty and the Temporality of Deity in Whitehead's Philosophy," *Journal of Philosophy* 58 (1961): 543–53, reprinted in *Alfred North Whitehead: Essays on His Philosophy*, ed. George L. Kline (Englewood Cliffs, NJ: Prentice-Hall, 1963), 168–78.

33. See Ivor Leclerc's excellent survey article, "The Problem of God in Whitehead's System," *Process Studies* 14(4) (1985): 301–15.

34. It might be thought that a ground is something that could not *be* creative. But the association of *esse* and creativity has been basic to process metaphysics and has been carefully defended. See Lewis Ford, "Creativity in a Future Key," cited above, and David L. Schindler, "Whitehead's Inability to Affirm a Universe of Value," *Process Studies* 13(2) (1984): 117ff.

35. The tendency goes back, of course, to Whitehead. Lewis Ford makes the same move in the famous trinity chapter in *The Lure of God*: e.g., 106f. Among many others, see also Joseph M. Hallman, "The Mistake of Thomas Aquinas and the Trinity of A. N. Whitehead," *Journal of Religion* 70 (1990): 36–47.

36. This tension has been brilliantly worked out in the thought of Werner Beierwaltes. See *inter alia Denken des Einen. Studien zur neuplatonischen Philosophie und ihrer Wirkungsgeschichte* (Frankfurt: Klostermann, 1985), and *Platonismus und Idealismus* (Frankfurt: Vittorio Klostermann, 1972).

37. See Ford in *Hartshorne: Process Philosophy and Theology*, 158, 162f., 171f.

38. Marjorie H. Suchocki, *The End of Evil: Process Eschatology in Historical Context* (Albany: State University of New York Press, 1988), 102. More recently, see her *The Fall to Violence: Original Sin in Relational Theology* (New York: Continuum, 1994).

39. This is also the view of Wolfhart Pannenberg, who identifies it as an orthodox Christian position; see *Systematic Theology*, vol. 1, trans. Geoffrey W. Bromiley (Grand Rapids: Eerdmans Publishing Co, 1988).

40. This was also Schelling's conclusion when he shifted in his final phase to a "positive Philosophie." See his *Philosophie der Mythologie*, vol. 12, and *Philosophie der Offenbarung*, vols. 13, 14, and, recently, Edward Allen Beach, *The Potencies of God(s): Schelling's Philosophy of Mythology* (Albany: State University of New York Press, 1994).

41. It strikes me as highly unlikely that we would be able to show this. Richard Swinburne has made the attempt on various occasions; most recently, see his *The Christian God* (New York: Oxford University Press, 1994).

42. Wolfhart Pannenberg, *Systematic Theology*, cited above; Pannenberg, *Grundfragen systematischer Theologie. Gesammelte Aufsätze*, vol. 2 (Göttingen: Vandenhoeck & Ruprecht, 1989); Jürgen Moltmann, *History and the Triune God: Contributions to Trinitarian Theology*, trans. John Bowden (New York: Crossroad, 1992); Moltmann, *The Trinity and the Kingdom of God: The Doctrine of God*, trans. Margaret Kohl (London: SCM Press, 1981); Eberhard Jüngel, *God as the Mystery of the World: On the Foundation of the Theology of the Crucified One in the Dispute between Theism and Atheism*, trans. Darrell L. Guder. (Grand Rapids, MI: Eerdmans, 1983).

Roland Faber
Trinity, Analogy, and Coherence

The following is a comparison of possible connections between trinitarian theology and process theology to show how they can supplement each other. The main thesis is that the concepts of analogy and coherence make it possible to translate each tradition in terms of the other, and in so doing, to shed light on peculiar problems within each tradition. For trinitarian theology, the problem is often understood as the problem of the "three" and their relations to each other and to the world. For process theology, the problem is whether to understand God as a single actuality or as a society. And for both together, the problem is how to relate God and the world so that God is not a part of the world, nor just its "idea," nor solely its untouchable, transcendental ground. The common basis of comparison is the question of an internal relationship between God and world. I show how analogy represents the process of coherence in a way that allows us to express how a structural possibility for the trinity exists within the process paradigm. The thesis, then, is that it is feasible to develop a trinitarian theological differentiation within the process paradigm that understands God as one actuality in everlasting self-differentiation.

In his famous chapter 11 of *Science and the Modern World* (*SMW*), with the laconic title "God," Whitehead compares his attempt at a concept of God with Aristotle's metaphysical model of the unmoved mover. When Whitehead observes an "analogous metaphysical problem" in Aristotle that "can be solved only in an analogous fashion" (*SMW* 174), he is not arguing for a reappropriation of Aristotle's unmoved mover. It is not the ancient solution that determines the analogy; on the contrary, it is the structure of the process of inquiry. God is required for the essence of the universe, as principle of concretion; or better: the Principle of Concretion is named God by Whitehead.

Thus, Whitehead treats the world and God under one combined view by determining the appropriate and even necessary categories for comprehending the world. In these categories, God's being gives expression to itself, and for that reason the categories frame the world. The question is not whether we need a concept of God to prevent a breakdown of the principles framing the world (*Process and Reality [PR]* 343), but which categories can be employed in a discussion of the concept of God that lead to comprehension of the world. The categories for comprehending the world are elucidated through the conceptualization of God. Likewise, the concept of God is illumined through the comprehension of the world within the same categories. For while Whitehead introduces God to illuminate the structures of the world, he actually understands God more as the expression of these structures, their uppermost realization, their pure gestalt. God's being embodies in itself the ground of these structures, and at the same time, as their reason, God is their actualization. This form of development of an analogy lets Whitehead establish a connection to Aristotle, insofar as he can give expression to the principle that everything that is in existence represents the categories of existence. To be sure, the resemblance to Aristotle's conception is limited, because Whitehead does not try to grasp God as the ground of the universe. The conceptualization of God, rather, must have the capacity for God's radical otherness, even if God represents the principle of the world.

Developing a notion of analogy for the relationship between God and the world unfolds a coherent concept of God that is suitable and not unreasonable to the Christian experience of faith and tradition. Theology tried to understand how God is related to the world, and whether God's relation to the world is a way to think of God as trinitarian. The categories gained in religious reflection were never intended to be a positive insight into God's mystery, but rather they made possible a new insight into the world. The aids for understanding the incomprehensible God extracted from secular reason serve at the same time to elucidate the world as one to which God is engaged. Thus, we can realize God's engagement with the world is not unreasonable.

It is this kind of development of analogy as a mutual explanation of God and the world that advances both trinitarian theology and a process theological view. Analogy and coherence can supplement, interpret, and criticize each another and, therefore, benefit both trinitarian theology and process theology.

The classical way of determining theologically God's world relation made the doctrine of God's one, substantial essence preeminent over God's trinitarian relational being.[1] God's being in relation to the world was as a "thought," or an external relation, in which God is not intrinsically touched by the world. This leads to the separation of God and world. However, the assumption of God's intrinsic movement requires a real relation of the trinitarian God to the world. This leads to criticism of that understanding of freedom and sovereignty by which God seems to be self-sufficient, producing a world through an arbitrary act of love. But can God be eternally self-sufficient in an untouchable glory? Does not God really need the one loved, in the suffering of God's love? Could a loving God ever have been without a world?

This requires that we determine anew God's world-reference in such a way that it could be named a real relation, but with a nonarbitrary reason within God. This is adequately found only in a trinitarian refinement. Thus, the crucial questions in a new determination of the relation of God and the world sharpen into the problem of whether and how and in what respect the category of an internal relation is constitutive for reality in such a way that it can determine the relation of God and the world, precisely because God is *in se* its prime realization.

In answering this question, a trinitarian conception of God can solve the problem of interpreting God's internal relationship with the world without denying God's primordiality over against the world. To speak within trinitarianism, God as Father is not primarily to be understood as in opposition to a world, but in relation with the *Logos*. Thus, it would be possible to interpret the world-relationship of God out of the intrinsically trinitarian self-relationship, and to see in the one relation a model for the other. The history of theology specifically offers the following perspectives.

The First Ecumenical Council in Nicaea spoke of the *homoousios* of the incarnated *Logos* with the Father; this meant a decisive change from the metaphysical categories of the ancient world. It implicated a revolution in thought, conferring on the category of relation an equal rank to the hitherto dominant category of substance. We can only observe this change in terms of the Middle and Neoplatonism that held sway in the time between 100 B.C.E. and the Council of Nicaea. A hierarchically ordered world was grounded in the inaccessible One in contrast to the principles of multiplicity (namely *nous*, "world-soul," and the unformed multiplicity of *hyle*). The absolutely undifferentiated One is, thus, strongly the prime-ground of the world, with no real relation to the other principles. *Nous* and world-soul are unneeded (although, in fact, given) manifestations in the pluralistic world with "nothing" in common with the absolute One.[2] Although this absolute unity, standing above all possibility of differentiation, became the image for a Christian understanding of the divine oneness of essence, in the concept of the Trinity the notion of *homoousios* undercut this monolithic understanding of unity.

In the trinitarian context, the possibility was open for a relational worldview. By means of the concept of "ex-sistence;" namely, to be by being grounded in another being, the category of a relational constitution of reality became possible. Richard of St. Victor developed the idea of the unity of the divine persons as *ex-sistentiae*, as beings who are intrinisic to one another, so that they are emerging out of one another. His now famous definition of person in this context is: *persona est divinae naturae incommunicabilis existentia.*

This concept no longer relies on a notion of a substantial *ens per se*, or *ens in se*, as the founding category of thought. Its "essence" consists in being not out of oneself, tantamount to a substance, but out of the relation with another. Each divine person is essentially only out of, and in relation with, the other persons. This nonsubstantial, relational understanding of God's internal, trinitarian being can now be understood as an element in the foundation of God's internal relationship with the world.

ANALOGY

Analogy is that element of the tradition where the quest for the relations in God, of God with the world, and the world itself intrinsically appears. The only "official" definition for analogy in a theological context was formulated by the Fourth Lateran Council

(1215) in the process of determining a relation between God and the world.[3] The Council comments upon a theological disputation between Joachim of Fiore and Peter Lombard about the correct understanding of the unity of the trinitarian community in God. Both the disputants and the Council agreed that God is to be understood not only as trinitarian, but also as one. The problem was *how* to determine this unity of the divine persons. Joachim reproached Peter Lombard for adding the one substance of God as a fourth person. The Council sided with Lombard in noting that God is one reality shared equally and totally by the three divine persons. It agreed with Joachim of Fiore that the unity of the divine persons is fundamentally unlike the unity of human beings within a community. Human beings ought to be "one" as the Son is "one" with the Father (Jo 17:22). But the meaning is transformed in a sense of divine analogy in which the oneness of the three persons is ever more dissimilar to human and mundane oneness. Because the understanding of unity has to be conceived as based in God and the assumption of the world in God's community, the analogy itself must be grounded in God. Thus, the Council could hold tight to a unity *sui generis*, which is not to be deduced from elsewhere, but is a natural oneness of the three persons, equal in the beginning.

Commonly, analogy is understood as a relation of similarity, a relation aimed at an abolition of dissimilarity. This understanding came to have such enormous influence that all attempts to think nonanalogously militated against analogy itself. I want to reverse this tendency in a way that is suggested by the Lateran definition of analogy. The formula runs, ". . . *inter creatorem et creaturam non potest tanta similitudo notari, quin inter eos maior sit dissimilitudo notanda*" (DH 806).

This is the core of the appeal to analogy: that the dissimilarity is ever more vast than similarity, and that this analogy beween God and world (and internally in the world) is founded in God's relational being, in the trinitarian community itself. In God's ever-vaster dissimilarity to the world, unity is not determined prior to the divine relations, but through them. An ultimately trinitarian horizon allows us to speak of an internal relationality of the world insofar as the world derives from God.

On dissimilarity, therefore, is bestowed a self-reliant weight vis-à-vis similarity in the "one" analogy: the dissimilarity is ever-vaster, not subsumable under similarity, inconceivable, ever ahead of it. And this is the challange: that this analogy beween God and world is founded in God's *internal*, relational being; in the trinitarian community itself. In God's innermost life, there must be the ultimate origin for this analogy that ultimately grounds the creational structure of being. The analogous relation between God and world is founded "in" God, *in* God's *intrinsic*, trinitarian relations, and it emerges *out* of the trinitarian origin. Because of God's intrinsic, analogous structure of ever-vaster dissimilarity, unity is not determined prior to the divine relations, but through them. And thus, the Lateran understanding of analogy realizes the classical, trinitarian concept of "person" in its deepest meaning. "Person," then, means all that, which is *not common* in God, all that, in which the persons of the Trinity *exclusively differ*; for in everything they don't differ, they *are* the one divine essence.[4] Thus, the divine analogy is intrinsically the analogy of the dissimilar, divine persons, and in their "oppositional relations" lies the ultimate root of the analogous structure as suggested.

Furthermore, the ultimately trinitarian horizon also allows us to speak of an *internal* relation of the world with God insofar as the world derives from God's dissimilarity, called into similarity with God. God's constitutive dissimilarity, in which God opens God's innermost self, transforms us into similarity. God remains the unsurpassible origin of the revelation of God's intrinsic life, but making itself recognizable through similarity. Analogy can now be understood as the internal relation of God to the innermost heart of the creatures. The being of God's creatures is an analogous being-from-God as ex-sistence, which biblically is characterized as a love-relation. In God's disclosedness, the ex-sisting creature in being dissimilar is called into similarity, and in this to its own self-being as free ex-sistence. Nevertheless, when God defines God in world-relations, in God's definition, God is in a certain sense always (dissimilarily) ahead of it while being (similarily) concrete within it.

PROCESS

The structure of the universe is to be in process; all complex realities in their multiple relations to one another are processual. The entire world can be analyzed as a process of organic processes. Each process is the creative realization of relations out of the world into a new relational creature. The universe is the whole of all possible and actual relations, and that means not only that more than that is not recognizable, but there is simply no more than that. Or seen the other way around: All that is communicable stands in connections, and is, therefore, in this sense relative. There is nothing that, insofar as it is, is not interconnected with all others in a permanently developing *universalis communicatio.*

In the working out of Whitehead's metaphysics of reality and actuality, this "communication in process" will find its expression in the three fundamental principles of reference for actualities: (1) the "ontological principle," where actuality leads back solely to actuality again, or the concrete is the reason for the concrete; (2) the "principle of relativity," which regulates the universal togetherness of all actualities, and finally (3) the "principle of process," which is that being is its becoming and is not to be understood apart from it. All that is, is experiencable; whatever is not "in" experience does not exist. And it is the concrete that gives itself to experience; when we experience, we experience the concrete actuality, the singleness, the unrepeatable, the unique itself, and not solely the general, attributes, universals, the repeatable.

Thus, the process paradigm can clearly support elements of the Lateran analogy formula and its mode of reference: the process of the world is grounded within God in a way that can interpret the relation between God and world. And this interpretation takes the irreducible concreteness into account as it grows out of dissimilarity and defines itself in similarity. This relation is one of inexhaustible novelty in a process of self-communication, self-revelation and attachment.

INTERPRETATION

Important elements can be named in which the coincidence of the doctrine of analogy and of Whitehead's thought will manifest itself in detail. Already in his early philosophy of nature, Whitehead drew attention to the distinction between dissimilarity and similarity in analogy. Against the conventional stress on similarity, he gave the primary weight to dissimilarity.

> Rational thought which is the comparison of event with event would be intrinsically impossible without objects (*An Enquiry Concerning the Principles of Natural Knowledge* 64).

Fugitive, unique, absolutely incomparable events that constitute reality as concrete are in their concreteness unrecognizable if there cannot be found an element whereby a comparison will be made possible. Dissimilarity has to interpret itself in similarity in order to receive durability as dissimilarity. This process is not just one of human cognition, but one of nature itself. The abstraction of thinking is just one mode of the essence of every natural interaction.

Obviously, the preeminence of actuality is due to dissimilarity; i.e., objects of perception solely exist in regard to events, because without them they are, so to speak, nothing. To be sure, a retroreference to similarity is required. For, while each act of realization is irreducibly concrete, private, ineffable, incommunicable, atomistic, perishing in becoming, perceived repetition of events is abstraction of the similar from the concrete, and for that reason, recognizable. Thus, neither events nor objects are independent, subsisting apart from each other. Their function to one another renders them both possible and actual. Despite a certain kind of independence from each other that makes them not reducible to one another, they are together or they are not at all.

However, how can such a structure of concretes and abstracts be made evident, which after all means that knowledge always aims at the concrete, the unprecedented, the irreducibly dissimilar, although cognition always happens in developing similarity through abstraction?

> But an event is just what it is, and is just how it is related; and it is nothing else (*PNK* 64). [F]or an entity which stands in internal relations has no being as an entity not in these relations. In other words, once with internal relations, always with internal relations (*SMW* 160).

With his conception of actuality as concrete, actual, becoming, and, therefore, concrescent, Whitehead can help to master this paradox, because for him organic relationality and concreteness irrevocably presuppose each other. Each single, processual actuality is a process of becoming, growing together out of already concrete actualities. Therefore, dissimilarity is essential for similarity. Concrete past actualities are objectified in the becoming actuality.

The process of objectifying past events renders possible the passage from public objects into the privacy of concrescence, and the passage from this intrinsic subjectivity into the new publicity of transition, and with that the passage from subject into object and reverse. That way, the retroconnection of the irreducible, analogous difference to similarity can be made intelligible by Whitehead, and he can express the rhythmical turn from one to another as the act of process that founds every reality.

Moreover, in choosing the process paradigm as a point of departure, the opposition between similarity and dissimilarity does not get stabilized into an ultimate antagonism. On the contrary, within the relative process structure of actuality, substance becomes dynamized, and, therefore, "unsubstantialized." The becoming of concrete actuality is the growing together of "concretes" and "abstracts" in one and in the same process, and the transition of one into the other is an everlasting turn. This twofold function grounds a kind of polarity in the process of every concrete actuality that has a physical and a mental side, with the physical side feeling actual entities, and with the mental side feeling eternal objects.

In the general process, the mentality of a prehended actual occasion becomes the content of the physical pole of another actuality. Just as events represent "unique–dissimilar"[5] and objects the "universal–similar," just so an event intrinsically is the perception of the dissimilar and its processual transformation into the similar. Events have the feature of being real potentials in other events and for them, and objects have an individual, dissimilar essence, because they are not entirely defined by their relations. Actual entities are perceived in physical feelings as dissimilar with reference to their importance for the process of appropriation. Therefore, they make the process, in which they ought to become consistent to one another and, therefore, similar, everlastingly go on by reason of their dissimilarity to each other.[6] On the other side, is the physical perception of nothing other than a conformal feeling of the predecessors and, therefore, the process of becoming similar (*PR* 164). Within the context of Whitehead's categories, the rhythmic passage of similarity and dissimilarity into one another gets transplanted into a complex matrix in which all elements condition one another in a certain mode of indefiniteness. This, on the other hand, renders our project feasible, because it avoids every dualism within the analogous structure.

On the other hand, "analogy" does not belong to the technical terms of Whitehead's philosophy. He uses it generally without specific intention, although he does use it in the context of the definition of congruence (*PR* 331), or in connection with the question of probability (*PR* 205), which does not have much in common with the issue treated here.[7] However, an important text referring to the notion of "analogy" appears in *Function of Reason* (*FR*)

> But why construe the later forms by analogy to the earlier forms. Why not reverse the process? It would seem to be more sensible, more truly empirical, to allow each living species to make its own contribution to the demonstration of factors inherent in living things.[8]

For our context, this means that analogy has to proceed out of what is dissimilar, not out of what is common in terms of a smallest common denominator. For Whitehead, this form of analogy seems implied within the notion of participation, particularly in *Adventures of Ideas* (*AI*):

> [A]n abstraction can be made and some elements of the complete pattern can be omitted. The partial pattern thus obtained will be said to be abstracted from the original. A truth-relation will be said to be objective contents of two prehensions when one and the same identical partial pattern can be abstracted from both of them. They each exhibit this same partial pattern, though their omitted elements involve the differences which belong to their diverse individualities. Plato used the term "participation" to express the relation of a composite fact to some partial pattern which it illustrates. Only he limits the notion of the partial pattern to some purely abstract pattern of qualitative elements, to the exclusion of the notion of concrete particular realities as components in a composite reality. This limitation is misleading. Thus we will speak of a pattern as possibly including concrete particular realities as components in a composite reality.[9]

Analogy is the process of participation, of *methexis*, wherein individual, dissimilar actualities are related to each other in reciprocal interpretation in terms of a common pattern of similarity abstracted from them. Decisive here are two elements: On one side, the process exactly does what was already emphasized regarding the relation between event and object; namely, allowing for mutual participation of individualities though an abstraction; thus, it is about an analogous relation. On the other hand, what Whitehead criticizes in Plato (namely, that he did not take the moment of participation of concrete actualities in the constitution of new actualities into consideration) is the reason for his giving priority to dissimilarity over similarity. For if the concrete events are integrated into the participation process, the relation of participation will describe exactly the process of development of actual entities out of their world's elements. In that way, the process of the emergence of concrete actuality from concrete actuality can be described with the help of abstraction as the process of analogy.

Thus, to summarize: Reality is the process of the development of concrete actualities through reciprocal participation and interpretation of dissimilar elements of the process (prehensions), so that through "similarization," which is mutually operative in these elements for one another, the end result will appear as nothing else than united dissimilarity.[10] Process is analogous, analogy exists as a process of actualities. The beginning point is the difference of the concrete; the end result is their contrast-enriched unity whose intensity will depend on the "analogous differentiatedness" of their components. Analogy within the process paradigm is the becoming of the *res verae*.

THE PRINCIPLE OF CONCRETION

In a series of antithetical remarks, Whitehead proposes that that which is the last reason, or even the ultimate principle of reasoning, has no reason itself. As the ground of this world, there rules not necessity and reason, but freedom. Reason becomes God as the principle of freedom and of the concrete that happens historically, in all its novelty. This finding leads Whitehead far beyond Aristotle's attempt to ground the world in necessity, and thus, in rational accessibility, in which God should be the necessary ground for the general character of things. If the concrete is the undeceivable dissimilar, then God as the reason of concreteness is the ultimate reason of dissimilarity. And God is this "reason" in a way that God's being does not allow one to reason about it. On the contrary, God gives reason out of unfathomable wealth. This givenness of God is at the same time God's self-giving as ground. The climax of this twist in Whitehead's thinking on analogy, then, is that God, because of God's being the ground of concreteness, can only be known in historical concreteness. God's metaphysical rank opens this way for a historical understanding of God, and a real relation with the world without dissolving in that relation because of God's dissimilarity.[11]

In *Process and Reality*, Whitehead comes back again to speak of God as Principle of Concreteness in the context of his innovative theory of subjectivity, in a passage that allows him to establish with all desirable clarity the connection with the inquiry concerning analogy:

> The immediacy of the concrescent subject is constituted by its living aim at its own self-constitution. Thus the initial stage of the aim is rooted in the nature of God, and its completion depends on the self-causation of the subject–superject . . . In this sense God is the principle of concretion; namely, he is that actual entity from which each temporal concrescence receives that initial aim from which its self-causation starts. (*PR* 244)

Subjectivity is, thus, not a "substantial" subject any more, but a "relational" subject that emerges out of its experiences, that constitutes itself within its experiences. The subject is an activity, a creative act of becoming one out of all its experiences, without being in advance of them (*PR* 26). Thus, the subject is in a certain sense forever "outstanding" and at the same time in the process of its becoming, is always already present as a final cause.[12] As initial aim and subjective aim, it is in its outstandingness still leading the process (*PR* 222), and is in its satisfaction perfected and now available for the becomings of other subjects. For Whitehead, the subjective process is the original happening of the creative, rhythmical turn from object into subject, from externality into immediacy and vice versa. By this means, the process fulfills the ultimate motion of the universe. It is always "subject–superject," becoming, standing in the immediacy of its own becoming, *and* being, which, deprived of its subjectivity, permanently acts upon others in order to enter them. As subject, its actuality is as subjective immediacy (*PR* 23), and as superject, its actuality is as objective immortality (*PR* 45).

Consequently, what should be noted here is that the subjectivity of each creature is, thus, grounded in the nature of God. Whitehead discusses this clearly in the passage cited above. The immediacy of irreducible subjects is grounded in the divine giving of a subjective aim, from which the otherwise *un*derivable subjectivity "derives." In a subtle paradox, God's nature is the *source* of the process of *self*-constitution for every actuality. This notion, in which the dissimilar God grounds independence and unsurpassable dissimilarity, and, with that, the self-reliance of creatures, proves to be a new variant of Richard of St. Victor's "ex-sistence" as relation, in which the incommunicable is founded as communicable in relation with others. According to God's "intrinsically analogous" being, dissimilarity does not found similarity, but dissimilarity; not dependence, but self-reliance; not necessity, but freedom. The initial subjective aim, luring the subjective process, is in its essence a complex eternal object. On the one hand, it represents essential novelty and freedom, introducing them in contrast to the fixed reality of the world (*AI* 83). On the other hand, in its dissimilarity in comparison with the past world, it is more the expression of analogous similarity, as argued above. The underivability of subjectivity, realizing itself in the decision-making process, therefore, paradoxically derives from somewhere else; namely, from creativity that is its process.

Thus, finally we ask: How does each becoming subjectivity originate in God's nature? Now we have arrived at that point where it is obvious how, in Whitehead's conception, the "analogous motion" of subjectivity is grounded in God, in a way happening almost as God's essence itself. God, in God's primordial aspect, is the active synthesis of inexhaustible potentiality in a process of self-actualization. God's concrescence itself, however, is directed by a divine subjective aim (*PR* 88) that is not to be derived from another ground, except out of creativity itself, herewith being the sheer expression of the undecisive primordiality and underivable disimilarity. God's subjective immediacy is not the eternal objects it unites, nor is it the creativity it enacts. Indeed, even eternal objects and creativity are expressions of God's godhead, but the ultimate root of God is God's unfathomable subjectivity that is not to be grounded in anything other than its own, irreducible act. By this means, in the process theological understanding of God, the Lateran preference of dissimilarity over similarity is grounded in God's nature itself, which realizes in its subjectivity the dissimilar actualization of similar objects. This is God's incomparability, providing for each analogy without being comprehended by it (*PR* 47).

Whitehead acknowledged this weight of God's underivable actuality himself in designating the subjective aim not just as expression, but also as limit of the ontological principle (*PR* 44). This is a remarkable assertion, if we consider the ontological principle to regulate the relation between ground (ratio) and principle, meaning that which can be grounded. One and the same reality is a concrete actuality *and* an abstract principle, realizing itself in actualities by means of being almost nothing in independence of them. Thus, God's primordial act is the ultimate reason, hence, not "reasonable" anymore. Yet such ungroundedness is not inconsistent with the system, but the proof of its ultimate consistency, because God's being is the underivable concrete, the ground of all rationality, and therewith the ultimate ir-rationality; i.e., ungroundedness. Ultimately, the Principle of concretion is God's *actus essendi*.

COHERENCE

This final section is an attempt to use these reflections toward a process theological understanding of the Trinity. Based on the concept of coherence and its use, I ask the question whether there can be a way, beside the traditional trinitarian analogies in Whitehead, to establish the Trinity. Similar to the inquiry concerning the Lateran analogy, we seek not the meaning of the "three," or the "functionalization" of the divine persons for any trifold character. On the contrary, our way of proceeding has the freedom to underline elements of structure within Whitehead's categories, and their structural unity with the Lateran analogy, rendering a trinitarian theological interpretation possible and meaningful.

Whitehead employs "coherence" in the following paradigmatic definition:

> "Coherence" . . . means that the fundamental ideas . . . presuppose each other so that in isolation they are meaningless. This requirement does not mean that they are definable in terms of each other; it means that what is indefinable in one such notion cannot be abstracted from its relevance to the other notions (*PR* 3). Incoherence, on the other hand, is the arbitrary disconnection of first principles. (*PR* 6)

Thus, analogy and coherence are structurally similar. Were abstraction not possible, there could be neither derivation nor difference from one another. The intrinsic connection to the other of that which is not derivable from the other without remainder involves a dissimilarity ever-vaster against each possible approximation. This nicely overlaps with Whitehead's understanding of reciprocity in which he states a presupposition of each according to their ever-vaster dissimilarity (*Modes of Thought* 46). In this sense, Whitehead knows that such formulations of ultimate principles are not able to be derived from each other, yet they achieve an internal, incorruptible togetherness. Examples are the polarity of events, subjectivity/superjectivity, givenness, potentiality, and freedom, and, finally, the category of the ultimate, whose three elements (many, one, and creativity) probably afford the final point of reference for a process trinitarian theology.[13] This ultimate togetherness in coherence itself performs a process:

> Thus "becoming" is the transformation of incoherence into coherence . . . (*PR* 25) . . . Creativity achieves its supreme task of transforming disjoined multiplicity . . . into concrescent unity . . . (*PR* 348)

The paradigm of process retains its final say even in the context of the concept of coherence. Process is the becoming of coherence, and this transformation is the supreme task of creativity. Coherence involves reality incarnating as the satisfaction of every process. The sole coherent outcome renders superjectivity possible in which coherent givenness gives itself into new processes of becoming. Coherence is the attainment of superjectivity in which every concreteness gets an element of ongoing creative process. Process, therefore, is systematically anchored in Whitehead's thinking, because of the everlasting rhythmical turn into one another of coherence into incoherence and, conversely, describing the character of the ultimate givenness of the world. And this transition is again indebted to the equally ultimate character of dissimilarity of the elements of process. Dissimilarity stands at the beginning of a creative unification of the dissimilar many, and as an element of ongoing process, the one, in its unique subjectivity, is, again, dissimilar to other processes of unification. The ultimate is not a fact, the ultimate is the process of concrete facts (*PR* 7; *AI* 190).

For Whitehead, the highest expression of dissimilarity pushing the creative process incessantly further is the contrasting opposition of God and the world (*PR* 348). This already coherently results in the ultimate irrationality; i.e., the ungroundedness of God both as primordial actuality and as the ground of this world (*PR* 75), in that God is both the ever-vaster dissimilarity in opposition to the world and, at the same time, its ground. This special dissimilarity expresses itself through the differentiation of the divine process from the world's process.[14]

In every respect God and the World move conversely to each other in respect to their process. God is primordially one, namely, he is the primordial unity of relevance of the many potential forms; in the process he acquires a consequent multiplicity, which the primordial character absorbs into its own unity (*PR* 349).

Significantly this *conversion* of process in God obeys the same principles and categories as any other process and, yet, subsists intrinsically in a completely dissimilar nature in every respect. Not only a so-called "reversal of the poles" is remarkable; i.e., God's primordial origination from the mental pole, but also the entire process progresses in the opposite manner to entities in the world and *intrinsically* conversed to it.[15] Thus, God is not just primordial subjectivity and infinite unconditionedness, but also the primordial superject of creativity; and God is this within the primordial, under-ivable, dissimilar actuality of God's subjectivity that represents perfect unification and validity of the objects in God's equally primordial satisfaction. For finite entities, the superjective self-giving to other processes means the loss of immediacy, but for God, God's essence is to give itself away in its givenness. God's objectivity (similarity) actualizes itself through God's immediacy (dissimilarity). Objectification (assimilation) is not the consequence of God's process, nor its end, but its actuality in the working out of God's subjective process. In the divine process, subjectivity and objectivity, dissimilarity and similarity attain supreme, coherent unity in the fulfillment of an analogous structure.

THE PRIMORDIAL ROLES OF GOD

Whitehead's twenty-second category of explanation now comes into play for developing the trinitarian implications of these features.

> . . . an actual entity by functioning in respect of itself plays diverse roles in self-formation without losing its self-identity. It is self-cre-ative; and in its process of creation transforms its diversity of roles into one coherent role. Thus "becoming" is the transformation of incoherence into coherence, and in each particular instance ceases with this attainment. (*PR* 25)

Every process is self-functional. In performance of such self-functionality, actuality combines self-identity and self-diversity. In such performance, actuality constitutes itself as immediate subject (*PR* 25). God's self-functionality is of such a structure as to project itself into a consequent multiplicity out of its primordial oneness. Thus, if the "conversion of the processes" really occurs, then God's process must begin as primordial coherence and proceed into a diversity that may not be shaped out of an incoherence of different roles, but construes itself into these roles as a sign of the dissimilar plenitude of God's oneness. To put it differently, the realization of God's subjective self-identity subsists in its continuous movement into self-diversity. This process is not the expression of an imperfection, of missing oneness, or underlying incoherence, but the expression of supreme wealth: in God, the inconsistent roles do not perish in finding coherent self-identity. In God, the coherent self-identity gains everlasting roles as an expression of the wealth of God's everlasting, self-diversifying, subjective process.

This is not contradictory to the theory according to which the process results in a coherent "one," which, in reaching coherence, turns again into "one under many," meaning new incoherence. The way of worldly being in process, or the world's processual, everlasting essence, is not cancelled in God through "conversion of the processes," although it is realized in a totally different manner. Incoherence is an expression of the ultimacy of dissimilarity. In God, contrary to the process of the world, the final, coherent role of the divine process is not shaping the *end*, but the *beginning* of the divine process. The everlasting unfolding of this ultimate being of God into many roles, embodying the expression of the process as incoherence, consequently is the *expression* of coherence without losing the *meaning* of incoherent dissimilarity. To put it differently, God's many roles are the expression of primordial coherence in the meaning of incoherence.[16] But this is not, as one might think, a contradiction within Whitehead's categories; on the contrary. Whitehead's concept of coherence, as explained above, does not demand that the terms that are conceived as coherent to one another are to be inferred from one another. In this case, God's Being is to be understood as an everlasting, coherent process within God's roles, which are undeducible from one another, having *ultimate character* in God.

The origination of such roles in God's process provides a structure that allows us to ground theologically a trinitarian interpretation within the following supporting features.

(1)   The process of an actual entity constitutes itself out of those elements it objectifies through prehension from its preceding actual world, and it proceeds to integrate these elements as a requirement of coherence. Each concrescent process passes through a functionalization of all prehensions in which all reach a defined, unmistakable self-consistent function, reaching a coherent state in satisfaction. In the "conversion of processes," God's becoming will articulate itself in such complex, self-consistent functions. With that corresponds the intrinsically divine process of the realization of trinitarian structures in which each divine person stands in an appointed, unmistakable relation with the other persons, defining them to some extent.

(2)   The origin and meaning of the word and concept "prehension" is explained by Whitehead with reference to the ancient word "appropriation":

> In a genetic theory the cell is exhibited as appropriating for the foundation of its own existence, the various elements of the universe out of which it arises. Each process of appropriation of a particular element is termed a prehension. The ultimate elements of the universe, thus appropriated, are the already constituted actual entities, and the eternal objects. (*PR* 219)

"Appropriation" means to make of something private property.[17] This is an ancient trinitarian theological term expressing the sense in which it is possible to assign the divine actions corresponding to the world's creation, redemption, and justification to the different divine persons, because these actions have a certain kinship to the "properties" of the persons that differentiate them from one another.[18] Theologically, in "conversion of the processes," the appropriation happens not for gaining coherence, but as the unfolding of divine plenitude within God's self-giving to the world. Appropriation is the development of primordial, coherent, multiple divine roles that represent everlasting, personal properties in God.

(3)   Each process runs through different phases of unification, of gaining coherence (*PR* 215). Each phase then is a part-process with its own task, its own depth, and its own importance:

> [An event] . . . suffers simplification in the successive phases of the concrescence. It starts with conditioned alternatives, and by successive decisions is reduced to coherence. The many feelings, in any incomplete phase are necessarily comparable with each other by

reason of their individual conformity to the subjective end for that phase. (*PR* 224) . . . The subject . . . passes from a subjective aim in concrescence into a superject with objective immortality. At any stage it is subject–superject. (*PR* 245)

It is remarkable that each process has to reach in each of its phases an unmistakable "subjective end," a point of coherence, even if it is imperfect, which at the same time means a certain self-reliance and completeness: each phase is peculiar in its own superjectivity. For God's becoming, in "conversion of processes," this has the consequence of a defined superjectivity for each phase of its process. Each of these phases, then, has its own "subjective end," and its own superjectivity, which establishes it as an unmistakable, coherent role in God's process. The everlasting roles of God form God's own superjectivity, and each role has its own unmistakable subjective end that characterizes it as permanently dissimilar to all others in the same process. If we further take into account all of this as a process of coherence, that means a reciprocal presupposition of nondeducible ultimacy, in which self-identity is realized *as* self-diversity. Then the way is paved for an understanding, not only of God's identity, but also of God's coherent, everlasting diversity as due to original and irreducible dissimilarity, such as would be demanded for a trinitarian theology.[19]

(4) For the divine "conversion of processes," God's "phases" and roles develop neither the seriality of temporal moments, following one another, nor are they ordered successively. If all processes of becoming are forms of nontemporal, nonserial concrescence, this holds, in a very real sense, for God's becoming, which is to be as a nontemporal actuality and, at the same time, as a nonderivative actuality (*PR* 32). This nonseriality of God also is a certain form of nonsuccessivity, insofar as it is based on God's unfolding into phases and roles as signs of God's infinite superflow of novelty, God's superplenitude. There is no reason why this could not have also the appearance of *multiple, simultaneous communication* of the roles. God's simultaneous roles, representing God's properties within God's process, become with one another in simultaneity, although they exhibit irreversible relations of origin, and with that equal succession.

Thus, a certain kind of "becoming within phases" can remain meaningful for the roles, considering the multiple unfolding of the process of the divine subjectivity. Entirely in the sense of the ancient trinitarian theology, it is the "one essence" that "subsists" in each divine person that permits at the same time "relations of origin" within God that are irreversible. This was formulated at the Fourth Lateran Council in context of the problem of analogy as follows: *Pater in Filium transtulerit suam substantiam.* (DH 805)

A text of Latin tradition, thus, reflects a Greek conception of the Trinity that lets the godhead find its supreme, intrinsic unity within the Father, because the Father gives his essence away to the Son who receives it as given. The Father is "Father" by reason of *diversity* of the persons, and at the same time, is the reason for *identity* of the godhead. In the Father, the one godhead gets the "head of God." This irreversible, logical "pre" of the Father in God, this form of "successivity" that expresses at the same time also a permanent, eternal simultaneity of the persons, can be process theologically interpreted through an everlasting communication of God's roles that proceeds within irreversible phases of everlasting origination.

(5)   In the diversity of the roles in God's process, there is an interesting terminological and material congeniality with the ancient term *person*. The Greek–Latin original meaning of *persona/prosopon* goes back to the Persian conception of a mask carried by an actor in the tragedy, embodying a role. Throughout the drama, the role "sounds" the identity of the character it embodies (*"per-sona"* etymologically means "sound-through"). Even Whitehead was guided by this original connection between role and character in his specific concept of person, because he defines a social nexus with serial order:

> It might have been termed a "person," in the legal sense of that term. But unfortunately "person" suggests a notion of consciousness, so that its use would lead to misunderstanding. The nexus "sustains a character" and this is one of the meanings of the Latin word "persona." (*PR* 35)

Based on the "conversion of processes," there is then a new meaning of role with respect to God; namely, the expression of an everlasting self-diversity, which in its own subjectivity develops its own character, and entertains it. This does not mean the emerging of subjects in the sense of different self-consciousnesses; this is excluded from Whitehead's use of "person." Nor was self-consciousness meant in the classical development of "person" in the context of trinitarian theological statements. For *"persona"* means *per definitionem* solely the uncomparable, the dissimilar within God, that which is not common, and consciousness belongs to all persons commonly. Similarly, in a trinitarian interpretation, Whitehead's understanding of the Latin original meaning of *persona* becomes the meaning of the roles in God. The roles in God's process are God's *personae* performing God's *primordial and everlasting self-diversity*.

(6) The question concerning seriality, which was explicitly excluded from the structure of processes by Whitehead, leads us to a last aspect illumining the roles in God's process. If, as discussed, God's process proceeds conversely to that of the world, then we are explicitly to pay attention to the new relationship between subjectivity and objectivity, or differently: to the meaning of primordial superjectivity. Since God is everlastingly "given away" in the wealth of self-identity *as* self-diversity, we must redefine the difference between seriality and successivity, or between actuality and nexus. For the objective efficiency of worldly actualities it means:

> Thus "perishing" is the assumption of a rôle in a transcendent future. The not-being of occasions is their objective immortality. (*AI* 237)

For God that means the contrary: The roles that God entertains in everlasting concrescence are already God's superjective roles through which God transitionally determines the world. In this manner, the transitional character of seriality turns into an intrinsically divine realization of concrescent successivity within the simultaneity of God's everlasting self-diversity of roles, allowing us to speak of persons in God.

CONCLUSION

I have attempted to show the meaningful possibility of fruitfully connecting different traditions of different ages and distinct origins. There are elements in the classical tradition of the doctrine of Trinity, and within recent trinitarian theology, that we can interpret in reference to an internal relation between God and the world. Therefore, a modified theory of analogy has been shown as a veritable, process-theologically founded structure. In its mediative role, it translates both trinitarian theology and process theology into one another with consistency. Thus, I have shown in what sense a process-theological understanding of Trinity is feasible and attainable in the context of Whitehead's categories.

By being the superject of creativity out of independent dissimilarity, God's innermost being can give itself into everlastingly coherent roles within an eternally ongoing movement toward novelty, and within the overflowing of God's existence. Therefore, God can stand in real relation with the world. The divine "persons" can express this real relation without forcing God to such roles as an outcome of God's relationship to the world. The everlasting roles of God are not a sign of imperfection, but God's primordial character of plenitude.

Within a process-theological perspective, it must metaphysically remain open in which kind of roles God would become concrete, and how such roles would appear. Not every individual prehension must develop a role; on the contrary, a complex of appropriations can also represent a complex structure that can unfold itself as a single role. And not every role is per se a primordial role of God's unfathomable, ultimate plenitude, in the emphatic sense elaborated above. Here, the principles and categories allow a huge flexibility. And it is also just this flexibility that allows us to draw a plain line between philosophical and theological speech of God in the context of the process paradigm. If to elaborate a doctrine of the trinity, one wants to appeal to the roles in the process of concretization, then, philosophically, there is an explanation coherent with the process of origination of the world as it realizes itself in the *res verae*, and primordially in God. But on the other side, of course, it is only a possible explanation. Therefore, from the perspective of process theology, it is not required to understand the structures of the world in a trinitarian way. Finally, this is a question of concreteness and, therefore, of the Principle of Concretion that is embodied by God. It is a question of history and experience, or theologically speaking, of God's self-revelation in history with the world.

NOTES

1. J. Moltmann, *Trinität und Reich Gottes*. (München: Christian Kaiser, 1980): 31–32: "Seit *Tertullian* wurde die christliche Trinität immer in dem allgemeinen Begriff der *göttlichen Substanz* abgebildet: *Una*

substantia—tres personae . . . Es ist verständlich, daß für *Augustin* und *Thomas von Aquin* diese eine, gemeinsame, göttliche Substanz als das den trinitarischen Personen Zugrundeliegende und ihnen gegenüber darum logisch Primäre galt."

2. Cf. the profound investigation in A. Grillmeier, "Jesus von Nazareth—im Schatten des Gottessohnes?," in *Diskussion über Hans Küngs "Christ Sein"* ed. H. U. von Balthasar (Mainz: 1976) 68: "Es ist das Bild einer hierarchisch gestuften Welt, deren oberste Spitze das "Eine," das "Hen" bildete, jenes absolut "Eine," das schließlich als Prinzip, als arché, über allem Sein schwebte. Darunter kam der schon depotenzierte, die Vielheit in sich enthaltende Logos oder Nous . . . Zwischen diesem Nous und der Hyle, dem Inbegriff der ungeformten Vielheit, stand an dritter Stelle die Psyche, die Weltseele. Wenn die griechische Philosophie der damaligen Zeit gegen etwas empfindlich war, dann gegen dies: als oberstes Prinzip, als arché etwas anderes zu setzen als das exklusiv-absolute "Hen" . . . Nous und Psyche sollten im Grunde gar nicht sein.—Eine göttliche Einheit in Dreifaltigkeit an die oberste Stelle als absolute arché zu setzen, war also für die Mittelplatoniker und die Neuplatoniker reine Torheit. Dies aber bedeutete die Annahme eines im Vater präexistenten Logos und Sohnes und des Pneumas."

3. *Cf. DH 803–808.* DH = citation of the corresponding digits in: H. Denzinger, *Kompendium der Glaubensbekenntnisse und kirchlichen Lehrentscheidungen.* ed. P. Hünermann (Freiburg 1991).

4. ". . . das Wort von "drei Personen" [bringt] dasjenige noch einmal unter einen quasi-allgemeinen Begriff . . . , worin Vater, Sohn u[nd] Geist sich *nur unterscheiden*, nicht aber übereinkommen, denn in allem, in dem sie übereinkommen, sind sie auch schlechthin eins in der einen u[nd] absolut selbigen Wesenheit," K. Rahner, "Trinitätstheologie," *Herder Theologisches Taschenlexikon* VII (1972): 359 (= HerBü 457). In God, then, the concept of person is not univocal, but analogous.

5. The essential nature of events to be dissimilar is due to their unrepeatability, not to their quality of being different from other events. Therefore, in repetition, the similarity of events could be perfect without losing the fundamental uniqueness.

6. A. N. Whitehead, *Process and Reality: An Essay on Cosmology*, ed. D. Griffen and D. Sherman (New York Free Press, cor. ed. 1978). (*PR*) In *PR* 164–166, Whitehead named the essence of the higher phases, treating physical feelings, "comparing" (*conceptual feeling*) and "comparing of comparing" (*propositional feeling*). That can be understood as development of analogous similarity.

7. Cf. Th. Beelitz, *Die dynamische Beziehung zwischen Erfahrung und Metaphysik. Eine Untersuchung der Spekulativen Philosophie von Alfred North Whitehead im Interesse der Theologie* (Frankfurt a.M. 1991) 163–170. He follows explicitly the question whether the Aristotelian–Platonic origin of the concept of analogy binds its contents in a way that Whitehead with his relativistic, nonsubstantial conception would be necessarily, and, in principle, beyond it. D. Emmet, *The Nature of Metaphysical Thinking* (New York: St. Martin's Press, 1966) 8–14 on the other hand, puts together five different kinds of analogy and investigates their connection with Whitehead's thought. Nevertheless, all these forms of analogy are actually overtaken by the Lateran kind of analogy.

8. A. N. Whitehead, *The Function of Reason* (*FR*), (Boston: Beacon, 1958) 15.

9. A. N. Whitehead, *Adventures of Ideas* (*AI*), (New York: Free Press, 1967) 242. Whitehead named this procedure of particular defined patterns "mutual interpretation"; cf. *AI* 250.

10. Cf. *PR* 26: *Contrasts* consequently produces in origination of dissimilarity an *indefinite progression* of categories.

11. Cf. R. Faber, *Freiheit, Theologie und Lehramt. Trinitätstheologische Grundlegung und wissenschaftstheoretischer Ausblick* (Innsbruck 1992).

12. Cf. M. Welkers idea to understand Whitehead's theory of subjectivity as the acting of "not-yet-beings" and in their becoming again "standing-out-beings:" "Whitehead's Vergottung der Welt," in *Whitehead and the Idea of Process. Proceedings of The First International Whitehead-Symposium*, ed. H. Holz and E. Wolf-Gazo (Freiburg 1984) 267f.

13. Cf. Hans Günter Holl, who has indicated this connection in a hint to his German translation of *PR* (Frankfurt a.M. 1987) (= stw 690); cf. *PR* 644: " 'Elementar' ist hier also logisch wie ontologisch gemeint und setzt in beiden Bedeutungen eine Grenze, die nicht überschritten werden kann. Wenn man so will, könnte man vielleicht sagen, daß sich hier die christliche Trinitätslehre in säkularisierter Form niederschlägt . . ." From this point, one is justly referred to the connection with this other "Trinity," God, world, and creativity (*PR* 348f), to see the relevance of this category. This connection is expressed in J. A. Bracken, "Process Philosophy and Trinitarian Theology—II," *Process Studies* 11 (1981): 85f.

14. I explicitly agree with the idea of "*reversal* of the poles" as developed by M. Suchocki for a reinterpretation of Whitehead's concept

of God. And, further, I do not agree with the idea of God as "society," because to think of God as one actuality seems to be more consistent *if* we are able to see the process of God as a very different process from that of other entities, without hurting the common categories through which we understand actualities. Cf. M. Suchocki, "The Metaphysical Ground of the Whiteheadian God," *Process Studies* 5 (1975): 237–246. Note, however, that Whitehead himself speaks of the "*conversion* of the processes." This mean more than a reversal of poles; namely, an intrinsic conversion of each aspect of the process of God in comparison with that of the world. Therfore, I prefer the concept of "conversion" to "reversal."

15. That means even for an interpretation of God as society, that because of the "conversion of processes" even a divine society will have a conversive meaning in reference to God.

16. This is the remaining Heraclitian side of Whitehead's thinking. Heraclitus' famous statement says that "*struggle* is the origin of the universe," insofar it makes the process ongoing and grounds the world as process: "*Polemos panton men pater esti* . . . ," *Fragment 53.*

17. Cf. M. Hampe, *Die Wahrnehmungen der Organismen. Über die Voraussetzungen einer naturalistischen Metaphysik Whiteheads* (Göttingen 1990) 113; 131 (= Neue Studien zur Philosophie 1)

18. Cf. M. Schmaus, "Appropriationen," *Lexikon für Theologie und Kirche* I (1957): 774.

19. Cf., for instance, the statement of H.U. von Balthasar in *Theodramatik. IV* (Einsiedeln 1983) 67f.: God is intrinsically " '*ewige Bewegtheit', da die göttlichen Hervorgänge und der darauf gründende Austausch der Personen nicht zeitlich begrenzt, sondern ewig aktuell sind. Ewig heißt hier zugleich unendlich, was . . . nur durch einen ins Je-Größere offenen Komperativ ausdrückbar ist.*"

Marjorie Hewitt Suchocki
Spirit in and through the World*

John B. Cobb, Jr., has made plain both in this volume and elsewhere that the ancient doctrine of the trinity is not a high priority on his agenda. He has a preference for a "binity" that focuses on the relation between God and the world: God transcends the world through the Primordial Nature, and is also immanent within the world insofar as the world prehends the Primordial and Consequent Natures of God. However, an overview of Cobb's works suggests an alternative development if combined with a Whiteheadian rather than Hartshornean understanding of God.

Cobb developed a doctrine of God in *A Christian Natural Theology (CNT)*, an anthropology in *The Structure of Christian Existence (SCE)*, and then, drawing on both, an innovative christology in *Christ in a Pluralistic Age.* (CPA)[1] Toward the end of that volume, he gave some attention to a constructive understanding of the trinity and a doctrine of the Spirit. On the whole, however, he gives no sustained attention to these topics that would bring the discussions of God and Christ into a full process interpretation of the trinity. Rather, the works since the christology have been devoted primarily to interreligious dialogue, ecology, political theology, economics, and education. But Cobb has often stated that the task of the Christian theologian is to give critical reflection on Christian faith, suggesting that creative transformation is particularly necessary for images that deeply form the Christian

---

*This article is an adaptation and expansion of an essay originally appearing in *Theology and the University*, edited by David R. Griffin and Joseph C. Hough, Jr., and published by the State University of New York Press (1990). Used by permission.

consciousness. "Trinity" and "Holy Spirit" well qualify as formative Christian images, and Cobb's theology offers fruitful possibilities for further development of both doctrines.

I argue that Cobb's works on the diverse topics mentioned above *are* his doctrine of the Spirit, with certain implications for a process interpretation of the trinity. The development proceeds first with a summation of Cobb's doctrines of God and Christ, and the implications for trinitarian thought. Questions are raised relative to the latter that push toward an alternative formulation of the Spirit. This, in turn, refines the position on the trinity.

GOD AND CHRIST

The major task of *A Christian Natural Theology* is to reestablish the viability of developing Christian theology in conversation with philosophy and the sciences, as well as with the religious data of the Christian community. The test case comes in the doctrine of God, for here, almost more than in any other area, Christianity faces the problem of establishing that there is indeed a referent for the word "God" beyond linguistic or psychological reductionism. Accordingly, and drawing heavily upon the conceptuality of Alfred North Whitehead, Cobb builds the analysis of experience that leads from existence as actual occasions to a conception of the human person as a responsible being in society. He focuses particularly upon the ground of novelty, especially as novelty takes us beyond the past in the direction of beauty and peace. Following Whitehead, Cobb suggests that peace includes but transcends beauty, with an ultimate breadth and depth that includes all values, becoming a "harmony of harmonies." Such peace is not achieved nor has it been achieved—it rests in no ideal past, and it eludes any immediate attainment. Yet, it functions as a lure within the soul toward civilization, toward some ultimacy of community that includes yet transcends all that we have experienced. It defies its own contradiction in our histories, functioning as something within the depth of things that continuously renews hope and energy toward some more pervasively satisfying mode of community. And with this allusive discussion of peace as the ultimate lure toward novelty, Cobb begins his discussion first of Whitehead's, and then of his own doctrine of God as the source of novelty.

The actual development of the doctrine explores the technical aspects of Whitehead's thought relative to God as the principle of concretion, of limitation, and of order. The arguments are by now familiar to persons acquainted with process philosophy and theology: God's primordial nature is the locus of all possibility, and source of the initial aim whereby the possibilities are adapted to the good of the world, providing at once a principle of limitation and a novel lure toward transcendence of the world's past. Cobb's revision of this doctrine is likewise technical, exploring the insufficiently developed unity of the primordial and consequent natures that comprise the Whiteheadian God, and arguing that God's own feelings of the world through the consequent nature are essential to the relevance of the aim of God for the developing world. This aim is then formulated within God as a propositional feeling, with appetition that it be realized in the becoming world.

Through the initial aim, God is creator *with* the world. The "withness" is taken in two senses: First, each entity in the becoming world prehends not only God, but also its entire past. Insofar as the past had intentions toward the future, these intentions can also be propositions for the new occasion, functioning analogously to the initial aim of God. God's aim is one among many, but its distinctive property is that it and it alone is the source whereby the present might transcend the past toward novelty rather than fall captive to the past in terms of sheer repetition. Thus, God as creator is associated particularly with the newness of things, and with the creative advance of the world toward more complex forms of order, whether in nature or the human community.

While God's creativity is exercised in conjunction with the world, and while God is prehended as past by the becoming world, God is nonetheless more appropriately associated with the future. If prehension of God is the route toward transcendence of the past, then God is the source of the world's future. The paradox obtains that while God is prehended because God is in the past of the becoming entity, God is prehended as that which is future relative to the entity. The doctrine of God, thus, focuses creativity in God through God as the source of the future of the world. Insofar as a becoming occasion's historic past also contains a propulsion toward the new, this was in its own time also derived from God— all novelty is associated with the primordial nature of God.

The understanding of God as the creative power of the future also entails important considerations concerning the nature of God's power. This power is fundamentally persuasive rather than coercive. Cobb develops this Whiteheadian thesis not only in *A Christian Natural Theology*, but also in *God AND the World*.[2] This development ensures not only the freedom of the world, but the freedom of God. If the nature of existence is to receive the influences of past and future, and creatively to integrate these as one's own novel becoming, then no occasion has the power totally to determine the being of another; freedom is within the essence of that which exists. One is influenced but not determined by that which is prehended. This applies even in the case of coercive force. How the force is received is in some respects—no matter how minute—variable within the affected organism. Relative to God, God is affected by the world through the consequent nature, but this effect is influential rather than determinative. God is free, exercising and experiencing power with others.

What, then, is the character of God for Cobb? Here the fact that Cobb introduced his discussion of God through the notion of peace is fundamental. God—as Creator, as Future, as Free—is the ultimate locus of that peace that is felt as the lure of the world. God IS peace, an ultimate inclusiveness of all values in a transcending, transforming, and everlasting beauty. Precisely this notion of the character of God lies behind the notion of God as future, for it is a future whose content is reflective of this peace that inheres in every initial aim toward novelty. God as peace is also God as creator, for it is the peace of inclusive complexity that functions to draw the world toward more complex forms of order. God as peace is the ultimate form of God as free, for it is the power of God's internal creativity, whereby God is able to receive the whole world through the consequent nature and to incorporate that world transformatively into God's own actualization, which is to say, peace. The notion of peace is, thus, central to Cobb's understanding of God.

And what of Christ? Ten years intervene between publication of *A Christian Natural Theology* and *Christ in a Pluralistic Age*; within that period, two other books were published that are critical to the christology. The first of these is *The Structure of Christian Existence*, where Cobb carefully builds on his earlier work in anthropology. The Whiteheadian conceptuality has already provided him with the dynamics of human existence; this is developed in the second and third chapters of *CNT*. What is needed is to integrate historicity into the anthropology, and this Cobb does in *SCE*. By analyzing the different structures of consciousness exhibited in the various religious communities of the world, he demonstrates the uniqueness of the Christian structure of consciousness and, thus, prepares for the fully developed christology that is to come. In fact, since christology presupposes clear doctrines of God and humanity, in one sense *CNT* and *SCE* can both be considered prolegomena to the christology of *CPA*.

However, the second book referred to interrupts the projected agenda, radically affecting the form of the christology to come. This book is the little study pamphlet prepared for the "Faith and Life" series of adult religious education, entitled *Is It Too Late? A Theology of Ecology (IITL)*.[3] This book, published in 1972 but written in 1969, merits for Cobb the Kantian phrase of being "shocked from dogmatic slumbers," for in it theology takes on a new urgency. Theology is no longer simply critical reflection upon one's faith for the sake of finding contemporary forms of faith; theology takes on an imperatively prophetic dimension in a milieu in which "the survival of life itself may be at stake" (*IITL*, 11). In previous books, there is a deep awareness of the interrelatedness of all life, but in this book that awareness takes on the existential knowledge that the vulnerability of interdependence can lead to planetary death as well as to richer forms of complexity. Process is not necessarily progress, and freedom allows the creative lure toward novelty to be perverted toward destructive ends. The human program, especially as developed by those whose structure of consciousness is formed around the paradoxical individualism of Christianity, is rapidly leading us toward ecological disaster. A radical ethical dimension is introduced into theology— it is no longer simply sufficient to reinterpret faith, one must transform it for the sake of the transformation of the world.

Cobb's consciousness of ethical responsibility conjoined with theology is not in itself new—consider, for example, the chapter, "Man as a Responsible Being" in *CNT*—but the urgency of this conjoining is new. Henceforth, theology must underscore one's radical responsibility for the well-being of the world. It is this sensitivity, as much as the careful preparation through *SCE* and *CNT*, that gives *Christ in a Pluralistic Age* its central theme: Christ is an image of creative transformation in the world, with implications for how we build our cities, how we engage in deepening human community through interreligious dialogue, and how we can foster hope within a desperate world.

The christology is deeply continuous with the doctrine of God formulated earlier, particularly in the central notion of peace. God is incarnate in the world through the initial aim, which is itself derived from God's primordial nature—the source of peace—and God's feeling of the world in the consequent nature, which, in integration with the primordial nature, is the actualization of peace. The initial aim draws the world toward relevant forms of peace, which in turn represent a creative transformation of the past toward wider forms of inclusiveness. Jesus of Nazareth becomes the one in history who fully constitutes himself through this initial aim of God, thus becoming the manifestation of God's peace in history. The abstract technical notion of God is clothed with the historical form of love, leading to hope. Jesus is the Christ in history, and Christ is the image of creative transformation.

The effect of Christ is to establish a field of force through which those who identify themselves with Christ become open to the risk of an identity radically informed not only by their own personal and cultural past, but also by the past and the future of others and, hence, toward the creation of more diverse modes of community that include the good of others as well as the self. This open identity is not restricted to the human scene; it includes an empathic association with the well-being of the whole created order. This openness of identity is itself the impulse toward acting for inclusive forms of the good, or peace.

Such an identity is fluid, dynamic, relativized. Its only absolute is that the lure toward creative transformation renders all absolutes radically open to question. While at times this value of creative transformation seems to border on valuation of the new for the sake of the new, this would be a gross distortion of Cobb's position. Peace is the aim of all creative transformation. The particular form of peace is always to be questioned, but its questioning is governed by inclusiveness of well-being—which is to say, by peace itself. The amazing hope that is offered by viewing Christ as the principle of creative transformation is not simply that God is at work in human history, working in us, with us, and through us, for the incarnation of peace, but that the peace that so draws us is not illusory. It is grounded in the very nature of God and is mediated to us in every initial aim.

The ethical force of this christology has many implications, not only for the religious pluralism addressed specifically within the book, but also with regard to cultural pluralism. Consider Cobb's discussion of memory and hope as constitutive of the self. Normally, self-identity is formed through owning a remembered past and through purposes and hopes for the future. Feelings about the self are extended to the various circles of others who share similar memories, and similar hopes—a family, a faith community, a culture. These groups share varying modes of kinship with the self and are accordingly more or less included in our notion of well-being. But what if we became open to memories of a past quite different from those of our kinship groups? Suppose, for example, an American of European ancestry sought to listen to the memories of an American of African ancestry. And suppose that, in turn, the person of African ancestry heard the stories of the Euro-American. A new commonality of shared memory could emerge, and with it, a critical concern for a common future. Community would be enlarged and new modes of peace made possible. The previous identification of our past would be creatively transformed to include a more complex history, creating in the process more complex selves, making possible a wider concern for the future, which would translate into forms of action in society that could make the new vision of the future actual.

It follows that the third portion of *CPA* is entitled, "Christ as Hope," for if there is incarnate in the world a force for peace in the sense described above, then no situation, however dire, dare be deemed final. What is required is that through the power of the Christ, we release the narrow past in openness to the future. This openness allows the possibility for a person—or community—to constitute oneself/itself in conformity to the transforming initial aim/s of God—the Christ—and so become a force for peace in the world. Peace is as possible as the persuasive power of God.

The doctrine of God, then, concerns the transcendent locus and power of peace; the doctrine of Christ is the application of that peace to the world. Where creative transformation exists, there the Christian discerns the Christ—God's initial aim toward peace immanent in the world. The technical aspects of Whitehead used to explicate this understanding are the primordial nature of God (identified extensively by Cobb as the *Logos*) and the initial aims of God for the world.

What, then, of the third aspect of God commonly understood in
the Christian tradition as the Holy Spirit? Unlike the extended treat-
ments of God and Christ, the Spirit receives but little attention.
There is, however, a powerful reference to the Spirit in the closing
pages of *Is It Too Late?*

> It [the power of hope] is not to be found somewhere outside the
> organisms in which it is at work, but it is not to be identified with
> them either. We can conceive it best as Spirit. It is the belief in this
> Spirit, the giver of life and love, that is the basis of hope. In spite of
> all the destructive forces [we] let loose against life on this planet, the
> Spirit of Life is at work in ever new and unforeseeable ways, coun-
> tering and circumventing the obstacles [we] put in its path. In spite
> of my strong tendencies to complacency and despair, I experience
> the Spirit in myself as calling forth the realistic hope apart from
> which there is no hope, and I am confident that what I find in
> myself is occurring in others also. . . . what makes for life and love
> and hope is not simply the decision of one individual or another,
> but a Spirit that moves us all . . ." (*IITL* 143–44)

In this passage, the identification of Spirit is remarkably similar to what will be named Christ in *Christ in a Pluralistic Age*. But
in the conclusion of that work, also, Cobb turns his attention
toward the distinctive doctrine of the Spirit, now associating Spirit
with "Kingdom of God." He has named the second person of the
trinity in a twofold sense: the Logos of God, which is the power of
creative transformation but not yet the incarnation of creative
transformation, and the Christ, who is the initial aim of God
become immanent in the world. Spirit is also named in a twofold
sense as the anticipation in history of God's full and final reign
(the Kingdom of God) and the fullness of that reign in the consequent nature of God. This follows the traditional distinction
between the "economic trinity," or the experience of God in history, and the "immanent trinity," or the inner dynamics of God.
Cobb's delineation of the immanent trinity is that the primordial
nature is the Logos, giving rise to the Christ as the power for creative transformation in the world, and the consequent nature is the
Spirit, or the world as received and creatively transformed within
God. There is no real third term in this formulation, so that the
binitarian view Cobb develops in this volume is consistent with
the earlier work.

A difficulty with the formulation thus far given is that there is no functional distinction between the notion of Christ and Spirit in history. The terms could be interchangeable, as in fact, they are in the extended passage quoted from *Is it too Late*. There is, of course, a distinction vis-à-vis God if they are identified with the primordial and consequent natures, respectively, but this leaves us with a binitarian view of the immanent God and a unitarian view of the economic God.

I suggest another way to view the Spirit (and, consequently, trinity) by utilizing John Cobb's system, one that is somewhat parallel with his christology. Cobb began the christology by recounting Andre Malraux's history of Western art in its movement from portraying Christ as the transcendent, remote deity, to a more humanized Christ as benevolent king, to a suffering and dying Christ on the cross. The movement continues with the introduction of human scenes into the background of the holy figure and the gradual movement into the foreground of human activity. There is an increasing personalization and individualization of the human figures and eventually the disappearance of the Christ figure altogether. The simply human has come to dominate, but with personal, emotional history now given witness. Cobb argues that the disappearance of the Christ is, in fact, the progressive work of the Christ, the incarnation of Christ into a principle of creative transformation that works through an interiorized pluralism. The principle calls for the relativization of all its forms in a restless movement ever beyond itself, expressed in our contemporary age in abstract art. The disappearance of "Christ" is the effective work of Christ.

There is a very brief parallel to this story in a fourteenth-century painting not of Jesus, but of the Spirit, in the angelic annunciation to Mary. Indeed, annunciation paintings may well have surpassed paintings of the crucifixion as a favored theme. In nearly all of the paintings, the Holy Spirit is represented as light or in the form of a dove, often hovering between Mary and the angel. But there is a significant exception. Giotto has painted typical annunciations, with the Spirit in the form of the dove. However, in one painting, the angel bows before the young woman, and where the dove was usually portrayed, there is a window looking out onto fourteenth-century Florence. Central in the bordered cityscape is a hospital—in fact, the Hospital of the Holy Spirit. The intriguing aspect about the painting is that in extant plans of the

Florence of that time, there was, indeed, a Hospital of the Holy Spirit, but not in the location portrayed by the artist. Giotto intentionally moved the hospital in his painting so that it would be midway between Mary and the angel, in the place commonly assigned iconographically to the Spirit. The Spirit had become incarnate in a work of mercy.

Cobb never followed his books on God and Christ with a parallel book on the Spirit. Rather, his publications since 1975 have taken on an ethical urgency relative to religious pluralism, ecology, economics, politics, and education. I suggest that these works, in fact, present Cobb's doctrine of the Spirit, given not in direct theological discussion, but in "works of mercy," or creative transformation. Like the dove replaced by the hospital, the theology of the Spirit requires implicit portrayal through works directed toward the good—the peace—of the world.

The Spirit facilitates the Christian community's openness to its own transformation. In our day, this can well be portrayed through interaction with other religions, through a new shaping of consciousness toward care for and with the earth, through political responsibility in a crisis-ridden international situation, through redevelopment of our economic life, and through education of leaders for the church who can facilitate the Christian community's own openness to God's call for creative transformation. This, of course, is the role of Christ in Cobb's christology, while the Spirit is the anticipation in time of the Kingdom of God. But what is such an anticipation, if not creative transformation? The two symbols are conflated.

If there is a desire to transform Christian symbols, giving them new meaning and power, would it not be better to give content to "Spirit" that is distinctive while yet consistent with the content of Christ? The unique content traditionally ascribed to the Spirit in Christian history has been that of a unitive, purifying force: The Spirit unites us with Christ and with one another in the formation of a community called "body of Christ." Hence, the Spirit is an indwelling presence, witnessing to God through works of love. Cobb's christology suggests a new dynamism that might be infused into the doctrine of the Spirit, with interesting consequences for the notion of the trinity.

Cobb associates the Christ with the initial aim, or the Logos of God become incarnate. We are called, like Jesus, to constitute ourselves according to this aim; that is, to integrate the aim into our own becoming, so that the initial aim becomes our subjective aim. We would then be coconstituted by God's aim for us and our own free response. The means whereby we appropriate the aim is prehension: God feels the aim for us, clothed in an appetition that this aim be realized. When this aim is toward more complex forms of novelty that allow richer modes of community in the world, then the aim is the principle of creative transformation, or the Christ. When we adapt that aim, we are coconstituted by the Christ, and creative transformation is incarnate once again in the world. Thus, Cobb names the aim *and* its incarnation the Christ.

In adapting this to a new formulation of Spirit, let us assume that God's appetition is itself creative, so that God does not passively await the nascent entity's prehension, but in fact, along with the world, evokes the new occasion, creating it through launching it on its brief but all-important journey. This is God as transcendent, persuasive creator, creating the world through a word for its good and inviting the world's own creative response. The fullness of God generates this word in recognition of the world's need; it is a particular word, fitted to the world. Thus far, this formulation is nearly a reformulation of Cobb's christology—it needs only the stipulation that those aims that result in the world's creative transformation are those that are particularly named Christ. However, it stops short of Cobb's christology by saying that aims toward creative transformation in themselves constitute that generative word from God that Christians can name as continuous with that which is seen in the one named Christ in history.

I propose that to speak of God's creatively transforming word is sufficient to name what Cobb terms "Christ," or principle of creative transformation. This Christ is the word that waits our response, and not yet the word integrated with that response. But it is a word combining God and world, since it expresses God's aim for us in light of our condition. Cobb calls it a "propositional feeling" in God, or an "eternal object" from God's primordial envisagement related to the particularities of our circumstances as felt by the consequent nature. God meets our condition, and in this sense, the aim has the twofold nature of God primordial and consequent, reflecting God and the world, divinity and humanity.

However, if the Spirit is traditionally understood to be "Christ in us," an indwelling force uniting us with God and one another, whose fruits are those things that build up the community, then the Spirit might well be that element of the aim that we allow into our becoming, or the subjective aim insofar as it conforms to the Christly aim from God. In traditional Eastern rather than Western language, the Spirit proceeds "from the Father through the Son." This would be the case in this process formulation, since the Spirit derives from the aim from God's own nature mediated to us through the Christ. Insofar as we instantiate that aim, the Spirit is born in us, becoming one with us in the creation of community. In other words, Christ *offers* creative transformation; the Spirit *is* creative transformation realized in the world.

In this case, of course, the Spirit is not manifest as Spirit per se, but only in "works of mercy," or the unitive work of God with us in history. There is no direct identification of the Spirit, only the indirect witness to the Spirit's presence through acts of creative transformation: openness toward one another involving our deepest identity in interfaith or ecumenical dialogue; open and concerned action for the well-being of the whole of this earth; empathic identification with others, so that their future good is as important as our own; and a will to move toward ever yet more complex modes of community. Under this reading, Cobb's works in these areas *are* his doctrine of the Spirit. But this has radical implications for a doctrine of the trinity.

TRINITY

There are interesting analogies between a process formulation of the nature of God and the more traditional formulation of the trinity. Traditionally in the West, the immanent trinity consists of the "Father" who eternally generates the "Son"; from the two proceeds the "Spirit." The "Son" is the logos of God, or God's own self-knowledge, and the "Spirit" is the will or love of God, whereby there is infinite union between "Father" and "Son." The works of God flow from this immanent trinity—or, the immanent trinity is the ground of God made manifest as the economic trinity. Creation is analogous to generation, incarnation is analogous to being generated, and redemption is analogous to divine union, being the community-building work within the world. While each work is chiefly associated with but one member of the trinity, the fullness of God is involved in each of the works. In every act of God, we have to do not with a "part" of God, but with the fullness of the triune God.

An analogous Whiteheadian formulation would call for the amorphous realm of possibilities called the primordial nature (or mental pole) of God to be likened to the traditional "Father," eternally generating from these possibilities the divine character in the primordial vision (or dynamically everlasting satisfaction of God). This vision is analogous to the divine self-knowledge traditionally attributed to the immanent "Son." In the process paradigm for God, God is *always* generating the primordial vision, or the divine character, and apart from such generation, there is no God. But while we might make this analogy regarding "Father" and "Son," it is not possible to extend the trinitarian formula so neatly to "Spirit."

Traditionally, the immanent work of the Spirit spoke only to the unity between the generative and generated aspects of God; the designation was entirely intratrinitarian. Thus, while we might be tempted to make a correlation between Spirit and consequent nature, inasmuch as the consequent nature does, in fact, proceed from the primordial in Whitehead's model, this does not take the full origin of the consequent nature into account. In the process model, the consequent nature derives both from the primordial nature of God *and* the world. The consequent nature is the "physical pole" of God, through which God receives the world and integrates that world into the primordial vision; the consequent nature is the initial locus of the prehended world in God. Thus, if the consequent nature be named as analogous to the Christian naming of Spirit, then the Spirit can no longer be understood to proceed from within God alone. Rather, Spirit everlastingly proceeds from God and the world. Through the Spirit and in the Spirit, the world is introduced into God.

A return to Cobb's works as interpreted above might clarify the force of this suggestion. The "economic" work of God is everlastingly to offer creative "words" to the world as "initial aims." These aims are the means of God's immanence within the world, and to the degree that the aims are adopted by the world, God becomes incarnate in the world. When such adopted aims deeply reflect the divine character, then God's own self is revealed within the world, and we can rightly say that the Spirit of God is manifest.

But this manifestation of the Spirit is the work of the world as well as of God: "God proposes, the world disposes." God offers the aim; the occasion in the world actualizes the aim. The resultant

Spirit combines God and the world, even in human history. Taking the event of Jesus to be the paradigm instance of such a revelation, those of us in the Christian tradition recognize God's incarnate Spirit wherever the Spirit may emerge. In the course of God's efficacious work, the Spirit is born again and again in the many forms of daily life.

But the work of God is not exhausted in birthing the Spirit in the world; the work of God includes as well God's prehension of the world in every moment of its completion into the divine life through God's physical pole, or consequent nature. Insofar as the actualized world, participating with God, brings Spirit into birth in the world, God's prehension of that world is at the same time the prehension of the birthed Spirit. Hence, the Spirit is thrice born: from God, in the world, and in God. To use more trinitarian language in however unorthodox a fashion, the economic work of God becomes the immanent work of God. The prehended Spirit is integrated into God's everlastingly dynamic primordial satisfaction, which in its own turn suggests yet new possibilities for the actualization of Spirit in the world. The consequent nature concresces into the primordial nature, bringing the primordial vision into continuous, everlasting, dynamic expression. This, in turn, continuously yields new aims for the world, and the cycle continues.

Thus, a process interpretation of the trinity that builds upon Cobb's implications for Spirit in the world forces the trinitarian distinctions of "immanent" and "economic" to fold into each other. Traditionally, the immanent trinity is the basis of the economic trinity in a unilateral motion. Many contemporary developments of the trinity focus solely on the economic work, leaving the immanent trinity to mystery.[4] But this process interpretation suggests that the economic work of God both flows from and to the immanent God. Thus, any discussion of the economic work of God requires reference to the immanent God, and discussion of the immanent requires reference to the economic. It plays on the double meaning of "immanent" within the Christian tradition to mean the inner structure of God on the one hand, and the sense in which God is in the world on the other. The "immanent" trinity yields an immanent-in-the-world economic work of God, and this work is taken into the divine life.

This process form of trinity parallels the trinitarian functions of the traditional doctrine in that it depends upon a generative function within God that produces God's own self-knowledge, integrating that dynamic self-knowledge everlastingly within the divine Self. Generation, wisdom, and love are as applicable to this process interpretation as to the traditional. However, the process mode suggests a further refinement, and this has to do with the somewhat problematic notion of person as applied to the distinctions within God.

Traditionally, God was understood to be a single rational nature, with three subsistences within this nature. These subsistences were not self-conscious beings, but three expressions within the single rationality of God. The word "person" was used to designate each of these three modes of the divine being, and for more than a thousand years the word was sufficient. However, as the word "person" began to assume more fully the notion of a singular self-consciousness in the seventeenth century, the trinitarian notion tended toward either unintelligibility or tritheism. This process analogy moves away from the tritheistic tendencies of the current use of "person," in favor of subsistences within the unity of God. There is that within God which everlastingly generates a primordial vision; there is that within God which is this everlastingly dynamic vision; there is that within God which everlastingly integrates the world into this vision. These are each subsistences within the fullness of God's own self—distinctive and irreducible subsistences that constitute the structure of God within this model.

With regard to the self-consciousness of God, the peculiar notion of Spirit as proceeding from God and the world offers an elaboration that goes beyond the traditional understanding. If God incorporates the world into Godself, and the world contains conscious creatures, then God incorporates these conscious creatures into the divine self. But God is one. Through God's own subjective aim, God directs the integration (concrescence) of the world into the primordial vision. The consciousnesses within the world are taken into the consciousness of God—not to their absorption and disappearance, but to their judgment, transformation, and salvation. Each consciousness is conformed to God's own will within the great consciousness of God. But if these implications of the model can be given any credence at all, then it is quickly apparent that our own small consciousness is but a poor model, indeed, for understanding the consciousness of God. God's consciousness would be highly multifaceted even while unified within God's overarching subjective aim.

Whitehead speaks of consciousness as evolving from the intensity of contrasts. If God holds the prehended actualized universe within the consequent nature, and all possibilities within the primordial nature, then the contrasts within God are maximal. There is yet a further contrast between the world as envisioned by God through initial aims, and the world as received by God through prehension. The intensity of these contrasts would everlastingly generate a maximal consciousness within God, but there is yet another complexity. If God prehends the world in its subjectivity, then God prehends every consciousness yielded by the world, and these are also retained within the consciousness of God.[5] Thus, the subjectivity of God would be multiply conscioused.

To speak not only of the world in God, but of the consciousness of the world in God, introduces a complexity into God far greater than mere threeness—for the world is many, and God is one, as Whitehead is wont to tell us. But if the world is immanent in God as Spirit, then is not God many and one at the same time? The fundamentally triadic structure of God (primordial nature, primordial vision, and consequent nature) would be the ground within God of a vast multiplicity barely symbolized by "trinity." The unity of this multiplicity follows from the work of the Spirit, born from God in the world and yet again in God, conforming the world to God. This conforming work is partial in the world, but would be complete in God, governed by God's own free subjective aim.

Earlier in this article, I referred to the importance of John Cobb's notion of "peace" relative to God. Given the above notion of God, the very reality of peace as actualized in God is a deeply communal image, requiring something like a world immanent and transformed within God for its realization. If the world, in fact, is all its teeming, buzzing manyness received into the nature of God, then peace is a transforming work in God, and a reality for which trinity is but a thin word, albeit the best the tradition offers. The very word "trinity" is itself creatively transformed to become a symbol of a vastly inclusive God, who somehow incorporates the received world into the divine being. So transformed, trinity names God not as three, but God as Peace, God as the transcendent/immanent redemption of the world.

The economic trinity is God experienced as gift, call, and responsibility for the future, as indwelling, empowering, community in the present, and as the deeper, pervasive sense of ultimacy and, therefore, ground of trust and hope. There is a trinitarian modalism in our experience—hence, the economic trinity. But when it comes to the immanent trinity, the ascriptions of a specific threeness are too reductionistic for the reality we intend. Trinity is a symbol drawn from time, but surpassed by eternity. God is a deep complexity, source of the world's future both as it comes to us as call, and as we go to it as destiny—for this God receives the world. Thus, we use the name trinity equivocally of God. In time, the economic trinity is experienced in three modes, and these three modes refer to the one complex God who generates these three modes in our histories. But in God's own time, trinity is symbolic of God's own threefold movement into an everlastingly deeper complexity that surpasses all number. God eternally generates the divine character, from which, in conjunction with feelings of the world, God generates purposes for the world that are themselves the potentiality of Spirit. Insofar as the world incarnates these purposes, Spirit is born in the world and, therefore, received into the divine character, everlastingly completing the divine being through the redemption of the world. The immanent trinity is rooted in this threefold action, but yields a complex unity beyond number. God is the deep reality of creative transformation: Peace.

This goal of peace has never been fully realized in history. The trinitarian understanding suggests, however, that this peace is grounded in the very nature of God, who offers us particular modes of peace suited to that which is really achievable in our own time. Insofar as we in our several callings strive toward this goal, quietly and without attention to itself will be the dynamic work of Spirit, witnessing to the source of all peace in our histories: the God who calls us.

NOTES

1. John B. Cobb, Jr., *A Christian Natural Theology: Based on the Thought of Alfred North Whitehead* (Philadelphia: Westminster, Press 1965); *The Structure of Christian Existence* (Philadelphia: Westminster Press, 1967); *Christ in a Pluralistic Age* (Philadelphia: Westminster Press, 1975).

2. John B. Cobb, Jr., *God AND the World* (Philadelphia: Westminster Press, 1969).

3. John B. Cobb, Jr., *Is It Too Late? A Theology of Ecology*. (Beverly Hills, CA: Bruce, 1971).

4. See, for example, Juergen Moltmann's *The Spirit of Life* and Catherine LaCugna's *God for Us*.

5. Because the subjectivity of God grounds each prehended consciousness, the perspective of that prehended consciousness is to know itself in and through its grounding in God's subjectivity. This, of course, becomes the basis for judgment, transformation, and salvation.

Bernard J. Lee, S.M.
An "Other" Trinity

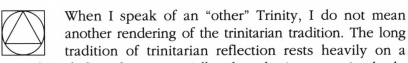 When I speak of an "other" Trinity, I do not mean another rendering of the trinitarian tradition. The long tradition of trinitarian reflection rests heavily on a *Logos*/Word christology, especially when the interpretative background for Logos is Stoic Greek philosophy. The "otherness" I propose consists in focusing upon the earlier Jewish *Dabhar*–Word meanings rather than Logos–Word meanings, and the ways in which Dabhar can mediate the christological meaning of Jesus. This shift of focus from Logos to Dabhar is what the otherness of these reflections is about.

It is helpful to remember that "Trinity" is not a biblical notion. It is second level reflection upon a particular Christian experience of God. While the categories of Father, Son, and Spirit are certainly biblical, a formulation of trinitarian theology begins to take serious hold of the Western Christian imagination in the third century. As the text of the Nicene/Alexandrine creed illustrates, the language of philosophy becomes more central than the language of scripture.

Why undertake this new interpretive venture? In the Second Vatican Council's *Nostra Aetate*, the Church attests that the Jewish people remain most dear to God, that God has not ever repented of the gifts offered to God's people. Although the church is a new People of God, this must not be interpreted as God's repudiation of the earlier People of God. (*Nostra Aetate*, §4). In a word, God's Covenant with the Jews as God's most dear people has not been abrogated. In the main, the christological tradition has been supersessionist: the new Covenant supersedes and replaces the old Covenant, which no longer obtains. One of the hardiest challenges to contemporary christological reflection is to understand Jesus in a way that is fully adequate to Christian experience (which is not the same thing as the accumulated second reflection upon the experience) and yet affirms God's continuing Covenant with the Jews. Whereas a supersessionist tradition has focused upon the discontinuities, we are now bound to retrieve the continuities. That is part of the motivation for these reflections.

I think we can say with relative certainty that the language of Ruach/Spirit and Dabhar/Word would have belonged to the assumptive world of Jesus and would probably have served His own sense of self-identity, while the Logos/Word probably would not have. If these Jewish religious understandings served Jesus well, they should serve us well. Therefore, I am making an effort to continue developing a Ruach/Dabhar christology and to interpret God, Son and Spirit from that perspective.

Metaphor

Sometimes metaphor is a deliberate literary embellishment. That is probably the most commonplace meaning, and it is a valid one. However, in my use of metaphor, I am following Paul Ricoeur concerning a more primordial function of metaphor:

> Metaphor, far from being limited to a linguistic artifact, is characterized by its epistemological function of discovering new meanings. What is at stake is still knowing in process but considered in its nascent moment. In this sense, metaphor is a thought process before being a language process.[1]

Metaphor mediates experience in the very moment of the origination of experience. When I hear God spoken about with the language of king, father, mother, word, breath, spirit, etc., I take these as metaphor, but not as "mere" metaphor. In this sense, metaphor is not an interpretation after the fact, but an enabler of fact in the first place and even a constitutive feature of fact.

Metaphor works because of an analogical bond: one thing is indeed like another. However, the one thing is also unlike the other. Ricoeur says there is always a secret "is not like" that helps guard the surplusage of meaning that belongs to all experience. One of the problems inherent in philosophical theology, which has been the theological tradition of Western Christianity, is that it ontologizes the "is like" feature of metaphor and forsakes the "is not like" feature, which is no less essential to mediated meaning. The doctrinal/dogmatic tradition manifests the same tendencies. I hope to keep in touch with the metaphorical origination of religious experience.

Hermeneutics

It was Nietzsche who first said that there is no such thing as uninterpreted fact. Our interpretation of anything bears the trademarks of our language, our culture, our social location , our personal histories, and even our vested interests (whether we know it or not).

Only with the rise of historical consciousness—and barely so, even now—are we learning how historically conditioned and thoroughly perspectival and partial is our tradition of Western Christian thought. This tradition has been effective, engaging, compelling, and filled with great beauty. But it is "a" take on Christian faith and not "the" take on it.

Empirical Process

One meaning of "empirical" is that second-level reflection is always under requirement to indicate how its articulation is respectful of the originating experience that it interprets. If Dabhar/Word and Ruach/Spirit are two central metaphors for the Jewish experience of God, we need to ask whether there are some family characteristics to the experiences that use each of these metaphorical names. It would seem likely that there are solid experiential reasons for having two names for the way God is experienced.

The way in which Spirit is used in the Christian scriptures is, in the main, highly consistent with its use in the Jewish scriptures. It is more difficult to sort out Dabhar, since the earliest manuscripts of the Christian scriptures are all in Greek. Therefore, the Hebrew word for "word" and the Greek word for "word" would turn up the same: Logos. I focus upon Dabhar.

I would like to indicate some correlations between the empirical meanings I develop and Whitehead's natural theology. In so doing, I suggest a different correlation between Word/Spirit and the primordial and consequent aspects of God than has usually been attributed by process theologians. I suggest the need for a development in the process interpretation of God as consequent in regard to God's providence for the world.

Ruach is one of the important words in Hebrew anthropology—along with Nephesh and Neshamah—for what we would call today "the human spirit," the depths of a person, the "who" of a person. In the Earlier Scriptures, Neshamah is used 24 times, Nephesh 754 times, and Ruach 378 times (nearly all of them postexilic). Ruach means both breath and wind, the common element being that of moved air. Hebrew anthropology is physiological in character. Because breath is so deep inside and so clearly essential to life, it becomes a metaphor for the depths of a person's inner reality. In the following passage, spirit names both the depths of the "who" of God and the depths of the "who" of human beings, and the transformative interaction between them:

> God had given revelation through the Spirit, for the Spirit explores the depths of everything, even the depths of God. After all, is there really anyone who knows the qualities of a person as well as one's own spirit knows, the spirit within a person. Well, in the same way, no one knows the qualities of God except the Spirit of God. Now the Spirit we have received is not the spirit of the world but God's own Spirit, so that we may understand the lavish gifts God has given us. . . . The natural person has no room for the gifts of God's Spirit and they seem as folly. Such a one cannot even recognize them, because their value can only be assessed in the Spirit. The spiritual person, on the other hand, can assess the value of everything, but such a person's own value cannot be assessed by anyone else. (1 Cor 2:1–16)

I offer, in summary, some of the generalizations I have formulated, based upon stories of the Spirit in the Earlier Scriptures.[2] The Spirit of Yahweh transforms the human spirit. The locus of that transformation is the heart. In Hebrew anthropology, the heart is the seat of personhood. Therefore, the Spirit goes right to the constitutive center of personality. The seat of personhood is affective in character, and so, therefore, is the ordering of history and the cosmos. This contrasts strongly with the sense of rational ordering implied in Logos, and implicit rational consequences for the Christian life.

Spirit effects change and conversion in the deepest reaches of interiority. The Spirit cleans and remakes the human heart, attuning it to the Spirit of God so that with sure instinct we can discern the things of God.

We are conditioned by God's Spirit in the valuational structures of our own spirit. We are transformed in our appetitive faculties to feel things accurately with the feelings of God and to yearn for them. Put simply, God's Spirit is where God's deep story is. Our spirit is where our deep story is. Through the immanence of God's Spirit in the human spirit, the deep story that is intended for history is transmitted.

AN EMPIRICAL THEOLOGY OF DABHAR/WORD

The closest English approximation for Dabhar is "word." However, that translation is impoverished. Dabhar also means "deed" and "thing." As word, it is never primarily an expression of a thought, idea, or image, which is the fundamental sense of the English word. When a person utters a Dabhar/Word, he or she concretely ex-presses [presses out] his or her reality in the stream of history. The word is a spoken thing/act. Speaking words (in the way just described) is a daily human action, one that becomes a metaphor for God's daily actions amidst humans.

In the expression "Word of God," Dabhar occurs 240 times, and an additional 20 times in the plural. The Dbr root also occurs in the verb form, with God speaking. The predominate usage of Word of God is in the word/event formula of the prophets: "The Word of God came to me saying . . ." The Word of God sometimes refers also to the Law, both as Torah in the broader sense, and sometimes in a more restricted way to the Decalogue.

The Word has a kind of historical particularity about it that does not so much characterize Spirit. God's Word tends to promote the historical transformation of a people by shaping them up in quite particular ways. If Yahweh's Spirit is valuationally and nonrationally transformative in the interior depth of the human heart or spirit, Yahweh's Word is more pragmatic and programmatic. It tends to be specific address to specific people with respect to the particularities of particular historical occasions. The Word, in both prophecy and law, specifies the shape which Israel's history is to take.

The constellated meaning which a phenomenological gener-
alization yields is that the Word of God is occasion-specific. It
takes people where they are in their own lives, their own times,
and their own histories. It then summons them on those grounds
to the creative transformation that Covenant offers. The occasion-
specific Word is efficacious and dynamic. It has consequences,
and thus, its name is "deed" as well as "word." The Word of God
accosts actual historical circumstances with concrete proposals
about how lives need to move in order for Covenant to unfold and
usher in a New Age. It is not as specific as: "blow your nose" or
"cook stew today." It does say, however: "move from way up
north back to the south," or "get going on building the temple," or
"these (Decalogue) are the behaviors you must do, while those are
the ones to avoid."

As God's Word, Dabhar suggests particular historical choices
that will be faithful to the deep story of God; i.e., God's Spirit. The
deep story itself is a kind of valuational structure that wants
events, whatever they look like, to be faithful to it. But it does not
require any specific course of events. Dabhar is God's particular
providence for particular occasions.

SPIRIT AND WORD AS CORRELATIVE

In my judgment, not only may the experiential meanings of Ruach
and Dabhar be described as I have suggested, but a reasonable
interpretation can be made about the relationship between these
two experiences of God's transformative presence.

The fullness of God's immanence and formative presence in
Covenant history are often experienced and described as Spirit
and Word. These are not two parallel models. Together they are
one model. Apart, each is half a model.

I want to suggest two analogies for the complementarity of
Spirit and Word. The first is a model of conversion, the second a
model from cultural anthropology.

Conversion

Most people believe that at any given moment, life is open to
improvement—that history can get better. Self-transcendence is
always a possibility: tomorrow can be better than today. These are
ways of talking about conversion.

The possibility for self-transcendence presupposes two factors. First, that there be genuine alternatives for tomorrow; that there are stories that might be told that contrast with the story now being told. Second, that there must be a valuational structure to allow for adjudication between alternative possibilities. Before an array of possibilities, a person needs a "nose" (really a heart) for "sniffing out" those possibilities that are, indeed, better tales to be told.

These two factors are natural components of creative transformation: the presence of genuine alternatives and a felt valuational structure that makes possible the discernment concerning which of those alternatives is/are truly better. If God is experienced as fully involved in the world's creative transformation, then God must be involved in both of those ways. God, trafficking with history as Word, has something to do with proposing particular alternatives for history to consider, as God did with successive transformations of Covenant and with the instructions from Law and prophets about how to live faithfully. Furthermore, God, trafficking with history as Spirit, makes available to the human spirit those powers of discernment that help us recognize the self-transcendence that is offered, urging us through the lure of qualitative increment, to go in pursuit of it. The empirically assessed meanings of Ruach and Dabhar support this analogy. These two efficacies together create a covenanted people living a covenanted daily relationship wherein conversion is God's relentless invitation.

Structural Anthropology: Deep Story and Particular Story

Deep below the surface of every culture is what is called, alternately, a narrative structure, a *mythos*, or a deep story. The deep story is so "deep" that it can never be surfaced in its entirety. It only shows itself in the particular stories that a people lives out. A people's stories, songs, laws, rituals, etc., all embody and reveal the underlying *mythos*. A culture instinctually preserves and hands on its deep story, and fights off, even fiercely, new stories that appear to contravene the deep story. Sometimes we find out where we do stand by knowing more clearly where we do not stand. Taboos function that way—they guard against violations of the deep story. Faithful denizens, of whatever culture, are faithful because they instinctually and accurately grasp the deep story and pragmatically live lives that embody it. Since no embodiment is timeless, they must know how to rebuild the story over and over.

In the Judaeo–Christian tradition, we hold that God has intentions for history and that it is our human task to collaborate with God in building all of our particular worlds in fidelity to God's intentions. In this framework, and building upon the empirical meanings of Ruach and Dabhar indicated above, I propose that Spirit is the self-gift of God that attunes our hearts to the heart of God with respect to the world's deep story, as God would have it. The Word is God's self-gift that guides our world-making by proposing a range of occasion-specific responses to historical challenges. This is God accosting our lived experience in particular ways. This is Dabhar.

THREE NEW TESTAMENT ROOT METAPHORS FOR GOD

There are several layers of God-meanings in the New Testament, each of which is used to express christological faith in Jesus. The older two metaphors occur in the Old Testament. The oldest metaphors are *Ruach* and *Dabhar*. These gain dominance in the prophetic period. In the several centuries before the common era, a new metaphor for God gains prominence: *Sophia,* or Wisdom. Ruach and Dabhar do not disappear, but they recede. Sophia, as a single metaphor, combines in herself the two kinds of agencies attributed to Ruach and Dabhar, but tilts toward Ruach. Matthew and Luke both use Sophia as well as Ruach and Dabhar; so does Paul.

The Logos/Word in John is also indebted to Sophia. What is attributed to Logos in the Johannine Prologue is also attributed to Sophia in the early chapters of Proverbs, in parts of Sirach and in many parts of the Book of Wisdom. Since John could use Sophia to promote his christological interpretation, but chooses to use Logos, whose stoic interpretation (as evidenced in Philo, for example) parallels Sophia, I would guess at the likelihood of some Hellenistic influence on the Johannine option. It is certainly the case that early Christian thought quickly avails itself of Stoic categories, as a result of which Johannine Logos christology virtually hijacks christological development.

Like Sophia, Logos tends to compress the two agencies attributed to Ruach and Dabhar into its single activity as Word. Philo was an Alexandrine Jew whose life overlapped the lives of Jesus and Paul. He interprets Jewish religious experience in categories of Stoic philosophy. He makes a Logos distinction that

Patristic theology appropriates to speak about the relationship between Jesus and the Father. Following Greek philosophical models, Philo speaks of a primordial sort of Unuttered Word (*Logos Endiathetos*), the rational soul of God in which order originates. This Unuttered Word plays a role similar to that of Spirit, but is thoroughly rational in character, rather than affective. The Uttered Word (*Logos Prophorikos*) provides the rationally ordered forms for created realities and, thus, has something in common with Dabhar/Word, except that it is far more formal. For Philo, the Logos Endiathetos pre-exists the world, from before all ages. This is God's unuttered Word. When that Logos funds God's creation of world, it is the Uttered Word, the Logos Prophorikos. There are similarities between the unuttered Word and Spirit. They are the deep story, deep within God. And there are similarities between Dabhar and the uttered Word. The uttered Word creates a specific world, forms a particular history. The Logos interpretation compresses these two aspects into one figure, Word.

I want to make a brief survey of similarities and differences among the three root metaphors. In the first instance, Ruach/Spirit is the deepest part of God as communicated to the deepest part of us. In Spirit is the origination of our relentless openness to a More. This restlessness is felt in the heart; i.e., the appetitive place in human life. In Spirit is rooted the world's urge toward transcendence. Spirit does not proffer a specific tale to be told. It is an openness to and appetite for any tale that is truly a More. It is God's presence as Dabhar/Word that helps give the More a specific content, a tale to be told whose shape is evoked by the particularities of history. Together Spirit and Word are modes of God's efficacious presence. These are modal presences of God, although Dabhar language occasionally borders on personification.

In the second instance, Wisdom is a single figure to which is attributed both kinds of efficacy that operate in Spirit and Word. Wisdom also begins to have a more intellectual configuration (but also retains a relationship to heart). The language of the Wisdom figure's kind of existence tends to be that of personification. Wisdom was with God before the world, but this seems to be a part of the personification of God's activity and reality, and not a real pre-existence of any kind.

In the third instance, the Logos, like the Wisdom figure, combines much of the two efficacies attributed to Spirit and Word. In Philo's version, Logos has an ideal pre-existence. Its mode of existence is an ideal (in a Platonic sense), personified pre-existence. The Johannine Logos is very similar, except that its mode of preexistence is real and personal. The Fathers of the Church sometimes availed themselves of Philo's work to elucidate an evolving Christian tradition. This was easy to do, because Philo speaks of the ideal, pre-existing Logos as God's Son and God's First Born.

Part of the clumsiness of trinitarian theology as it developed is lack of philosophical clarity about the Holy Spirit. I surmise that this clumsiness reflects the fact that a binitarian metaphor (about Unuttered Word/Father and Uttered Word/Son) has already assimilated many of the Spirit's activities into the Logos Endiathetos. Attempts at a Spirit Christology vis-à-vis Logos will probably not work. I become more and more convinced that a fully elaborated Spirit christology needs to be in tandem with Dabhar christology.

In recent decades, there has been an upsurge of interest in Spirit christology, partly because Spirit christology is more attentive to the humanity of Jesus (which Logos makes difficult to elaborate). Roger Haight has offered an insightful summary of efforts at Spirit christology.[4] The Western tradition has, in fact, not found it easy to develop a pneumatology that is readily coherent with the Logos tradition. The Nicene Creed plays out the relationship between Father and Son in a detailed philosophical way. The inclusion of Spirit, however, is largely a liturgical and not a philosophical inclusion (the Spirit, as the Father and Son, is worshipped and glorified), very different from the philosophical categories that elaborate the Father and Son. I hold to the great importance of a new development of Spirit christology, and I contend that it can most fruitfully be elaborated in tandem with a Dabhar christology and not with a Logos christology.

I want to return now, however, to a comparison/contrast between Ruach/Dabhar and the process relational modes of thought of Alfred North Whitehead.

A WHITEHEADIAN/PROCESS CORRELATION

From early on, process thinkers made a correlation between Word and God's primordial nature, and between Spirit and God's consequent nature. This was Dorothy Emmet's suggestion long ago.[5]

John Cobb[6] and David Griffin[7] have both affirmed this correlation. Emmet and Cobb make clear that their proposals interact with the doctrinal traditions of Western Christianity (Patristic literature, Creeds of Nicea and Constantinople, doctrine of Nicea and Chalcedon). It is not my conclusion that Cobb, Emmet, Griffin, et al. were wrong, only that they came to their conclusions based upon the mainstream Western theological tradition, rooted as it is in the Logos root metaphor and its concomitant narrative structure. My proposal is to reverse the correlation, associating Spirit with the primordial nature and Word with the consequent nature.

WHITEHEAD'S THEISM

Alfred North Whitehead's philosophy caught the attention of Christian thinkers from early on, and for two reasons. The first is his interpretation of the world as relational and as pervasively interconnected and interdependent. The second is his natural theology, which interprets God in relational terms as well, and also as pervasively and causally interconnected with the entire universe and interdependent with it. God is not interdependent for the fact of divine existence, but for the shape of divine existence, since the world and God act upon each other.

Whitehead described two aspects of deity: God's character as primordial, God in whom order primordially emerges; and God's character as consequent, God, the shape of whose concrete existence is consequent upon God's experience of the world. In Whitehead's work, the burden for both novelty and order seems to rest upon the primordial nature of God. I turn our attention to God as primordial.

God as Primordial

Whitehead apparently concludes that some of the novelty that occurs in the world is so stunningly new—so simply unprecedented—that it cannot be accounted for by a rearrangement of the old. Therefore, as of yet, unrealized possibilities must be, as it were, waiting somewhere in the wings for their ingression into the actual world when the unfolding drama gives them their hour upon the stage. That "somewhere" is God as primordial.

Every thing must be somewhere; and here "somewhere" means
"some actual entity." Accordingly the general potentiality of the
universe must be somewhere; since it retains its proximate relevance to actual entities for which it is realized. . . . Thus "proximate
relevance" means "relevance in the primordial mind of God."
(*Process and Reality*, 46).

God, then, holds "the absolute wealth of potentiality" in God's primordial envisagement (*Process and Reality* [PR], 343). Every entity
receives from God an "initial aim" for its becoming (something
partly analogous with the traditional "will of God"). That initial
aim is rooted in an entity's experience of God as primordial, and
novelty depends upon it.

Now I turn to the issue of order. Whitehead has coined a
technical term to refer to any act of experiencing: prehension.
Subjects prehend objects. Whitehead also recognizes that no two
subjects ever prehend the same object in absolutely the same way.
Each subject's experience and vested interests color how it experiences anything. The "how" that clothes every experience is a
very loaded "how." It is freighted with valuations and with emotional feelings. Our decisions finally rest upon a felt choice.
Reasons may help elucidate a decision, but we finally do what we
do "just `cause," as children sometimes very insightfully say.
Sometimes two persons who can give nearly identical pros and
cons about the same issue will still act differently, because how
they feel about those reasons differentiates one from the other.
Our "hows" are right at the heart of our identities. "How an actual
entity becomes constitutes what that actual entity is" (*PR*, 23).
Subjective form is the name of the technical category Whitehead
uses to name the "how" of our prehensions.

When Whitehead talks about God's envisagement of the full
wealth of the world's potentiality, he insists that these prehensions, like all prehensions, have a subjective form. Each of God's
envisagements of possibility has an emotional texture laden with
qualitative features. And, here is the point I want to underscore:
God's valuational/affective responses are primordial. They are
first. They are not responses to values already there. They make
the values. Whitehead indicates that the subjective forms of God's
envisagement do two things: they create the value of each possibility, and they also constitute the mutual sensitivities of values to
each other (*PR*, 344).

This structure, affectively constituted, is the deep story of God's own heart. It is also the structure that generates the ideal deep story for the world. The order that should obtain in the world is grounded in the primordial affect of God. Because it is affective in character, it is with the "heart" that we resonate with God's self-gift as primordial. In the scriptures, Jewish and Christian, the heart is regularly the location of the Spirit's formative presence.

In *Process and Reality*, Whitehead is very clear that the primordial aspect of God is experienced in history as an "urge" toward the future and "appetite" in the present (*PR*, 33). In *Adventures of Ideas*, published some years later, he invokes a new thematic metaphor to describe God's primordial character and God's presence to the world under that aspect: the new motif is "*Eros*." In language reminiscent of "Spirit" in the biblical tradition, Whitehead talks about the importance of being attuned to God's *Eros*: must we not ask, Whitehead wonders, "whether nature does not contain within itself a tendency to be in tune, an Eros urging towards perfection."[8] He identifies God's primordial nature as the basic *Eros*, which when immanent in the world, is "the Eros of the Universe."[9] Analogous to Spirit in our tradition, Whitehead speaks of God's *Eros* as "indwelling" in the soul.[10]

Now to the problematic. Until the final pages of *Process and Reality*, Whitehead does not attend to the other aspect of God's reality—the consequent nature (and even there at the end, the treatment is brief and unsatisfying). Whitehead considers the immanence of God as primordial to be "the primary action of God on the world," sufficient for accounting for the world's definiteness (*PR*, 345). But the primordial nature envisages possibility that is exactly "pure possibility;" that is, it tells no tales about the actual course of things. Whitehead is quite specific about this: "the primordial nature of God does not relate to the given course of history" (*PR*, 44). "God's 'primordial' nature is abstracted from his commerce with 'particulars' (*PR*, 34). The will of God as the initial stage of an entity's aim for its becoming) then, results "from the inevitable ordering of things, conceptually realized in the nature of God" (*PR*, 244) Are we, then, to presume that God acted freely one time only (the primordial evaluation), and that God's will for history ever after is the inexorable logic of that once-only free choice? Do not both Jewish and Christian traditions insist that God's will for the world adjusts event after event to the intimate particulars of each moment, as an expression of God's love and God's conscious choices? Process philosophers and theologians early sensed the problematic, and have addressed it in different ways.[11–14]

It is the logic of relationality as a metaphysical characteristic that necessitates the consequent nature of God. All entities act upon all other entities and are acted upon by all other entities. God receives the world's experience into God's experience. This is the "reaction of the world on God" (*PR*, 345). God really (*relatio realis*) experiences us, and God's concrete being as God is shaped by the experience. God's concreteness is in some measure dependent upon what God experiences. That "experienced God" is God as consequent.

The same relational reasons that demand God's experience of the world also require that the world, in turn, experience this experienced God. I do not mean to play with words, but the issue is most important. What difference does God's experience of us make to us? Early in *Process and Reality*, Whitehead says that God is immanent in the world with respect to both his primordial and consequent nature (*PR*, 32). He then proceeds to be preoccupied with the efficacy of God as primordial. Only on the very last page of *Process and Reality* does he once again state clearly his conviction that God's experience must pour back into the world, making a difference in the story of the world. But there is no hint in his systematic work at precisely how he thinks this occurs.

The first phase of creativity is God's activity as primordial. Second, there is the origination of individual entities, receiving their initial aim from God's primordial nature. Third, these many individuals are experienced by God and are integrated into a single experience in God that assures the everlastingness of the world and the possible relevance of any past fact to any new fact. Let me cite the pertinent text affirming the efficacy of God as consequent:

> In the fourth phase, the creative action completes itself. For the perfected actuality passes back into the temporal world, and qualifies this world so that each temporal actuality includes it as an immediate fact of relevant experience. . . . The action of the fourth phase is the love of God for the world. It is the particular providence for particular occasions. (*PR*, 351)

Whitehead never attempts to say how this particular providence for particular occasions directs the flow of God's love into a formative role in the emergence of new fact.

Whether Whitehead's system requires that or not, the Judeao–Christian experience of God does. God's will in the world reflects God's consciousness of us and love for us. When the ancient Hebrews reject the Judges and want a king, Yahweh refashions the character of the convenant and deals with the nation on the basis of the decision they have made (1Sam.8). In Jeremiah, Yahweh makes clear that how God relates to a people depends upon the choices they make; and when they change their minds and act in new ways, God changes God's mind, too, and comports God's self with them in a new way (Jer 18:7–12).

The Dabhar/Word of God is a key metaphor for the particular providence of God for particular occasions, spilling out of God's love. As I indicated earlier, the Word of God is occasion-specific. It is a Word of address to particular people in particular situations. The form of the Word is often the prophet who tells a people how they must fashion their story; sometimes the Word is the particularity of the law.

The philosophical category that becomes relevant to this discussion is that of the nonconformal proposition. Nonconformal propositions are "tales that might perhaps be told by actualities" (*PR*, 256). The proposition is an imagined alternative. The proposition functions as a lure for our feelings (*PR*, 187). "In their primary role, (propositions) pave the way along which the world advances into novelty" (*PR*, 187). Now, if God is to be understood as interacting with history out of God's own concrete consciousness (which indeed is what Dabhar/Word reports is the case), then God must have some on-the-line role in fashioning the propositions which lure history.

I believe there are hints in Whitehead's work that suggest how this Dabhar function might proceed. I want to develop those hints. Whitehead speaks of God as "the lure for feeling, the eternal urge of desire," in respect to God's "particular relevance to each created act" (*PR*, 344). I want to suggest that there might be a good reason for the double-edged statement with its two differing prepositions: for feeling and of desire.

In an earlier section of *Process and Reality* in which Whitehead addresses the role of subjective form in making certain possibilities lure the process of becoming, he speaks of the subjective forms as lure of feeling (*PR*, 88). This seemed different enough from Whitehead's accustomed "lure for feeling" that the editors of the corrected edition needed to justify retaining it as a reading rather than correcting it as a mistake. They cite the fact that Whitehead used "of" in the table of contents that describes the chapter in which the expression is then used. On the same page on which he speaks of the "lure of feeling," Whitehead also speaks of an entity's own decision for how it responds to a lure for feeling. I am suggesting a hint here in Whitehead that God's efficacy as primordial moves us by causing in us the "urge of desire," and that his efficacy as consequent addresses us through a nonconferral proposition that functions in us as a "lure for feeling." (Conformal propositions prehend what is the case, nonconformal propositions prehend what might be the case). In these two, the lure of feeling and the lure for feeling, are functions akin to the activities of Ruach and Dabhar.

RUACH AND DABHAR—PRIMORDIAL AND CONSEQUENT

What the world gets from God as primordial is a structured appetition—a formed urge. But the urge is object-less. That is why this metaphor can only be half a model for God's efficacy in history. The primordial ordering does not require of history ahead of time any particular way in which history should tell its tale, only that whatever tale does get told be in conformity to the deep story of God. The urge, therefore, does generate a feeling of urgency about some future that will be satisfying. The urge as primordial may be object-less, but the structured nature of the urge makes it possible to adjudicate among the many tales that might be told. I am suggesting that God's gift as primordial is a structured urge, a lure of feeling, and that this function of God has something significant in common with God's efficacy as Ruach.

I am also suggesting that God's gift as consequent is his implication in the formation of the tale that might be told (Convenant is such a tale). The function of God as consequent has something significant in common with God's efficacy as Dabhar. God must be implicated in the propositions offered history if God's providence is, indeed, directed to particular occasions. This functions through nonconformal propositions, through tales that might be told which act as lures for feeling—at which point the object-less formed urge can function occasion-specifically in the world.

Whitehead says that conscious awareness always involves elements of contrast. To know what something is presumes some sense of what it is not, what it might have been, or what it could yet become. Consciousness presupposes a contrast between "in fact" and "might be" or "might have been" (*PR*, 267). Since God as consequent is precisely God as conscious of each historical reality, God's consciousness will always involve an awareness of contrast between what God experiences as fact, and what that fact can become in its next moment of becoming. God's consciousness is the ground for an objective lure for feeling for an occasion. The concrescent occasion feels God's propositional feeling of itself from its last moment of experience.

This matter is not as complex as the language about it sounds. We see ourselves reflected in the faces of those who know us well and love us deeply. We see in their eyes not only who we are but who we can become. We experience them experiencing us and feel their feelings of us. Furthermore, the stature of their spirit rubbing off on ours often gives us the urgency to pursue what we might become. They feel us with their own spirit, and we feel them feeling us that way.

Addressing the efficacy of God in civilization, A. H. Johnson, one of Whitehead's former students, has made the same suggestion:

> . . . in God's consequent nature, data from the world of ordinary actual entities can be harmonized in accordance with his subjective aim. This aim involves the selection and realization of the best possible pattern from the realm of eternal objects, as envisaged in his primordial nature. The harmonization is made available to the world of ordinary actual entities by the function of God's superject.[15]

Although Johnson does not specify further, a proposition about an entity's ideal new version seems the logical way in which God as consequent is made available to the world of ordinary actual entities. Will Beardslee suggested "proposition" as the key process category for describing what Christians intend when they call Jesus "the Christ."[16] In this context, Beardslee says that God gives an occasion its initial aim in the form of a proposition.[17] This tale to be told is a Dabhar function. Let me now bring the pieces together.

Based upon what Ruach and Dabhar report upon God's efficacy, I suggest that we speak of an initiating impulse that each actual occasion receives from God. Its two components are: a feel for the deep story, an Eros, a lure of feeling; and a feeling of the particular way in which this new moment of history might tell its tale. These two components name the immanence (superjectivity) of God in us with respect to both the primordial and consequent aspects.

To speak of "two" components is to follow Whitehead's "distinction of reason" as he describes the "two natures" of God. The two natures themselves are technical, philosophical categories that, according to Whitehead's insistence, are metaphors mutely appealing for an imaginative leap. (*PR*, 4) No scientist has seen an electron or a quark. No process philosopher has seen an actual entity, or an initial aim, or an initiating impulse, or a nonconformal proposition. No theologian has literally seen God's Spirit or heard God's Word, for God has neither lung nor larynx. To correlate Ruach and Dabhar with the superjectivity of God as "primordial" and "consequent" is to engage in hermeneutical conversation. It is to try to hear *Ruach* and *Dabhar* as we think Jesus probably heard them, then to hear God described as some people in the late twentieth century are wont to do, and, based upon similarities in the metaphors, to "fuse horizons," as Gadamer calls successful interpretation.

RELATIONSHIP AS CONSTITUTIVE: TWO NEW TAKES ON AN ANCIENT ISSUE

The great mysteries of Christian experience have such surplusage of meaning that they outrun articulation. Eucharist and Trinity are such experiences. Interpretations about them compete. Argument and debate around them are very old. One of the struggles has been to interpret the ancient notion of person so that Trinity does not turn into a tritheism (which has been a Jewish objection to Trinity). The extreme avoidance of tritheism looks like unitarianism, which does not do justice to the trinitarian experience of God. Trinitarian interpretations of God must not, of course, violate monotheism. A unitarian interpretation is the extreme avoidance of monotheistic violations.

Modalism has haunted trinitarian understanding as a heterodoxy. In the philosophical world view within which much of the debate took place, relationships were considered an accidental. Substance names what one is, and one then has relationships. But relationships do not impinge upon identity. Modalism attempted to use relationship to explicate the trinitarian experience of God, but was found wanting, because there is something so essential about that experience of God that categories of accident are insufficient.

The two new takes I am offering are: (1) carrying on a discussion on a Dabhar road rather than along a Logos avenue; and (2) using relationship as a constitutive rather than an accidental category in accounting for the reality of anything, including the reality of God. Charles Hartshorne has shown well, I believe, how a Greek worldview (not the biblical experience) required the interpretation of God as immutable.[18] Within that interpretive framework, immutability is necessary to the affirmation of God's perfection. Given the necessary and interactive function of God with respect to every creature in a process relational interpretation, Hartshorne calls God pan-relational, the most relational of beings. Pan-relationality is necessary to the affirmation of God's perfection.

In this interpretive framework, nothing first exists and then has relationships. Actual existence is an emergent from relationships, not once but always. Relationships are constitutive, not accidental! My colleague, Michael Cowan, observes that relationships are the perpetual womb of our becoming. In the technical system of Whitehead, subjectivity does not precede the experiencing of objects. Rather, experiencing is what makes subjectivity. In the receiving of an initial aim from God, the experiencing subject is created.

Spirit and Word are co-creatively at the center of every world. The only God we know is the God we experience in history. That does not exhaust God. Every being is more than what is disclosed in its immanence. Otherness and witness are correlative categories. "Total otherness" is a contradiction, because anything totally other would not be in my world of experience, and, therefore, I could not report upon it. ("Totally other" is perhaps a useful poetic category for indicating the utter greatness of God). Our starting point is God-with-us. The tradition has been fascinated by speculation about who God is without us, but the only God we know is the God who is with us. An empirical commitment leaves us with God-with-us as the only context for our knowledge of God. World-with-God is equally our context, for it is the only world we know. We can speculate on otherness beyond the witness, but the speculation is only as good as the hints of otherness embedded in the witness and unfurled with imagination.

Ruach and Dabhar are metaphors that for us human beings in a particular sweep of cultural and linguistic tradition mediate our experience of God-with-us, or, as Catherine La Cugna has developed (not in a process-relational framework), God-for-us.[19]

It is the Judaeo–Christian experience that Spirit is not an arbitrary presence of God that might or might not occur, but a necessary and constitutive presence. It is like God to be that kind of a God in our kind of a world—the only God and the only world we know. It is the Judaeo–Christian experience that Ruach/Spirit is not an arbitrary presence of God that might or might not occur, but a necessary and constitutive presence. Ruach/Spirit is the Who of God in whom the deep story of the world is founded. Similarly, it is the Judaeo–Christian experience that Dabhar/Word is not an arbitrary presence of God that might or might not occur, but a necessary and constitutive presence. Dabhar/Word is the particular providence of God for particular occasions. It is like God—the only God we know—to care for the world in that incredible detail. Ruach and Dabhar are essentially Who God is, not accidentally.

CHRISTOLOGY

Trinity is a reflection upon the Christian experience of God. The trinitarian imagination is funded by the experience of God whom Jesus and Christian communities call Father, by the experience of Jesus as God's Son—the Incarnate Word (Logos), and by the experience of Spirit in connection with Jesus and with Christians. I am offering a reflection that retrieves Dabhar as a category of Word and thinks about God trinitarianly with a Dabhar/Ruach christological understanding of Jesus funding the religious imagination. There is space only to hint at the barest indicators of a Ruach/Dabhar christology.

In Luke's Gospel, Jesus is conceived by the Holy Spirit, as a result of which He is to be called Son of God. The baptism of Jesus is something of a paradigm for Father, Spirit, and Word/Son. The Spirit of God comes upon (Mt) or into (Mk) Jesus, and then the filiating Dabhar is spoken: "This is my Son." If Dabhar "filiates" Jesus; i.e., makes Jesus God's Child/Son, this filiation implies the Fatherhood/parenthood of God. In the Good News recalled and announced by the Markan community, God is called Father 4 times, and the Kingdom of God is announced 18 times.[20] In Matthew, Father appears 37 times, and the Kingdom of God 47 times. In John, the latest Gospel, God is called Father 173 times, and the Kingdom of God is mentioned only 5 times, clearly indicating the extent to which the Fatherhood of God shows development as a way of indicating the Kingdom's tale to be told.

In Luke, when Jesus gives his inaugural address in the synagogue, he invokes Isaiah to claim that the Spirit is on him and has anointed him to proclaim good news to the world. The Good News is the historically specific shape of human behaviors that belong to God's Kingdom. This is the Dabhar the anointed one speaks. To be anointed is to have oil poured on oneself. Jesus is filled with joy by God's Spirit and then prays to the Father (Lk 10:21). The anglicized Hebrew word for an anointed one is *Messiah*, and the Greek work for the same is *Christ*. The claim, then, is that the activity of Spirit in Jesus is a christologizing act, an act that constitutes Jesus as the Christ. The deep story of God's heart and the deep story in the heart of Jesus are experienced by Paul as so identical that he can interchange Spirit of God and Spirit of Christ. (With a Logos christology, it is more difficult to locate a christologizing Spirit in the reality of Jesus, because Jesus is christologically constituted in his pre-existence.)

There is a pattern in Paul that suggests a similar process for Christians. The gift of Spirit into our hearts leads us to cry out (to recognize the Dabhar/Good News): "Abba, Father!" If Spirit is christologizing in the reality of Jesus, the same spirit is analogously christianizing in our case. In both instances, the efficacies of Spirit effect God's redemptive work in history.

Jesus presents himself as both the proclaimer and initiator of the reign of God. His teaching is a communication of the content of God's reign, the specific ways that we must be together in the world with each other and with God because of who God is. In many ways, Jesus functions, thus, in the prophetic tradition, speaking the Dabhar of God. The expression, Good News, is the New Testament way of naming God's address to human history. While Jesus is presented as announcing the Good News—the Gospel—he is also present as the Good News. This is a christological claim: Jesus is the Dabhar of God. This Dabhar christology far transcends the prophetic claim.

CONCLUSION

To begin with, I want to call attention to something strange about process philosophy and Christian faith as dialogue partners. Our belief in God as trinitarian is contingent upon our experience of Jesus as the Christ of God. As the Christ of God, Jesus makes God known. Our faith is contingent faith. Whitehead understood his philsophy to be a search for necessary categories of understanding—for that is the character of metaphysics. Necessary categories (if they are that) cannot establish contingent fact. All we can do is establish correlations that provide from philosophy some additional intelligibility for our faith. And because, as Whitehead said (*PR*, 337–338), philosophy must not suffer from narrowness in the selections of evidence ("the fairies dance and Christ is nailed to the cross"), contingent faith can also address metaphysics with its evidence about God, in this case, suggesting that philosophy adjust its natural theology (with respect to the efficacy of God as consequent in God's providence for the world).

I have approached a sense of trinity that gives central attention to Ruach/Spirit and Dabhar/Word. This is an "other" sort of trinitarian reflection that focuses upon Dabhar/Word rather than upon Logos/Word.

I have engaged Whitehead's philosophy as a conversation partner, a contemporary worldview. Whitehead's presentation of God under primordial and consequent aspects has been used to interpret the efficacy of Spirit and Word. This has rebounded back into process philosophy by suggesting a development of God as consequent in order to account better for God's Dabhar/providence for particular occasions.

Process relational modes of thought also frame relationships as constitutive rather than accidental, offering a new way of understanding the experienced reality of God as Spirit and Word.

There is much more that needs to be said than what I have suggested in this paper as an "other" way of understanding an "other" trinity. I have tried to find within the religious experience of the Judaeo–Christian tradition a way of interpreting God as Father, Dabhar/Word as Son and Holy Spirit that is faithful to Christian faith and does not violate what was probably the assumptive world of Jesus himself. What remains is the tickling question of a messianic interpretation of Jesus that is adequate for Christian faith and also responsive to the "fact" (at least as I understand it) that Jesus never stepped outside his Jewish faith to be what he was, do what he did, and say what he said. Which is to say that God the Father did not step outside that trajectory in his relationship with Jesus. Nor did the Spirit of God. Nor did the Word of God.

NOTES

1. Paul Ricoeur in *The Metaphoric Process: The Creation of Scientific and Religious Understanding*, ed. Mary Gerhart and Allan Russell (Ft. Worth: Texas Christian University, 1984), xii.

2. Bernard J. Lee, *Jesus and the Metaphors of God: The Christs of the New Testament*, (New York: Paulist, 1993), 80–119; and "God as Spirit," in *Empirical Theology: A Handbook*, ed. Randolph Crump Miller (Birmingham: Religious Education Press, 1992), 129–141.

3. Lee, *Jesus and the Metaphors*, 110–122.

4. Roger Haight, "The Case for Spirit Christology," *Theological Studies* 53 (1992): 257–287.

5. Dorothy Emmet, *Whitehead's Philosophy of Organism* (London: Macmillan, 1932), 252–255.

6. John B. Cobb, Jr., *A Christian Natural Theology* (Philadelphia: Westminster, 1965), 225.

7. David Griffin, *A Process Christology* (Philadelphia: Westminster, 1973), 192.

8. Alfred North Whitehead, *Adventures of Ideas* (New York: Free Press, 1967), 251.

9. Whitehead, *AI*, 253.

10. Whitehead, *AI*, 275.

11. Delwin Brown, "Freedom and Faithfulness in Whitehead's God," *Process Studies* 2(2) (1972): 137–148, esp. 143–145.

12. Cobb, *Christian Natural Theology*, 155 ff.

13. James W. Felt, "The Temporality of Divine Freedom," *Process Studies* 4(4) (1974): 252–262.

14. Lewis S. Ford, "The Non-Temporality of Whitehead's God," *International Philosophical Quarterly* 13(3) (1973): 347–376.

15. A. J. Johnson, *Whitehead's Philosophy of Civilization* (New York: Dover, 1962), 180–181.

16. William Beardslee, *A House for Hope* (Philadelphia: Westminster, 1972), especially chapter VIII.

17. *Ibid.*, 166.

18. Charles Hartshorne, *The Divine Relativity: A Social Conception of God* (New Haven: Yale University Press, 1948).

19. Catherine Mowry La Cugna, *God-for-Us: The Trinity and Christian Life* (San Francisco: Harper, 1991).

20. The figures in this section are from James D. G. Dunn, *The Evidence for Jesus* (Philadelphia: Westminster, 1985), 34, 44.

Concluding Remarks

A number of issues have been raised by the preceding essays that will need further reflection on the part of anyone working within this field in years to come. The first issue has to do with the relationship between reason and revelation, especially when the content of revelation is itself a matter of debate among Christian theologians. The second issue focuses on the understanding of the relationship between the One and the Many and on the way in which a given philosophical understanding of this relationship influences our understanding of the doctrine of the Trinity. The third issue is akin to the second and has to do with the relationship between the Infinite and the finite. If God is infinite, then can God be simultaneously personal; that is, responsive to others on an interpersonal basis? Finally, the fourth issue lays open the question of the ongoing relationship between classical and neoclassical metaphysics in the light of the current antimetaphysical bias of much contemporary trinitarian theology. It asks, in other words, whether or not the two rival metaphysical approaches to reality can be somehow combined so as to offer a more convincing explanation of the God–world relationship than those that offer a purely experiential or phenomenological understanding of the doctrine of the Trinity to present-day Christians.

The first issue, as noted above, has to do with the relationship between reason and revelation, specifically, between Whitehead's metaphysical conceptuality and the traditional doctrine of the Trinity. Which of these two forms of knowledge ultimately serves as the criterion of truth for the other? Ideally, they should complement one another as two approaches to one and the same objective reality. But, if they at least appear to conflict in their truth-claims, does one modify one's understanding of the Trinity so as to be consistent with Whitehead's metaphysical scheme, or does one modify Whitehead's metaphysical scheme so as to remain faithful to the received doctrine of the Trinity? A case can be made, it seems to me, for the legitimacy of both alternatives.

On the one hand, it can be argued that metaphysical schemes are inherently fallible and, therefore, revisable; whereas, revelation constitutes a privileged form of knowledge about suprasensible reality; e.g., God and the God–world relationship. Hence, if the one must be somehow adjusted to the other, it is evident that Whitehead's metaphysical scheme must be rethought in the light of what we know about the triune God and God's relation to us creatures. Furthermore, one can point to a historical precedent in this matter; namely, the way in which Thomas Aquinas revised the philosophical scheme of Aristotle so as to make it compatible with his own understanding of Christian revelation, specifically, the doctrine of creation. That is, whereas Aristotle specified that substantial form or essence is the first category of being, that which exists in and for itself, Aquinas argued that over and above form or essence there is the actuality of existence. All creatures owe their existence to God as the Subsistent Act of Being (*Ipsum Esse Subsistens*). How they exist is in large part determined by processes of generation and corruption, as described in the philosophy of Aristotle. But this is subsidiary in Aquinas's mind to the more fundamental question of their factual existence. Why is there something rather than nothing at all? This philosophical question, once raised, demands an answer quite independently of its starting point in the theology of creation.

In similar fashion, Gregory Boyd in his essay raised strictly philosophical questions about the adequacy of Charles Hartshorne's metaphysical scheme that deserve consideration quite apart from their pertinence to the doctrine of the Trinity. The question, for example, whether experience is exclusively asymmetrical (that is, only inclusive of events in the past of the current subject of experience) or whether it is also in some respects symmetrical (that is, likewise inclusive of events taking place contemporaneously with the current subject of experience) has a much broader range of application than simply to the doctrine of the Trinity. The problem of actual occasions being unaware of their contemporaries has significant implications both for God's relations to us and our relations to one another.[1] A justification of God as triune along the lines suggested would, thus, be the occasion for a much deeper rethinking of Hartshorne's metaphysical scheme in its entirety, as Boyd's other two points in his essay likewise make clear.

Furthermore, my own rethinking of Whitehead's doctrine of societies has not only the goal of justifying a specifically trinitarian understanding of God, which Whitehead himself never envisioned, but also of drawing attention to what many Whiteheadians concede is a lacuna in the latter's thought. For, as I point out in my essay, from Whitehead's own remarks in *Process and Reality* and elsewhere it is not clear what is the ontological basis for the agency of societies as corporate entities with enduring characteristics, above all, if these same societies lack a "soul" or regnant subsociety of personally ordered actual occasions. My own solution to this problem; namely, that all societies without exception possess a corporate agency derivative from the interrelated agencies of their constituent actual occasions, would have a range of applications, if accepted, far beyond the question of God as one or God as triune. It would, in effect, force a basic rethinking of Whitehead's metaphysics in the same way that Boyd's proposals would force a rethinking of Hartshorne's metaphysical scheme.

On the other hand, confronted with the rival truth-claims of process-relational metaphysics and of traditional Christian belief in the doctrine of the Trinity, one could just as readily choose to submit the traditional understanding of the Trinity to critical scrutiny and revision. This, moreover, seems to be the approach taken by John Cobb, Lewis Ford, and David Griffen in their essays. John Cobb, for example, begins his essay by taking note of four different ways in which the doctrine of the Trinity has historically been conceptualized. He then adds that Whiteheadian metaphysics can be used in support of each approach, but "there is no one doctrine of the Trinity that is dictated by that conceptuality." It would seem, therefore, that compatibility with process-relational metaphysics is the tool Cobb uses to assess the usefulness of various approaches to the doctrine of the Trinity. This is not to say, of course, that revelation is in every instance subordinate to human reason in Cobb's mind. But in any case, it awakens the suspicion that Cobb is much more convinced of the truth-claims of Whiteheadian metaphysics than he is of any individual systematic approach to the doctrine of the Trinity. As Cobb himself says, "my concern is not to argue strongly for one Trinity or another. My concern is to recognize the usefulness and authenticity of threefold formulations of what we experience and know of God alongside others, while showing that more than one such formulation is possible." What remains the same for Cobb through these different formulations is, of course, Whiteheadian metaphysics.

In similar fashion, Lewis Ford in his essay, after conceding that his own earlier efforts at a process-oriented understanding of the Trinity were basically unsatisfactory, offers a new understanding of Trinitarian doctrine ("contingent trinitarianism"), which is, to say the least, revisionary. But the connecting link with the earlier essay is once again fidelity to the basic tenets of process-relational metaphysics. This is not to pass judgment on the merits of Ford's proposal but only to make clear that in the conflict of truth-claims made in the name of traditional Trinitarian theology and with respect to process-relational metaphysics, Ford, like Cobb, favors the latter alternative. Ford, to be sure, argues that metaphysics and revelation cannot be in conflict, since metaphysics deals with necessary truths applicable to all beings everywhere and in every cosmic epoch; whereas, revelation is based on historically contingent truths. "By revelation, we normally mean the manifestation of God as expressed in the contingencies of history, such as the exodus from Egypt. If revelation outruns reason, it should not be because theology proposes self-contradictory or inconsistent 'truths.' It is because the necessary concepts of philosophical reason abstract from the concrete contingencies making the revelation possible" (pp. 52–53).

In support of this contention, Ford offers in the second part of his essay a new explanation of the historical origin of the doctrine of the Trinity within the early Church. As he sees it, early Christians basically experienced God as Christ but could not affirm this transformation of God into Christ because of unconscious philosophical assumptions about the reality of God as timeless and unchanging. Ford, to be sure, distinguishes here between the earthly Jesus and the Christ. Only in his passion, death and resurrection does the earthly Jesus become the Christ; namely, God as experienced by Christians. For Jews, on the other hand, God remains the God of the Hebrew Bible, the God of Israel. The Father and the Son as Christ are thus co-equal ways for Jews and Christians to approach the invisible reality of God. Ford then concludes: "trinitarian concerns have no place in God considered all by Himself, but only in the way we, specifically the way Christians among us, are intimately related to God, and how we conceive other salvific communities to be related to God. Trinitarian thinking concerns contingencies essential to our salvation, and not to some eternal threeness of the abstract divine nature" (p. 64).

Finally, David Griffin in his argument for a "naturalistic" Trinity likewise reveals that his deeper loyalty is to the metaphysical scheme of Whitehead rather than to the classical tradition of trinitarian theology. This is not to say that Griffin may not be fundamentally correct in his penetrating critique of "supernaturalistic" theism as the theoretical source of much that is wrong with contemporary Western society; e.g., a proneness to violence rather than persuasion as a way for human beings to settle disputes with one another, the ravaging of nature's resources for short-sighted and self-centered goals, etc. But the "immanent" Trinity in naturalistic terms that he sets forth at the end of the essay bears a remarkable resemblance to Whitehead's understanding of God in *Process and Reality*. Creative Love would seem to be another term for the divine primordial nature; Responsive Love, for the divine consequent nature. Moreover, because Whitehead himself said that God is a "creature" of creativity (*Process and Reality [PR]*, 88), it is easy for Griffin to associate creativity with the third functional principle within the immanent Trinity. Last, Griffin's insistence throughout the essay that God works exclusively through persuasion, never through coercion, can conceivably be traced to the fact that there is no place for divine coercive activity within Whitehead's metaphysical scheme. To be consistent with Whitehead, accordingly, Griffin has no choice but to claim that God works exclusively through persuasion in dealing with creatures.

Once again, this is in no way to repudiate Griffin's hypothesis, but only to "deconstruct" it; i.e., to bring to light its underlying presuppositions. Furthermore, in support of the approach taken here by Griffin, Ford, and Cobb, it should be noted how difficult it often is to decide what constitutes divine revelation to which human reason must simply submit and what is even within the pages of Sacred Scripture already a conceptualizing of the data of revelation in the light of some antecedent philosophical understanding of reality. This is especially the case with respect to the doctrine of Trinity, which is not formulated as such in the Gospels or the other New Testament writings. What validity, therefore, should one give to the declarations of the Council of Nicaea and other early ecumenical councils of the Christian Church? Here the centuries-old debate between Protestants and Roman Catholics about the role of tradition in the transmission of the Gospel message reappears in another form to set off from one another different contributors to this volume. Yet, it is no longer strictly a Protestant–Roman Catholic debate, as a careful reading of the different essays should make clear. All the contributors, whether

Protestant or Catholic, regularly refer to the doctrinal heritage of the Church; but some use it more consciously and authoritatively than others.

The second issue raised by the essays in this volume likewise has to do with the relation between reason and revelation. That is, several of the contributors have reacted negatively to the notion of tritheism and strongly reaffirmed monotheism as alone consonant with Christian belief. Certainly, the pages of the Bible bear witness to belief in God as one. But is the unity of God proposed here the unity of an individual entity or the unity of a community as a specifically social reality? Furthermore, is one's response to this question grounded in divine revelation about the nature of God or in an antecedent philosophical understanding of the relationship between the One and the Many? Is the One, for example, necessarily an individual entity that transcends the Many, that is, the plurality of entities in need of order and coherence? Or can the One also be understood as somehow emergent out of the dynamic relationship of the Many to one another?

Certainly, the tendency within ancient Greek philosophy since Plato was to think of the One as transcendent of the Many. Moreover, linked with the traditional Hebrew belief in God as one, this philosophical assumption unquestionably had a strong impact on the Greek and Latin Fathers of the Church in their efforts to "explain" the doctrine of the Trinity. As John Cobb points out in his essay, Western theologians tended to think of the triune God in basically modalist terms; Father, Son, and Holy Spirit are simply interrelated "modes of being" within God as a unipersonal reality. Even among the Greek Fathers who placed more emphasis on the plurality of the divine persons, the transcendence of the One over the Many was still evident in their tendency to subordinationism; that is, they located the unity of the Godhead in the person of the Father with the logical consequence that the Son and the Spirit owed their being and activity to the person of the Father.

Moreover, this tendency to either modalism or subordinationism is present among many contemporary Trinitarian theologians. Bernard Lee, for example, in his essay for this volume seems to endorse (unconsciously perhaps) the modalist approach to the Trinity. That is, for Lee "Father" is the name for God in a primordial sense with "Word" and "Spirit" as the names for the personalized activities of God in dealing with human beings. Lee contends, however, that this is not Sabellianism or classical modalism, since within a process-relational perspective Spirit and Word along with the Father are "constitutive presences" within God rather than simply time-bound manifestations of the one eternally hidden God. Yet how are these "constitutive presences" within God related to one another as well as to us humans?

The subtitle of this book is "A Relational Theology of God," which echoes the classical notion of *perichoresis* (mutual coinherence) as used by the Cappadocian Fathers and St. John Damascene. In this classical term, there seems to be implicitly operative a new process-oriented ontology, a new way to understand the relation of the divine persons to one another without the danger of either modalism or subordinationism. Likewise, Thomas Aquinas's notion of the divine persons as "subsistent relations" carries within it the germ of a new approach to the problem of the relationship between the One and the Many. Roland Faber's and Marjorie Suchocki's essays in this volume do much to update Aquinas's insights here. That is, both Faber and Suchocki indicate how there must be antecedent structural differentiations within God, which ground God's trinitarian presence and activity in the world. Suchocki, to be sure, likewise argues that the reality of the world is likewise necessary for the reality of the "immanent" Trinity. God as Spirit comes into being as the world continuously responds to the divine initial aims. Furthermore, it is clear that both Faber and Suchocki take issue with Boyd and me over the notion of God as a primordial divine community. Especially for Faber, this is to forget that the similarity between God and creatures is clearly outweighed by the ever-greater dissimilarity. The three divine persons cannot be said to possess individual self-consciousness without a relapse into tritheism. But does this not, once again, raise the purely philosophical issue of how one understands the relationship between the One and the Many?

The third issue for further reflection and research, namely, the relation between the Infinite and the finite both in classical Trinitarian theology and in process-relational metaphysics, is prominent in Philip Clayton's essay. Classical trinitarian theology has always affirmed the infinity of God but without adequately explaining how creatures, above all, human beings can be genuinely other than God, involved with God in something like an I–Thou relationship. Process-relational metaphysics, on the other hand, has always struggled with the notion of infinity, since all actual entities (including God) are at any given moment determinate and, therefore, finite. Perhaps the only candidate for infinity within Whitehead's metaphysical scheme is creativity, since creativity, by definition, transcends all its instantiations (including God). Yet, as Clayton points out, the relationship between God and creativity remains ambiguous within Whitehead's thought. Since creativity is not itself an entity but exists only in its instantiations, where does it primordially exist except within God as presumably the *ground* of the divine being? But that raises the further question of the relation of creativity to the primordial and consequent natures of God within Whitehead's scheme. In brief, then, if Clayton is right in proposing that the Infinite, however understood, is the necessary presupposition for a proper understanding of the finite, then much more reflection and research must be done on the role of the Infinite both in trinitarian theology based on the metaphysics of Aquinas and in any trinitarian reinterpretation of German Idealism (e.g., Schelling) or Whiteheadian metaphysics.

This leads, finally, to the fourth and last issue raised by these essays on trinitarian theology and process theology, namely, whether the different metaphysical systems can be somehow combined to form a common front against the contemporary tendency to do systematic theology, specifically, trinitarian theology, from a largely phenomenologial or existential basis. Admittedly, as Catherine LaCugna and others have pointed out, the classical doctrine of the Trinity has proven to be more of a "museum piece" than anything else because of its abstractness and lack of connection with the faith-life of the Christian community.[2] Yet, if one shifts to a phenomenological understanding of God as exclusively "for us," there is an equally grave danger that the reality of God will be eventually seen simply as a projection of human wishes and desires. God will become nothing more than a function of our human strivings for self-understanding and understanding of the world in which we live. Metaphysics, in other words, which addresses the issue not simply of human being, but of being as such, would seem to be in the end necessary to justify belief in God as an ontological reality quite independent of human existence and activity.

Yet, classical and neoclassical metaphysicians have engaged more in warfare with one another over the rival truth claims of their respective systems of thought than with their more logical opponents, namely, all those who for various reasons are sceptical of the validity of the entire metaphysical enterprise. Perhaps it is time for those same classical and neoclassical metaphysicians to concede that no single system of thought (be it Thomistic metaphysics, German Idealism or process-relational metaphysics) contains the whole truth about reality. Each world view, in other words, possesses strengths which its rivals lack. Hence, only an artful combination of insights from them all will produce a system of thought truly responsive to contemporary desires for ultimate meaning and value.

On the other hand, one might well take the opposite tack and argue strongly for metaphysical pluralism; namely, the belief that a middle-ground position incorporating such diverse world views as medieval Thomism, German Idealism, and process-relational metaphysics is impossible and that one must, as a result, simply choose one or another approach and live with the consequences. Certainly, along the analogy of work currently being done in the relatively new discipline of comparative theology, it would make good sense to be firmly grounded in one system of thought and then to try to find ways to incorporate insights from the other metaphysical systems into one's own chosen world view. The result, accordingly, would then not be some three-headed "monster" but a systematically organized world view with strong appeal to at least some believers.

Naturally, only time will tell which approach will actually be used by theologians trying to articulate the doctrine of the Trinity in process-oriented terms to their readers/hearers. Moreover, these same theologians will surely have to make still other preliminary judgments about the scope and direction of their work as they try to work out a fully consistent process-oriented Trinitarian theology. The point of this concluding essay has simply been to mark out those areas where careful reflection is clearly needed and where ultimately a conscious decision with respect to methodology will inevitably be required.

JOSEPH A. BRACKEN, S.J.

NOTES

1. Cf. on this point an intriguing essay by J. Gerald Janzen, "Modes of Presence and the Communion of Saints," in *Religious Experience and Process Theology*, eds. Harry James Cargas and Bernard Lee

(New York: Paulist Press, 1976), 147–72, esp. 154, in which he distinguishes between "presence in" and "presence to": another human being is present through causal efficacy in my consciousness in terms of what he or she was an instant ago, but the same human being is present to me here and now by virtue of presentational immediacy, and it is this latter sense of "presence to" another that governs my behavior from moment to moment.

2. Cf., e.g., Catherine La Cugna, *God for Us: The Trinity and Christian Life* (San Francisco: HarperSanFrancisco, 1991), 1–18.

Index of Proper Names

Index of Topics

immanent vs. economic, 6, 11–12,
18–19, 21, 25, 34–39, 40n. 13, 55,
123, 138–39, 161, 180, 184, 186,
188–89, 219, 221
naturalistic, 23–40
necessary, 51–55, 117–19, 126
social, 4–5, 43–44, 47–48, 50, 73–88,
100–101, 105, 109, 112n. 24, 126,
149–51, 171nn. 14–15, 220–21
(cf. also God as divine
community)
temporal, 126, 171, 19
tritheism, 5, 37, 46–48, 166, 187, 208,
220–21
truth, 123, 140n. 3, 156, 215, 217–18,
222–23

Ultimate/ultimacy, viii–xi, 39, 52, 161,
163, 189, 223
Ultimate Efficacy (cf. God as Ultimate
Efficacy)
ungroundedness, 157, 159, 161 (cf.
also Ground)
Unitarianism, 11, 37, 208
unity:
homogeneous, x–xi
in contrast, 79–80, 151, 157
objective, 97–100, 106, 127, 129,
150–51, 157, 162, 220
subjective, 105
universality/particularity, 153–55, 181,
195, 197–98, 203, 205–06, 210,
212

valuational structures, 197, 202–03,
206, 223 (cf. also aesthetic
experience, value)

Western vs Eastern theology, 5, 7,
200–01, 220
Whole/part relation, 77, 99, 106, 110n.
12, 121, 124, 129–30, 136, 140n. 10,
141n. 11, 153
Word/*Logos*, 3, 19–20, 29, 51, 183,
191–93, 198–201, 208–13
occasion–specific, 196, 198,
205–06
Word/*Dabhar*, 191–93, 195–200,
205–13
world:
as "body" of God, 95
as "consequent" to God as
"ground", 133
as contingent, 86, 88
as immmanent in God, 44, 97,
101–02, 109, 110n. 3, 112n. 24, 127,
135, 180, 185, 188–89
as similar to/dissimilar from God,
151–52, 157–62, 167
as transcendent of God, 45, 221
future of, 175–179, 189 (cf. also
eschatology)
world view, philosophical/scientific,
34, 119, 150, 212, 223
worship, 106, 200

Yahweh, 195, 205